Ferry Command Pilot

FERRY COMMAND PILOT
by
Captain Donald Moore McVicar, KC, OBE

Words on Wings Press

Edited, Designed, and Illustrated
by
Donna Margaret McVicar Kazo

Foreword
by
Air Commodore Griffith Powell, CBE, RAF (retired)

2015 Edition
Published by
Words on Wings Press, LLC
ISBN 0692447148
ISBN/EAN 978-0692447147

Adapted primarily from the First Kindle Edition
Published 2012
© 2012 by Donald Gordon McVicar
and Donna McVicar Kazo
Illustrations © 2012 Donna McVicar Kazo

Originally published by Airlife Publishing Ltd. as *Ferry Command*,
© 1981 Don McVicar
ISBN 0-906393-12-4

Ferry Command was divided into two books
and self-published by the author in 1990:
Ferry Command Pilot, ISBN 0-9696229-2-9 and 0-9696229-3-7,
and *South Atlantic Safari*, ISBN 0-9691416-0-4
with changes and new material added to both.

www.wordsonwingspress.com
www.donmcvicar.com
www.donmcvicaraviationbooks.com
www.donnamcvicarkazo.com

Dedication

Dad never did actually dedicate any of his books to anyone, although he would write a nice personal dedication in books that were going to live in new homes. I really don't know why.

As his editor, favorite artist, and best of all, daughter, which gives me a bit of an advantage, I'd like to make up for that.

First, I am dedicating this book to my mother. Since they met during the war, it was fascinating to read the original *Ferry Command* in 1981 and speculate on her identity! She definitely inspired him. Dad was a great guy, but tough to live with, as demanding in his writing as he was in his flying. Dad's writing/researching/publishing/marketing basically took over their home. Dad relied upon Mom's excellent memory, and she supplied him with details that brought life to the scene. They were quite a pair.

I firmly believe that my brother Donald Gordon McVicar made these books happen. He was there for Dad no matter what. I could write a thousand words, but they'd be inadequate expressions of my love and gratitude to Gord for all he did for Dad and Mom.

Without him, dear reader, you would not be reading Don McVicar's words.

Over the years, as Dad continued to write, many good folks helped him with photographs, logbooks, clippings, letters, and their memories. My sincere thanks go out to them.

This book is also dedicated to those brave souls in the Royal Air Force Ferry Command. Until Dad wrote *Ferry Command*, their vital contribution to the war effort was almost unknown. And now most of them are gone. Will we ever see their like again?

—Donna McVicar Kazo

Praise for Ferry Command (published 1981) and Don McVicar

Aviation News, Calgary, Alberta, January 11, 1982
Review by Publisher-Editor H. Richard Engel

Some books leave you with more questions than answers. Not so, *Ferry Command*, one of the most interesting Canadian aviation books I've read. An exciting story of a little known part of World War II.

Ferry Command is the autobiography of one Don McVicar (a well known Canadian aviator) who joined Ferry Command very shortly after its inception with 2000 hours in his log book, gleaned as a young bush pilot in Northern Alberta and Saskatchewan.

Ferry Command gives the reader a very human look at the lives and difficulties experienced by pilots and crews, pioneering and welding links in the chain of aircraft delivery to all theaters of action during World War II.

A book I couldn't put down until I had finished it.

The Gazette, Montreal, Saturday, January 23, 1982
"Ferry"'Amends RAF History by John M. Ross

Ferry Command of the Royal Air Force (RAF) hasn't received much attention in the histories of wartime flying, yet it was a highly significant factor in the Allied war effort from 1940 to 1945.

Based at Dorval, the first flight of seven Lockheed Hudsons, crewed by Canadian Pacific Air Services personnel, made its way across the Atlantic in November, 1940. This later became the RAF Ferry Command, which delivered more than 10,000 combat aircraft to the war zones by the time peace came.

Don McVicar was one of the early pilot-navigators and in this book, he tells his personal story of his adventures from 1940 to 1942. It is an airman's account from the cockpit of a variety of aircraft and will be particularly appreciated by the now old hands of the Command, whose home was Dorval and the Piccadilly Club in the Mount Royal Hotel.

Scores of names are mentioned that will bring back many memories of hazardous flights over long distances to Britain and elsewhere that didn't get the attention received by the combat fliers of fighter, bomber or coastal commands but, nevertheless, were an important chapter in the RAF's history.

This book is a labor of love on McVicar's part and one of the most fascinating sections deals with his key role in laying out the flight paths from Dorval to Goose Bay, to Baffin Island, to Greenland, Iceland, and Britain for the delivery of bombers in the early years of the war.

For history buffs on wartime flying this is an intriguing volume.

Airforce: Air Force Productions Limited, Volume 6, Number 1, March 1982
Reviewed by Mike Kowalski

...The story of the Ferry Command from its inception in 1940 until September 1943; the formative stages, recruiting of competent personnel, civil and military training are very well described by Capt. Don McVicar.

The author was a pioneer in establishing the routes across the high Arctic, North and South Atlantic and over the hot terrain of Africa to Cairo in Egypt. His love of flying and determination to perform to the utmost satisfaction for his superiors, his superb handling of a variety of airplanes including the B-26, popularly called the "Widow-Maker" make very interesting reading.

His description of the various routes and aircraft used reminded this reviewer vividly of the difficulties and adventures each delivery encountered. McVicar's erotic adventures on the ground are typical of the relief sought by aircrew from the tension of wartime flying.

Readers of both sexes will find the book most interesting.

The AHS Journal, published by the Canadian Aviation Historical Society, Spring 1982
Reviewed by F. W. Hotson

Don McVicar has done what many people promise themselves, but never get around to. He has put down in writing, the recollections and details of the high point in his career – his association with the wartime Atlantic ferry service. Like many such attempts, it is in a unique style that is very much a part of the author's personality. In this case, the style follows the pattern of tavern conversation, full of airmen's jargon and amusing colloquialisms. The result is an easy-to-read account of what life was like in one of the little known services of World War Two.

McVicar was an ambitious young man from Western Canada who had started a career in aviation radio when war broke out, but was working his way to a pilot's job. His brief sojourn with the BCATP Air Observer's school in Edmonton under "Wop" May only added fuel to his ambition and he decided there were bigger planes to fly and more of the world to see. The story begins as he "jumps ship" and leaves Wop May for a try at the highest ring on the pilot's merry-go-round of the day: Ferry Command.

The author's determination not to let anyone or anything stand in his way is quite clear, but that was the modus operandi of the day. He makes his way to Dorval airport which was the headquarters of the Command and continues a detailed account of how he made the grade as Captain. Chance happenings played vital roles in those days, for good or for bad. A meeting with a western pilot acquaintance, Louis Bisson, not only gained him a one-of-a-kind chance at Arctic flying, but put him into the team that developed the north staging route: enough to win him the King's Commendation.

As an Air Observer School pilot who stayed longer than average and who got to Ferry Command much later, I found the story accurate and interesting. McVicar describes the people and places well and fits them neatly into the narrative. He is predominantly telling his own story, but as one of the very few accounts written of the Ferry Command in the first person, it is a valuable addition to the overall story of World War II aviation. His description of the Mount Royal's Piccadilly Club and the Music Box are very accurate and the author's escapades away from the airport read like a Robbins novel. In this case, he gallantly states that "only the ladies' names are changed to protect the guilty." Underneath it all is the story of a typical ferry pilot's life, from the easygoing bravado to the emotion of the close calls—and the ever present drive to beat out the other guy...

Like Air Commodore "Taffy" Powell who wrote the foreword, I found it "a darn good read."

**Aircraft Flown by Capt. Don McVicar
(as mentioned in *Ferry Command Pilot*)**

Boeing 247
Boeing B-17 Flying Fortress
Bristol Fairchild Bolingbroke
Consolidated Catalina PBY/Canso
Consolidated Liberator B-24
deHavilland Moth
Fairchild 24
Handley-Page Hampden
Lockheed 10
Lockheed Hudson
Lockheed Ventura
Noorduyn Norseman
North American B-25 Mitchell

Autobiographical Aviation Books
by
Captain Donald M. McVicar, KC, OBE

Ferry Command (1933-1942)

Ferry Command Pilot (1933-1942)

South Atlantic Safari (1942)

North Atlantic Cat (1942-1943)

A Change of Wings (1943-1945)

Mosquito Racer (1945-1948)

More Than A Pilot (1949)

A Railroad From the Sky (1948-1954)

Distant Early Warning (1954-1957)

From Cuba to Oblivion (1961-1965)

Dorval Airport (1940-1996)

The Grass Runway (a novel)

Table of Contents

List of Illustrations

Preface: Flying With My Father
by Donna McVicar Kazo

It was 2011 when I realized that technology had finally caught up to my father. Don McVicar was always ahead of his time, the earliest of early adopters. At the age of twelve, in order to escape a mundane existence on the Canadian prairies, he fashioned a radio from peanut tubes that was good enough to catch signals from faraway American cities. That was in 1927. Nine years later, in the depths of the Great Depression, he managed to earn his Canadian Private Pilot's Licence; and sixty years later, in 1996, Dad correctly predicted the value of the then-mysterious Internet to authors, artists, and independent publishers.

Aviation has always been in the forefront of technology. Although today many scoff at the primitive features of aircraft from those wild first years after the Wright brothers' triumph, they were truly the bleeding edge of technology. Reading Dad's memoirs gave me a lot of respect for those flying machines, and even more for the people who dared to fly them.

Dad said he had to write 2,000,000 words before selling his first 60,000. In 1981 *Ferry Command* was published by Airlife in the United Kingdom. Four books quickly followed, but then Airlife decided they weren't interested in non-British aviation, leaving Dad without a publisher and many more adventures to share with us.

So my father, showing the same sort of resourcefulness and persistence that kept him alive in the air, found a way to self-publish, when he received an order, the books he wrote of his amazing life in the Golden Age of Aviation, and completed his story. In 1990 he divided the by-then-out-of-print *Ferry Command* into *Ferry Command Pilot* and *South Atlantic Safari*, adding new material to both.

In other words, this aviation pioneer had now become a pioneer in independent, print-on-demand self-publishing! Considering that his computer was primitive, with a tiny screen and a total of 30 megabytes of memory, his printer was dot-matrix and he relied on a Montreal printing company, Whiteprint, to physically manufacture the books, this was an astonishing accomplishment.

Meanwhile, in 1991, I had taken a position as Art Director and co-Editor with a small magazine. Didn't pay much, but thanks to the new field of desktop publishing, I could work from home while my daughters were young and never had to place them in daycare. How often I wished that Dad could have been able to use the state-of-the-art tools at my disposal: a powerful Macintosh SE and QuarkXPress! But there were a lot of miles between my Florida home and his in Dorval...but I vowed that one day, when the time was right...it just took a lot longer to get here than I thought.

I still recall that exciting moment in 1981 when I first cracked open my very own copy of *Ferry Command*, my dad's adventures finally in a real book! (Which girlfriend was my mother?) What a disappointment to find it rife with typos, and me such a stickler about that in my editing. Could be that's when the seed was planted for me to give it a makeover.

Getting back to 2011...that's when I saw a guy intently looking at his iPhone, asked him what was so interesting, and he told me he was reading a Kindle book. A bolt of excitement struck me: *it was time!*

I knew Dad would have been very proud of me when I figured out how to edit, format, prepare and publish *Ferry Command Pilot* on Kindle later that year, two decades after *Ferry Command* was published. My intention was to keep going, get *South Atlantic Safari* published as soon as possible. But something held me back. For one thing, realizing I was a bridge back to that important time in history, I felt compelled to read and research and to fill in some gaps. I am keenly aware that I'll never attain Dad's level of scholarship on the subjects of WW2 and aviation (among many others) but I do my best, because Dad and the others in his books deserve it. I've often wished I could have learned from him by sheer osmosis!

On the Internet I sought kindred spirits, and am delighted by the ones that have appeared (so far!). I created Facebook Pages for *Ferry Command Pilot* and Captain Don McVicar, OBE, which have brought to me some wonderful folks such as fellow Ferry Command historian and aviation journalist Ted Beaudoin in Ontario.

But what truly made this printed, "real" book possible was a connection, through Ted, to Bob and Jan Care; Bob's father, Captain Fred Care, flew in Ferry Command, and also knew Dad: small world, no surprise! To publish *Ferry Command*, Dad had had to sacrifice his copy of the commemorative book written by Air Commodore Griffith "Taffy" Powell, *Per Ardua Ad Astra, A Story of the Atlantic Air Ferry*. Only 500 copies were printed. Airlife had to basically destroy Dad's copy in order to scan the photographs.

At some point, Dad obtained photocopies of someone else's book; all I had to work with in 2011. It is very important to us that every photo used in Dad's original books (plus others!) is placed in our new editions. Fortunately the Kindle requires small image files, so Photoshop made his photocopies passable. We also placed them on my website, donnamcvicarkazo. com, in an Aviation Gallery so they can be viewed in greater detail.

But, for a printed book, *high-quality* digital images are required. So all of us owe a huge thank-you to Bob Care, for scanning in his dad's book and emailing it to me as a PDF, with his blessings, Jan for being our liaison, and Ted for putting ten years of his life into researching and writing about the "earth angels" of that unique organization, RAF Ferry Command, and sharing so generously with us and the world.

What this means is that the Kindle edition of *Ferry Command Pilot* will soon be revamped to include these better photos and new ones added to this edition. In the generous spirit of Captain Don McVicar, it is important to show as many of the people and aircraft mentioned in his books as possible. Most people within his books were not honored elsewhere for their contribution to victory.

Another new friend is renowned filmmaker William VanDerKloot, Jr., son of one of Ferry Command's most famous pilots, Captain William VanDerKloot. This twenty-seven-year-old American was chosen to fly Prime Minister Churchill on several top-secret missions in *Commando*, a B-24 Liberator. Bill Jr. honored his dad and Ferry Command with his excellent documentary, *Flying the Secret Sky*.

Other kindred spirits have appeared, too numerous to name here. The main thing is, as I once again "fly" with Dad, I am blessed with my own wonderful "aircrew" that have strengthened my resolve.

But my greatest happiness comes from my partnership with my amazing daughter, Christianna Cannon. Together we have founded Words on Wings Press, LLC, in order to publish her grandfather's books (and others, eventually) and she will keep the legacy alive. Christie is an artist, writer, editor and web designer extraordinaire who loves history and research; seems to be a family trait!

June 21, 2015 will be Don McVicar's 100th birthday, and we know there is no better way to celebrate than with the publication of this new edition of *Ferry Command Pilot* in paperback. 2015 is also the 70th anniversary of the end of WW2, and the 75th anniversary of the beginning of Ferry Command, with the first daring, experimental deliveries taking place in November, 1940. We are pleased to have the opportunity to honor so many fine individuals.

And now a few words from Himself:

Author's Notes to the Self-Published 1990 Edition of Ferry Command Pilot

The painting on the front jacket, "Frigid Fires," was created by my daughter, Donna McVicar Kazo. It is her portrayal of my Catalina Canso aircraft FP533 shrouded in St. Elmo's Fire over the desolate Greenland icecap as described in Chapter 16, titled "Crimson Route East."

My first book *Ferry Command* sold out, and is now out of print. Numerous readers have told me how much they'd like to buy a copy, but to date no publisher has seen fit to republish it.

So, I have taken the first steps toward self-publication. I had every intention of copying the original text, word for word, to disc on my computer. It didn't work.

Donna again:

Why didn't it work? Well, after writing several books after *Ferry Command*, Dad had a lot more confidence in his abilities. I find *Ferry Command Pilot*, and *South Atlantic Safari* to be more expansive, and truer to the unique spirit and voice of the rough-hewn but good-hearted Captain Don McVicar. So Dad let himself loosen up a bit, and *that* did work.

We'd be delighted to hear from you in any regard. Did you have a relative who served in Ferry Command? Do you have any pictures, letters, clippings? Please share them with the world. There are too many unsung heroes! Email us: **editor@ wordsonwingspress.com**

About the Illustrations

The wonderful illustrations of Lynn R. Williams, Airlife's artist, were not used in this new version due to copyright issues. Dad always encouraged me to draw and paint the planes he flew, and was my biggest fan, so I've tried to do justice to them in these pages.

And again, heartfelt thanks to Ted Beaudoin, Bob and Jan Care for sharing RAFFC Captain Fred Care's commemorative Ferry Command book in order to honor these heroic souls.

So, as Don McVicar was fond of saying, let's get the show on the road!

Don McVicar, D.C.T. Bennett, "Punch" Dickens and "Taffy" Powell, skilled pilots and aviation heroes all, share a toast at the 1980 Ferry Command Reunion held at Dorval, Quebec.

Foreword
by Air Commodore Griffith "Taffy" Powell,
CBE, RAF (retired)

Formerly Operations Controller of ATFERO, Ministry of Aircraft Production, then Senior Air Staff Officer of RAF Ferry Command, Dorval, Quebec, Canada.

I first read the draft of Ferry Command on Friday, June 13, 1980 in Montreal, when I was suffering from jet lag after my flight from France to attend the 40th reunion of the RAF Ferry Command.

Because sleep would not come, the tale was at first a handy means of dealing with some sleepless hours, but later as the chapters unfolded it developed a compelling attention and I finished my reading the same day.

Of course the series of adventures and misadventures of Don McVicar and his colleagues had "for me" the special effect of reviving old memories, but I could at the same time apply a critical eye. I use the words "for me" because for a long time I was in charge of the operations of the ferry organizations under its various Canadian Pacific Air Services, Ministry of Aircraft Production, Ferry Command, and finally No. 45 Group RAF Transport Command with headquarters in England.

This was a span of more than three years and I had been a member of the original ferry project since it started. Perhaps an historical note will help set the scene for readers who may not grasp at once the many civil aspects of what became the huge Royal Air Force operation.

Scene One Act One was in Washington, D.C. when the British Air Attache was studying the means available to transport aircraft procured in the United States to the battle front. The Lend-Lease procurement is in itself a tremendous story but for the moment this note can state that the Air Attache's first problem was a batch of Lockheed Hudson twin-engine bombers and a handful of four-engine Boeing B-17s—the "Flying Fortress."

Sea shipping was only practical for small aircraft and at the time not an insurable risk! The RAF was fully stretched on the home front and the United States was not at war. The solution was proposed by Mr. George Woods-Humphrey, the veteran Managing Director of Imperial Airways, who said he could do the air ferrying job, provided he could get the use of some of his old Atlantic pilots plus management assistance. To flesh out this skeleton, he arranged with Canadian Pacific in Montreal to use their premises, organization, and above all their "clout" on the Canadian scene.

I must quickly pass from the earliest days to set the scene for the McVicar story. Great contributions from "Punch" Dickens, OBE, DFC, the ageless doyen of Canadian aviation and from the Canadian Department of Transport who released first a dozen, then a flow of their radio operators. But it was the pilots who were the big problem.

The original handful of Imperial Airways pilots was augmented by borrowing from the RAF and the RCAF. But civilian recruitment was to provide the need for massive expansion. There were therefore contract pilots, navigators, flight engineers and wireless operators—hundreds in all who bore the brunt of the ferry programme. Towards the latter part of the war the RAF and the RCAF were able to release trickles of aircrew that had completed operational tours and were being rested, or had special qualifications; for example, flying boat experience. There was a later powerful surge of aircrew trained by the British Commonwealth Air Training Plan at Canadian stations.

When the flow of trained aircrew from the BCATP became sufficient the recruitment of purely civilian aircrew became unnecessary, but the civilians remained the backbone of an aircraft delivery system which eventually spanned the North Atlantic, the mid- and South Atlantic, and the Pacific.

There was no way by which the normal administration of the Royal Air Force could control and train the immense and far-flung force, so many supervisory functions were taken over by civil contract ground staff, especially the vital functions of flight training and testing which will explain references to, for example, Captains Hunter Moody, Al Lilly and the late Captain Wallace Siple.

Don McVicar arrived after the early recruitment problems, and although it may not read like it, many facets of the ferry business had settled down to routine. Whether McVicar's experiences rate him as a typical ferry pilot/navigator is not for me to say.

This book is the tale of his own deeds and I would not seek to alter a word of it.

What I can say is that he was a skillful and courageous pilot and he and his colleagues completely satisfied the Allied requirement of getting much-needed aircraft—the tools of war—to the battle front. Their efforts were a substantial aid to final victory.

—Griffith Powell, 1981.

Endless Triangles in the Sky

Only the thumps from late afternoon updrafts disturbed our ancient English Mark I Anson's flight as we sailed along towards our home base of Edmonton. We were completing a navigation exercise on that hazy, not-very-lazy day of August 25, 1941. I squinted as the red ball of the setting sun suddenly peeked around a towering white cumulus cloud, and said to my copilot, "The smoke from these damned prairie grass fires sure makes it tough to pinpoint."

"Sure does," Don Jamieson replied, "but our two Aussie navigators seem to be right on the ball."

I checked the slip of paper which one of our trainees had just passed up to the cockpit.

"Yep, this course correction and new ETA look like they could be bang on," I chuckled cynically, "and anyhoo, the worse the weather, the better the training."

"Up to a point, skipper, just up to a point."

"You've got a point there," I replied, at the same time thinking how terrible it was to be addicted to the lowest form of humor called a pun.

Even a copilot is entitled to complain about puns.

"Jeeze, that's lousy..." Jamieson began, but stopped abruptly as a genuine emergency invaded the cockpit.

"Goddam," I shouted as the port engine of the wooden Anson suddenly got so rough I thought it was going to jump out of its mount. I quickly closed the throttle, but still the vibration persisted. Was the rogue Cheetah engine going to vibrate right off the wing? When it finally shuddered to a halt its ugly black fixed pitch prop became starkly visible.

"Serve me right for taking this bloody 6048," I said bitterly.

"Yeah, 6047 never bit us once," Jamieson replied. Each crew had their own favorite aircraft.

This crew's immediate problem was to stay in the air. The Mark I Ansons the school flew had actually seen active service in England. Not quite "clapped out" but definitely worn. I pulled the lever controlling the good engine fully *back* which enriched its mixture. It seemed back-asswards, something like only a Frenchman would do. Then I pushed the throttle of our precious good engine fully forward to the EMERGENCY position. At the least the throttles weren't back-asswards. The engine roared reassuringly as I reached over my head and cranked on full rudder trim.

But the roar was deceptive and we began to lose altitude, even after I had let the airspeed decrease from our normal 120mph cruise to 90mph. It was a relief when we leveled off with the altimeter needle indicating we were just below 4,000 feet. That might have been a nice ground clearance back in the U.K. where the Anson was built, but it wasn't so good here, because there were hills up to 2,500 feet on our flight path.

Up on the panel the cylinder head and oil temperatures were holding just below the maximum limits but the very important oil pressure was slowly drifting down towards the *minimum* allowable 35 pounds. I reached forward and tapped the strangely shaped vertical instrument, willing it to remain high.

"We better watch that."

Jamieson was also staring at the offending gauge.

"Right."

He was obviously wishing as much as I to see the numbers stay in the green. He knew as well I did that if any of the temperature or pressure readings got out of line there wasn't a damn thing we could do about it.

"Take a look out and see how our fuel pressure is doing."

This instrument was mounted on the inboard sides of the engine nacelles. He reported that the needle was pointing straight up. Good enough! I put it out of my mind. If the fuel pump on the good engine packed up we'd get the message soon enough.

Slowly, painfully we passed Beaverhill Lake, then Cooking Lake. I was shouting into my microphone, but our usually reliable radio was failing to raise our company ground radio station or the DOT control tower. I wanted someone, somewhere to share our misery.

Finally, just before we crossed the North Saskatchewan River, and with the airport in sight, the control tower answered.

"Anson 6048 ten miles east, on one engine," I said, "declaring an emergency."

Without asking any stupid questions the man in the control tower cleared out some conflicting traffic and gave us number one to land. On the downwind leg I told Jamieson to crank the landing gear down.

He puffed his way through 160 tedious turns of a handle under my seat until the red warning light on the panel went out. Twin green knobs on the right side of the pedestal protruding from their covers also indicated the wheels were locked down. As I began final I selected "flaps down" with a lever right in front of me and told Jamieson to pump them all the way down.

I overshot a bit on purpose, because I believed it would be better to run off the runway rather than crash on an undershoot. With the good engine throttled right back, for a few seconds it was eerily quiet. I let the airspeed bleed down to the stall of 50mph.

Then, with a small bounce the trainer was safely on the ground. I reached down and carefully lifted the brake lever. Carefully, because there was only so much brake available from the bottle of compressed air. When it was used up you were in for a long coast, because there was no engine-driven compressor to refill the bottle.

We slowed down and I let the wooden bird coast clear of the runway, wondering if I looked as relieved as my copilot. Our Aussie students were grinning, obviously believing the whole operation was a great lark. I thought how marvelous it was to be young and ignorant! We were lucky to make the landing on the first try, because our Anson wouldn't fly on one engine with the landing gear hanging down.

And even strong young arms took a hell of a long time to turn that damn handle more than 160 times.

Jamieson and his brave captain were soon settling our nerves in a local beer parlor. He was a farm boy from Manitoba with a reddish complexion and light blue eyes, almost as tall as me at six foot even. He had a great sense of humor which made him a pleasant drinking companion. After we had knocked back a couple of cold drafts each, I leaned back.

"Too bad we weren't carrying bombs."

He stared at me, almost spilling his beer.

"Bombs! What in the hell do you mean?"

I hid my grin behind my hand so he wouldn't figure out I was pulling his leg.

"Well, the thing is designed to carry two 100 pound bombs and eight twenty-pound bombs or smoke flares."

"So?"

"So that would improve our single-engine performance, dummy."

In the West the occasional insult never hurt a friendship. In fact, under some circumstances being called a "bastard" was considered to be a sort of compliment.

He stared at me, obviously puzzled.

"But we were already down to our empty weight without bombs."

He'd picked the flaw in my beery logic. My little joke had fallen flat. I took the usual captain's revenge.

"You want any more landings, Don?"

"Sure do."

"Well then, you'd better laugh at my jokes."

"Ho, ho," he said.

"Better."

"Ho, ho. Ho fucking ho."

"Now you've got it."

For a time our conversation sort of dried up, and then he said, "You sure are cracking in the hours."

"Yeah, I've been trying to do two exercises a day. Since each exercise is about three hours long, even when Norm Forrester scrubs the odd one for weather I'm averaging better than 100 hours a month."

"Why work so hard? Hell, we get paid by the month no matter how much we fly."

"You talk like one of those Yank pilots who came up here to help out. I thought you knew I want to join the Royal Air Force Ferry Command. The more hours I've got the better my chances of being accepted."

"It's a pretty nice life here," he answered slowly.

"Yeah, but the Ferry Command is where the action is."

"What about those Liberator accidents at Prestwick the local newspapers have been headlining for the past couple of weeks? They sure wrote off a lot of pilots."

That very question had been bothering me, of course, so with some false bravado I answered, "That's a one-shot deal. The law of averages means it'll never happen again." I felt my fingers crossing themselves out of sight under the table.

"What about Ruth?"

Ruth was my wife. Like a lot of wives she liked a pilot's good pay, but not the risk.

"I hid all the newspapers with their damn big black headlines."

Jamieson laughed.

"Nice try. But don't worry, one of your so-called friends will be sure to tell her."

There was no answer to this remark, and sure enough one my "friends" did tell her. After a big dust-up I told her I was going away. She retorted that I seemed to be the only pilot who wanted to go. I suppose she was right, but the thought of spending the rest of the war making endless triangles in the sky didn't appeal to me. Our marriage began to deteriorate.

I had wanted adventure and had been seeking it for years. When I was twelve I took two peanut tubes and turned them into a shortwave radio so I could listen to such exotic places as KDKA in Pittsburgh. At seventeen I enrolled in the University of Alberta. At eighteen I got my ham radio call, VE4PH, which led to me enlisting in the local half-company of the Royal Canadian Naval Volunteer Reserve. About the same time I found out about girls. The competition was too much, so something had to give. Much to the distress of my father, I dropped out of college.

I decided to seek my fortune with the McInnis Fish Company. They used Grant McConachie's Ford Trimotor and a couple of Fokker Super-Universals on skis to fly whitefish caught in Peter Pond Lake in northern Saskatchewan. The aircraft landed on a small lake just east of Cheecham, about 200 miles north of Edmonton. There the fish were loaded into horse-drawn sleighs which were heated with potbellied wood-burning stoves. Then the horses forced their way through the bush to a siding of the Northern Alberta Railroad. When each heated reefer car was full, the fish would be rushed to the big Jewish market in the States, especially around Chicago. Fresh whitefish was considered to be a great delicacy. I couldn't figure it out, but frozen fish just didn't satisfy these gourmets.

Weather and position reports were vital for the operation and I was hired to act as radio operator at Cheecham. My duty was to communicate with our station at Peter Pond Lake, as the aircraft didn't carry radio. I believe that the fact that I supplied my own home built receiver and transmitter was the deciding factor in me getting that job, which was my first.

Or maybe the fact that my father was traffic manager for the little railroad might not have hurt my chances. My pay was $25 a month, plus bed and board. The "board" was heavy with fish, morning, noon, and night. My shackmate was a young pilot named Len Waagen. He was getting $75 a month with bed and board. I decided to become a pilot. For that kind of money, I'd learn to like fish.

I got my Private Pilot's Licence in 1936 after eight hours of instruction in a deHavilland Moth owned by the Edmonton and Northern Alberta Flying Club. My instructor was the sometimes patient, sometimes irascible English war veteran Maurice "Moss" Burbidge. He was an excellent instructor, who nicknamed me "Leopard" because of the color of my eyes. When he received the McKee Trophy, awarded annually to Canada's outstanding pilot, I always said it was really for having enough guts to turn me solo. Somehow he never called me a liar.

Earning a license is one thing, the first essential step, of course, but it took the better part of six years before I was paid to fly. The problem was the Great Depression. Money was tight and expensive flying time had to be carefully budgeted. Jobs were scarce and nobody wanted a pilot without experience. To get flying hours I took any job I could get.

One of them was in Los Angeles at Mines Field where I worked as a line boy for a flying school called American Flyers. The job called for swinging propellers, wiping down and refueling planes, sweeping the hangar floor, even cleaning toilets. The pay was a meager five dollars a week, but in addition, I got five hours per week in a Kinner-engine Fleet biplane. The only way to get ahead in aviation was to get more flying time, and in Canada the Fleet time would have cost me almost fifteen dollars per hour.

Food came second, of course. However, aided by ample supplies of oranges which could be plucked from convenient groves, a ten cent hamburger once a day, and free lodging in the loft of a friend's barn, I survived. The CAA flight test was tough and the inspector was tougher, but finally I qualified for an American private pilot's license.

Back home again, for some time I worked as a radio operator for Leigh Brintnell's Mackenzie Air Service. He paid $35 a month with no room and board, but being based in Edmonton helped. On weekends, when the weather allowed, I hopped passengers on a joyride for the Flying Club. The Club got the money, I got the time and my lucky passengers got a thrill.

In October 1938, the knowledge gained through the courses I had to pass to attain the rank of Leading Telegraphist in the Royal Canadian Naval Volunteer Reserve enabled me to write both Second Class and First Class Civil Radiotelegraph licenses at Victoria, British Columbia.

This led to a job with the Department of Transport as a radio operator at Cranbrook, deep in the Rocky Mountains, on the new Trans-Canada Airway. We handled flight plans and observed the weather which we hammered onto a teletype circuit. Very occasionally we had the pleasure of talking to a passing aircraft on 3105 kilocycles.

Aided by my new-found friend Don Revie, who owned a 40-horsepower Taylorcraft, on December 4, 1939, I passed the flight and ground tests to gain Limited Commercial Pilot Certificate No. C-1658.

Then I passed a tough Civil Service acceptance test for Canada's first Airport Traffic Controller's course. After a couple of months training in the first control tower at St. Hubert, Quebec, I passed all the tests, so that on March 26, 1940, I was issued ATC Certificate No. 9. I was sent to Winnipeg as chief of the first air traffic control tower in western Canada. This was a grand-sounding position with only one drawback— the tower had yet to be built.

But a few months later that had all changed. Using the common control tower frequency I was controlling the Ansons of No. 5 Air Observer School and the Lockheeds of Trans-Canada Air Lines and Northwest Airlines. My free hand operated the green, red, or white light to control non-radio-equipped aircraft and the Tiger Moths of No. 14 Elementary Flying School who were waiting for the mud to dry at their real base at nearby Portage la Prairie.

The war changed everything. Anyone who knew the difference between prop wash and a rain shower was suddenly in demand. I used my Limited Commercial Pilot's license to escape from my glass cage to fly for No. 2 Air Observer School back in hometown Edmonton.

But it was in Winnipeg that I got hired by a really nice World War One pilot turned bush pilot, Tommy Thompson of Canadian Airways.

I was twenty-six years old, with an intense desire to fly anything, anywhere.

After I had built up my flying hours, with the lure of the Ferry Command always in mind, I tried hard to get out of the AOS. No luck. With pilots at a premium on the prairies my manager had decided we were all too valuable to be let go. His name was Wilfrid "Wop" May and his main claim to fame was that it was he whom "The Red Baron" was trying to shoot down when that World War One German ace was killed by another Canadian, Roy Brown. Somehow I didn't think nearly as much of this claim to fame as he did.

He was one mean son of a bitch, a real martinet who just sneered at me and my dreams. I decided to put some pressure on him to secure my release. It seemed that somehow as we pilots got our night endorsements, this increase in pay we were entitled to never found its way into our pockets. I got right on the mat with him and threatened to form a pilots' union. One of the first things this union would do would be to find out what was happening to the missing money. Later I heard that the matter had been brought up in the House of Commons, but by that time it didn't matter to me, because I was long gone. May called me into his office and glared at me with his good eye as he swore I'd never get my release.

So I took the train for Winnipeg and unloaded my troubles on Thompson, May's boss. He saw it my way. Good man!

Back in Edmonton, May called me to his office and chewed me out for going over his head. Then, with great reluctance he signed my release, and I was so pleased I took the precious bit of paper without comment. But he still hadn't given up, and snarled that if I washed out with Ferry Command there sure as hell wouldn't be a job for me in the whole British Commonwealth Air Training Plan if he had anything to do with it. It took some effort not to punch the bastard.

Had I stayed, my future would have been secure. Like welders and machinists, AOS pilots were employed in what were considered to be war-essential jobs, so were exempt from Army military service.

Had I stayed, my marriage also would have been secure. War or no war, my wife wanted a constant, reliable husband. My signing up with Ferry Command ruined all her plans. She was so upset she refused to come to the railroad station on that November day of 1941 when I took the train for Montreal.

So the only people to wish me luck were my father, Don Jamieson, and "Westy" Westergaard, an old-time bush pilot, now the assistant operations manager of the AOS.

The Canadian National Railways Continental Limited took three days and three nights to steam into Montreal. After a while I got used to the continual swaying and was able to get to sleep in my cramped upper bunk. As we clanked and puffed along, the scenery was not spectacular; first the unrelieved, interminable flatness of the prairies, then the rocks and pine forests of northern Ontario, then the grey towns and cities of the east.

It was a time of reflection. What was I heading for?

*Pilots of No. 2 Air Observer School, Edmonton, Alberta, June 1941, with Mark I Avro Anson. Rear L-R: Ted Birch, Doug Littlejohn, Bill Cormack, Morris Fry, Ginger Coote, **Don McVicar**, Les Shears, Ab Coyne, George Johanneson, Gordon Latham, Art Irwin, Roy McHaffie, Don Jamieson, Dave Dyck, George Fletcher, Ralph Oakes. Front L-R: Spence Addeman, Bill Hodgin, Ab Hill, A. "Westy" Westergaard, Norm Forrester, W.R. "Wop" May, George Frank, Dave Kennedy, Frank Holdridge, Stan Seaton.*

Dorval Airport

In a very real sense the idea of delivering aircraft by air across the North Atlantic was a product of desperation. The British, holding out alone against Hitler, had to have warplanes. American factories were now producing them in quantity, but not enough were getting across the ocean. German U-boats were decimating the convoys across the North Atlantic, sending ships, seamen, and cargo to the bottom. An important part of that cargo was military aircraft. For much of the year, ships were the only means of delivering aircraft to Europe.

That was the case until November, 1940, precisely a year before I got into the act. The North Atlantic had never been flown in winter. The path to Europe was thought to be blocked by towering ice-filled clouds that could dump an aircraft into the sea. But the war effort was in dire straits and a decision was made by Lord Beaverbrook to make an attempt to deliver bombers by air— winter weather notwithstanding.

Aircrew from first Hudson deliveries, Gander, 1940, in front of one of the railway coaches used for sleeping, eating, and offices: Standing, L-R, W.M. King, J.C. Mackey, Snailham, D.J. Dugan, Unidentified, H. Carveth, H.A. Sweet, F. Pearce, A. Gilhousen, H.F. Parker, G.P.M. Eves, D. Anderson, J. Silverthorne, R.H. Page. Kneeling, L-R: A. Finch, J.D. Bledsoe, G. J. Byars, J.R. Fraser, D. Raine, J. Howard, F.G. Godfrey.

Photo (and the two to follow) by Griffith Powell, Royal Air Force, then-manager of the just-constructed Newfoundland base.

Aircrew in Gander from first Hudson deliveries, 1940: Standing L-R, W.B. Lyons, D.L. Gentry, R. Adams, C.M. Tripp, W.C. Rodgers, J.A. Webber, J.D. McIntyre, S.T.B. Cripps, N.G. Mullett, A.M. Loughridge, A. Andrew, N.E. Smith, G.R. Hutchison, J.W. Gray, D.C.T. Bennett. Kneeling L-R, D.B. Jarvis, H.G. Meyers, J.E. Giles, E.F. Clausewitz, K. Garden, W.T. Mellor.

The British were willing to take terrible losses in the attempt. If just fifty percent—fifty percent!— of the aircraft made it across the losses would be no worse than by sea. And three or four precious months would be saved in delivery from factory to fighting front.

Canadian Pacific Air Services was told to assemble flight crews who would attempt to deliver twenty-one Lockheed Hudsons fitted with long-range fuel tanks. The company hired a mixed bag of airmen: American, British, Canadian and Australian. They were to be the guinea pigs and they understood the risks. They were given intensive training at St. Hubert airport near Montreal, then sent on their way.

Aircrew from first Hudson deliveries, 1940: Back row standing L-R, R. Allen, R.F. Campbell, W.C. Hunt, S.H. Dekantzow, J.W. Allison, J.A.S. Hunter, F.C. Cornish. Front row, standing L-R, J.N. Wilson, A.G. Store, F.W. Coughlin, R.S. Leroy, F. Mitchell, N. Jubb, M.A. Alden, R. L. West, N. Steen. Kneeling, R.C. Jude, D.N. Rennie, F.L. Graham.

On November 10, 1940, the first flight of seven Hudsons, led by D.C.T. Bennett— the Australian long-distance record holder— took off from Gander, Newfoundland.

They were supposed to cross in formation, but the North Atlantic weather soon scuttled that idea. Yet to everyone's surprise, all seven landed safely at Aldergrove, Northern Ireland, on their own. Radio bearings and old-time pilotage had led them in.

A week later, a second group of seven also arrived safely. One aircraft of the third flight crashed, but the crew escaped unharmed. It was a successful conclusion of the first part of a great effort.

Now the effort became even greater in Montreal where the initial ferry group was rapidly expanded. Ground maintenance men were hired and Trans-Canada Air Lines provided valuable engineering assistance. Marconi Radio and the Department of Transport provided trained radio operators. Experienced pilots were hired from around the world.

In New York, the Clayton Knight Committee recruited shamelessly, despite the fact that America was not in the war. Scheduled airlines lost some of their best pilots until this bleeding was stopped by management.

British Overseas Airways loaned key personnel. Survivors of nations overrun by the Nazi war machine, such as Poles, Norwegians, Belgians, Czechs and Free French found their way to Montreal. There was even a Cuban on the payroll. Ferry Command became a truly cosmopolitan gathering of top-notch aviation talent.

Through the winter of '40-'41 deliveries continued through good weather and bad. More Hudsons, along with monstrous B-24's, the four-engine Consolidated Liberator, were joined by Boeing B-17 Flying Fortresses. The Liberator had enough gun turrets to defend itself, but the early Forts had been built lacking a tail turret, which meant it was cold meat for a fighter attack from the stern. Later models corrected the mistake, but it made a person wonder who made the blunder in the first place.

Catalina flying boats made the longest delivery flights: more than 3,000 long miles from Bermuda to the Firth of Clyde in Scotland. During that winter, losses of all types of aircraft were only four aircraft out of 185 dispatched.

Flight crews were returned by ship, a voyage that was often more hazardous and uncomfortable than the flight eastwards. Twenty-four hours over to Prestwick and twenty-four days to get back was common. Seasick men looked forward to the day when they would be returned by air. Only a Liberator had the range. Yet, amazingly during the return by sea, Ferry Command never lost a life. The U-boats might have been concentrating on traffic going the other way.

In the spring of 1941 the ferry group was officially named ATFERO,

First B-24 Liberator through Gander airport

short for Atlantic Ferrying Organization. Bennett left and CP lost control.

The name was short-lived. In June, President Roosevelt decided that Lend-Lease military aircraft being delivered to Canadian airports must be accepted by a military organization. So the RAF Ferry Command under the leadership of Chief Air Marshal Sir Frederick Bowhill came into being.

The change was purely cosmetic as far as the flight personnel were concerned. They retained their civilian status and by VE Day had delivered nearly 10,000 warplanes.

St. Hubert airport was proving to be too small, so the construction of a new airport at Dorval was pushed hard. In the blink of a government eye, relatively speaking, its three runways and spacious hangars were ready to accept and dispatch aircraft in September.

The air brakes squealed as the long train, packed with military personnel, began to slow down for Dorval. I pressed my nose to the window, taking in all I could of the giant base. In the distance I could see a line of twin-engine bombers, Lockheed Hudsons, the aircraft which would determine my immediate fate. I would have to pass a flight check on the Hudson, and I'd never even seen one before.

I had good health, exceptional reflexes and about 2,000 hours of flying time. But most of that time was on single engine types. And it was a long step up from the friendly Avro Anson I'd been flying to a hot modern aircraft like the Hudson.

The Continental Limited ground to a stop and I straightened my rumpled Harris tweed jacket, grabbed my bags and lugged them onto the wooden platform. I was one of the few to get off. Most of the men were continuing on to Halifax where a troopship would try to run them through the gamut of U-boats to England. I hoped they would make it safely and was glad I wouldn't be on board to find out.

There was a short line of taxis outside the station. I jumped into the first one. "Headquarters, Royal Air Force Ferry Command," I said, much impressed with my own importance.

The driver stared at me in his rear-view mirror.

"New pilot?"

I just grunted. It wasn't any of his business whether I was a new pilot or an old pilot, and I certainly didn't want to reveal that I was indeed a new pilot. The driver was unfazed.

"They've been having quite a few accidents, you know."

I didn't know. Such things were rarely published. Nor did I really want to know, so I kept quiet. But the driver kept on talking.

"Training, mostly, I hear. Those Hudsons they use got a nasty habit of ground-looping." He pointed at the airport infield.

"Take a look over there. Yesterday one of 'em burned to a crisp. Not much left, eh?"

I could see the lonely outline of a smoke-darkened wing sticking up from a pile of twisted metal. I forced out, "What happened to the crew?"

"Oh, they got out just by the skin of their teeth." He seemed to relish the thought.

"Great," I said, hoping I would do the same someday. We were now passing rows of Hudsons in their factory-fresh grey-and-white camouflage of Coastal Command.

Aircraft at Dorval airport awaiting overseas delivery by RAF Ferry Command

The taxi driver continued.

"You'll be checking out on Hudsons. One thing's for sure, they've got plenty to play with."

"Really?"

He pointed to a Liberator and imparted more wisdom.

"If I was in your shoes I'd get checked out on one of them. They're ugly bastards, but they've got lots of range." He chuckled to himself and added, "Those four engines'll put you in clover."

"Oh."

I thought, what is it about taxi drivers anyway? How come they all seem to know everything? Here we were at a supposedly secret wartime military organization with a cabbie who could have served as its briefing officer. If I ever have my own spy system, it will be based on taxi drivers.

He had more gloomy news to impart.

"British Overseas Airways uses Libs to bring you guys back. They call it the Return Ferry Service and this summer they had three crashes in Scotland and killed forty-four, I read. I used to drive a lot of I used to drive a lot of the Yanks, and quite a few of the guys who were left went back to the States. Too bad, they were good tippers."

I felt I had to say something.

"I read about those crashes out West."

My driver was off on another tack. He gestured to the right.

"Biggest hangars in Canada, maybe in the world, for all I know. That brick one up at the end is for Trans-Canada Air Lines. All the rest are for Ferry Command." Then he waved his arm to the left.

"They've got their own cafeteria and a hotel they call the Airport Inn. Plain but cheap."

"Yeah," I said, making a note about the cheap part.

He swung around a small loop and stopped in front of a sprawling two-story grey wooden structure with the RAF winged emblem displayed proudly over white, colonial-style doors.

"Here we are. This is the Admin building. Fare's a buck and a half."

As I paid, I thought that seemed a lot of money for a ten-minute ride. Well, maybe he was entitled to charge for the briefing.

I went inside and asked the uniformed guard where I could find the supervisor of civilian flight personnel. As he gave me the instructions, the way he looked me over somehow made me feel like I was a log about to be thrown on a fire.

Shrugging off this strange reaction, I followed his instructions down a long corridor and found myself outside a freshly painted door with only a number to identify it. I paused, summoning up my courage, then knocked three times. A brusque voice said, "Come in, it's open."

I found myself facing a man in civilian clothes who was seated behind a plain wooden desk. He had penetrating but rather withdrawn blue eyes. Although his face was a little jowly he looked very stern. He stood up and we shook hands.

"Welcome aboard. I'm Captain Wallace Siple."

"Glad to meet you," I managed to reply. He shot out his right hand.

"Well, let's have 'em."

I looked at him stupidly. He frowned.

"Your log book and your flying license, I mean. We don't hire just anyone off the street here."

"Yes, sir."

Had I already prejudiced my chances? I dove into my bag and produced my RCAF flying log book. He took it without comment and began to leaf through it from back to front.

I could hear him mumbling, "Two thousand hours total. Good. Five hundred hours multi-engine day. Just okay. One hundred and twenty hours multi-engine night. Good."

I was becoming more confident by the minute, but then he looked up.

"But it says here you've got only thirty-two hours instrument time. How come?" I rubbed my cheek as I sought an answer.

"The weather is always pretty good out West, I guess. But I've got nineteen hours Link time too."

That meant practice instrument flying time under the hood of a simulator devised by a genius named Ed Link. Most pilots hated it because it was more difficult to fly than an aircraft, and left a permanent trace on recording paper of all their goofups. Naturally all the ground types loved it.

Siple shook his head and my heart dropped as he said, "And just Anson time, too, except for a few hours in a Boeing 247 and a Lockheed 10. Most of the pilots we're hiring have lots of heavy twin time."

"I can learn," I replied, quite upset.

"Of course, of course." He softened his tone.

"Quite a few Canadian pilots like you have made the grade."

He looked at me keenly and added, "As a matter of fact that's exactly how I did it. I flew at No.1 AOS in Toronto with Peter Troup and "Babe" Woollett."

He snapped my log book shut, then handed it back to me. I felt a little more confident.

"Now let's see your flying license. Your medical better be up to date."

I was glad I had taken a recent medical as I handed over my red cardboard license, which was held together with a black shoelace. Below the first page heading, which told the world that I was entitled to hold a Limited Commercial Air Pilot's Certificate was an ID passport-type photograph of me glowering out at the same world.

Siple looked at me, then back at the photograph, and checked the date of my last medical. He nodded, then smiled. I realized I had passed one of his tests and immediately felt better, quite relieved, in fact. He apparently wanted to put me further at ease as he said, "Did anyone ever tell you that you look a lot like Douglas Fairbanks, Junior?"

I felt the blood rising in my face. This wasn't the way interviews for pilots were supposed to go!

"Naw," I mumbled as I squirmed on my hard wooden chair. Siple stared at me for a moment without saying anything. Then his voice hardened as he returned to business.

"This is the way we do it here. The first week you'll spend brushing up on navigation and meteorology. The second week you'll find out what makes a Hudson tick. You'll be examined after each course. If you don't make 85 per cent—OUT—no second chance. Understand?'

"Yes sir." Technical exams I didn't fear.

"Good. On the third week you'll get your flight checkout on a Hudson. We'll schedule you for some Link too. If you pass muster, we'll measure you up for your own Hudson and you'll be on your way over. Any questions?"

I thought a moment.

"About the Hudson checkout. How much dual will I get?"

"Six landings or two hours dual, whichever comes first."

I took a deep breath. Only two hours! Barely enough time to get the feel of it, let alone go solo. But this was no time to show my anxiety, so I kept a straight face.

"Right. Anything else I should know?"

"You'll get ten dollars a day while you're on probation."

This was quite a comedown from my Air Observer School pay of $450 per month. Well, I had no choice. I just had to make Captain.

"And after I check out?"

"When you check out you'll get a thousand dollars a month."

He paused to observe my reaction.

The mention of this really big money cheered me up. Not only that, but he'd said, "*when* you check out," not "*if* you check out." Little things like that are very reassuring.

Then he proceeded to let the air out of my balloon.

"Of course you were born on the wrong side of the border. The American captains get ten percent exchange and don't pay any income tax up here. But we Canadians sure do! You'll be giving more than half back to the government."

To me, pay was the last of my worries. I'd fly a Hudson for nothing! So I just nodded.

*R/O Hodgson, Captain Al Lilly, Air Vice Marshall Marix,
Captain Wallace Siple*

Siple added in a friendly tone, "I suggest you check into the Airport Inn right here on the field. It's a little rugged, but it's cheap. Now go along the hall and look on the notice board to find out when the first navigation class starts."

We shook hands again, and I left his office in a daze.

At the notice board I found my first lucky break. A navigation class was due to start the following morning. This was one course I was confident I could handle. I'd done plenty of navigation getting my lost students back to the Edmonton airport. But in addition, a friendly RCAF navigation officer at the AOS had helped me with the difficult tables essential for astro navigation. I'd volunteered for a lot of night navigation exercises where I'd let an up-and-coming copilot fly the Anson while I memorized the stars and took my shots.

Sextants were unavailable, so I'd used a small surveyor's level. Copilots liked flying with me because they got plenty of hours while I struggled to make the "cocked hat" of three position lines fit on my plotting board. The important things I'd been able to master were star identification and how to work the complicated tables against my timepiece, which had to be accurate to the split second.

I'd been led to believe that Ferry Command required astro-navigation capability from its Captains. Now I found this was not so. A normal flight crew consisted of a pilot, a radio operator and a navigator.

I was an oddity: all three rolled into one. The additional knowledge surely wouldn't hurt me; in fact, some day it might save my life.

The Airport Inn was constructed along the lines of an army barracks. After checking in, I dropped my bags on the floor of the spartan room they'd issued me and slammed the door. After I flopped down on the lumpy mattress of the iron-framed bed I gave a great sigh of relief.

I really felt that I was halfway to my goal.

Dorval airport in summer, circa 1941-42

The Checkout

I was dozing when someone rapped sharply on the flimsy wooden door. The face that poked itself into my cubicle was movie-star handsome. A hawk nose, deep-set blue eyes, flaming red curly hair, white teeth. All this over a pair of wide shoulders on a tall, lean, rawboned frame. Mr. Hollywood introduced himself in a Texas accent.

"Hi. I'm Johnny O'Neill from Fo't Wu'th. Saw you comin' out of Siple's office. I guess we're on the same course." He grinned.

How can you get rid of a friendly guy so you can catch up on some sleep? I didn't even try. I introduced myself and invited him to sit down on the room's only chair. If we were on the same course, maybe we could help each other through the rough spots. Besides, I couldn't help liking him. He was earnest and open.

O'Neill had been a barnstormer, then a pilot with a charter outfit hauling anything and anybody anywhere. We shot the breeze all afternoon, pilot talk, then walked over to the cafeteria for supper. Like similar setups it was an argument against eating. Lined up in the steam tables was a selection of thin stew, ground meat of unknown ancestry, greasy gravy, potatoes and last summer's carrots. Followed by Jell-O, which at least was colorful. O'Neill and I shook our heads. With food like this, it was going to be a long three weeks.

There were seven of us in the class, all experienced pilots, all folded absurdly into wooden desk-chairs that had last seen action in some third-grade classroom. The navigation instructor wasted no time. If we wanted to go from here to there we knew enough to draw a line on a map, measure the degrees from true north and allow for magnetic variation; and if the wind blew from over there at some assumed speed, we knew how to allow for drift. We all nodded.

He displayed a Dalton flight computer. On one side was a circular slide rule that had a little window for temperature and altitude corrections. When properly used they would convert the aircraft's indicated airspeed into true airspeed.

Right?—Right! we chorused. Old hat.

Then he turned it over. This was new. With a roller to set up true airspeed and a bezel to set up wind direction and speed, the eternal mystery of the wind triangle solved by a mere pencil dot.

Then we did a couple of days of meteorology. Types of clouds and their meaning. Depressions and highs complete with lines of equal barometric pressure called isobars. Cold fronts, warm fronts and occluded fronts. Dew point and fog. And so on. All seven of us passed.

Now the weekend stretched ahead. O'Neill and I had a debate. I took the position that now was the time to charge out and celebrate the first hurdle overcome. He argued that celebration was premature. He did have a point, so that weekend we sat around drinking Black Horse Ale and telling airmen's lies.

But as we lowered the level of the brown glass quart bottles we established a principle. Call it the Principle of Instant Access. When (no ifs allowed) we passed our flight check we'd both move into the Mount Royal Hotel. The Mount Royal contained the Piccadilly Club. The Pic was where the senior captains did their drinking. We'd be on top of the action in case some beautiful girl wandered in. We raised our glasses and drank to the future.

The next Monday we had a different kind of instructor. He grumbled that he was really a flight engineer who'd been railroaded into this lousy job. However, he'd provide us with the aircraft manuals, the diagrams of the fuel and hydraulic systems and the safety provisions. The rest was up to us. He slammed the door as he stalked out of the classroom.

It reminded me of when I was a student at the University of Alberta. Some profs provided only a few clues as to where the information his class needed was hidden. The rest was up to the students.

We all buckled down to learn the technical data. Our lives could well depend on how well we knew the guts of our Hudson. In the process we learned a lot of details that a pilot could never use, but at the same time we learned how to cope with emergencies.

We lost one man on the Hudson technical examination. He was a somewhat supercilious Englishman, the blue-blooded type who considered it unnecessary to study with mere Yanks and Colonials. Ferry Command thought otherwise. Now we were six.

That weekend O'Neill and I stuck to our resolution. The lights of Montreal beckoned, but we drowned our lust, which was getting pretty intense, in more of the stuff from the brown quart bottles.

Jack Parkinson, one of our classmates, joined us. He was another westerner with a quick sense of humor. His nickname was "Indian Jack." He was tall and slim with bright black eyes and black shiny hair. His face had an uncanny resemblance to that of a rhesus monkey. He'd made his escape from No. 3 AOS at Regina.

Later I found out that Parkinson's manager was a fighter pilot who had served in the Royal Flying Corps in World War One. Before managing the AOS he'd set up Prairie Airways on a scheduled run in Saskatchewan using twin Beechcraft. His name was Richard W. Ryan, and unlike Wop May, he had not tried to block his Anson pilots' departures for the big time. Maybe he wasn't as hard up for pilots—or maybe he had something against rhesus monkeys.

On the Monday when our Hudson flight checkout was due to start, the clouds were on the deck.

O'Neill cracked, "Even the birds are walkin'." I forced a wry grin.

We reported to No. 2 hangar where Civilian Flight Training had just been established. There we checked in with Captain Russ West, a thickset gruff man, almost the archetype of a veteran American barnstormer. His seamed, weather-beaten face looked as if it had been eroded by the waters of a thousand rivers. I learned that Parkinson and I would check out together. We presumed this was because we were the only Canadians on the course. The rest were Americans.

Parky and I were soon introduced to the man who would control our destiny, instructor Captain Hunter Moody. We had been told that he had been flying since he was twelve years old. Not only that, but that with his brother Humphrey had set the world's endurance record for light planes in 1939, a record they still held. They'd taken off in a Taylorcraft from their father's farm near Decatur, Illinois. Their Continental engine had kept them in the air for an unbelievable 343 hours, 42 minutes and 43 seconds. A truck racing along the ground below at the same speed as their aircraft had used a rope and a five gallon milk can to pass up fuel, oil, food and water. I never had enough nerve to ask what they used for a toilet.

Humphrey Moody

Hunter C. Moody

Happily enough for us, Moody was no prima donna. He was a sandy-haired man of powerful build, average height, penetrating hazel eyes and two buck teeth. We discovered he had already made several deliveries and had gained the reputation of being a fine pilot. He was also said to be a tough but impartial instructor. Each Monday he accepted two fresh students whom he injected with a quick and thorough flight course. By Friday, only four days later, on his sole recommendation, Ferry Command would have two urgently needed new Captains.

But if the two trainees weren't up to his standards there was no second chance. They would quickly be sent back to wherever they'd come from.

Now, in his sparsely furnished office, he stared at Parky and me with the usual cool appraisal of an instructor towards men who had a good chance of killing him.

"No flying today. They say the weather won't lift until tonight. But your Hudson's in the hangar, let's go down and do a runaround check."

"Yes, sir," we chorused, while I thought, my Hudson! This was real progress.

In the cavernous hangar we started our careful walk-around inspection of the stubby converted airliner. We knew at their factory in Burbank, California, Lockheed had whipped the Hudson together from the carcass of its twin-engine Model 14 airliner when the British Purchasing Commission had come shopping on June 23, 1938. We also knew that the 200 the Brits had ordered had filled an urgent need for light bombers while new designs were still on the engineers' drawing boards. A bomb-bay had been added, but the passenger windows were still in place. The distinctive twin rudders seemed to be almost touching the floor.

The parking areas at Dorval were usually well filled with aircraft awaiting delivery, modification, or allocation to overseas theaters.

Moody showed us where to look for trouble. Stains from oil or fuel leaks. Loose pipes or wires in the engine nacelles. Binding flight controls, cut or worn tires, and so on. As Captain of Aircraft we would have to sign the RAF Form 700 for each aircraft before we flew, certifying that we agreed with the maintenance people that it was serviceable for flight. Of course we knew that. Only when we were airborne would we find out the hard way if the bird was really serviceable. However, a good walk-around inspection before taking off by us, the pilots, whose ass was at risk, might catch something the ground engineers had missed.

Then we entered the side door and made our way up the fuselage into the cockpit, edging past the long-range fuel tank which, aided by the big tank in the bomb-bay would enable us to make a nonstop flight across the North Atlantic. Moody knew we had studied the controls and instrument dials long before, so now he told us exactly what he had in mind when the weather improved.

"I'll sit here," he said, wriggling around in the canvas-backed copilot's seat, "and I'll demonstrate just one takeoff and landing."

Parky and I had no comment, and none was expected. Still, I couldn't help thinking, this wasn't what could be called a hell of a lot of dual instruction.

Moody continued, "Watch out for a ground loop. This thing can swap ends so fast it'll make your head swim. That's due to the tail down position and the short coupling between the main gear and the tail wheel. Got it?"

"Yeah," we both said, although I really hadn't.

Jack Parkinson

Then he became even more serious.

"The brakes are powerful and damn sensitive, even vicious," he said.

I had noticed there were no toe pedals on the rudders. Just like the Anson. There was a lever sticking out of the pedestal but just to make sure, I asked, "How do you control them?"

Moody demonstrated as he talked.

"You pull out this lever here." I heard a sort of racheting noise. Then he said, "The more you pull the stronger the brake. Some people call it the Johnson Bar because it looks like a train engineer's control. The rudders react in the usual way."

"I've heard a lot of the ground-loop accidents are caused by the Hudson's brakes," Parkinson offered.

"You're right. But I've heard that Lockheed are building an improved model which will have toe-brakes and we'll get them soon. But for you two it's the Johnson Bar." He made a noise between a laugh and a snort which for some reason made me feel quite nervous.

"Jeeze." I said.

He looked at me quizzically, then quickly continued, "Don't get me wrong. The Hudson is an honest aircraft with damn good single-engine performance. If you handle it like the Thoroughbred it is it'll treat you just fine. Abuse it and it'll bite back. Ferry Command figures it's the perfect aircraft for checking out new pilots, because the guys who can fly her can fly anything ever built."

We climbed out of the fuselage considerably sobered, and I, for one, didn't sleep too well that night.

The next morning the sun rose on a clear day. A cold front had moved out all the low cloud. It had also provided a brisk, gusty wind from the northwest. We would be using runway 28; the numbers indicated the magnetic heading with the last digit. This would give us a cross-wind from the right of about 30 degrees. Would Moody cancel our training flight? With such a stiff cross-wind many training schools would have scrubbed the exercise.

Not Ferry Command.

Parky and I tossed a coin and I lost. So I climbed into the left-hand seat and looked over at Moody. He signaled to start up the engines. He seemed completely unconcerned as I tried to not forget any of the complicated routine. Lock brakes, crack goose-necked throttles, pump up fuel pressure, prime, engage starter, then prop blades, then both mags on. Mixture controls forward to auto-rich and adjust throttles as the Wright engines coughed their usual clouds of blue smoke before setting into a steady, powerful rumble.

After they had warmed up, Moody got taxi clearance, then waved away the chocks. He used his left forefinger to indicate I should start taxiing. I unlocked the tail wheel, then reached down and released the brakes. I could feel Parkinson's hot breath on my neck. He was taking it all in as we moved away from the parking ramp.

Just as I had feared, I found the hand brake awkward, as I taxied to the downwind end of the runway. The Anson's hand brake was nothing like this! Moody had told me to not use the tail-wheel lock, which would have helped me keep straight. He wanted me to become accustomed to using the brakes, throttles, and rudders together. As a result, I over-controlled and reeled down the taxi strip like a drunken pelican before I got stopped at ninety degrees to the end of the runway.

I sneaked a glance over at Moody. He seemed calm enough and just pointed to the engine instruments, indicating he now wanted me to do an engine run-up. I breathed an involuntary sigh of relief. Apparently I'd performed within his limits so far. So I went through the engine check-out, exercising the props and checking their feathering buttons. With the throttles forward to 43 inches of manifold pressure the engines roared smoothly as the cockpit shook and vibrated. Back to thirty inches of boost where I checked the carburetor heat and each mag. The drop was normal. All the other instruments were normal as well. Moody called the tower.

"Hudson 9069 ready to take off."

The tower gave us clearance and my instructor signaled that he wanted me to take position on the runway. When I got more or less lined up, over the roar of the engine, he shouted the famous flying instructor's phrase.

"I've got it!"

I raised my hands and drew back my feet to show I'd relinquished control. He got properly lined up and reached forward and engaged the tail-wheel lock, then braked to a stop.

"This is the most important part," he proclaimed, his voice serious. "Get lined up straight. If you start off at an angle you'll never get straightened out. Understand?" Parky and I chorused, "Yes, sir."

"Okay, now follow me through."

I gently placed my feet on the rudder pedals, left hand on control wheel, and right hand just behind the throttles. Moody now began to open the throttles, explaining as he went.

"I'm going to lead the left-hand throttle to take care of the torque. The Hudson's bad for that, but with this cross-wind I won't need much of a lead. The tail wheel will keep her straight until I get about fifty knots."

He applied power a lot more quickly than I had expected and I felt the acceleration forcing me back in my seat. We were going down the runway as straight as an arrow and I saw the airspeed indicator begin to flicker. As it passed through fifty Moody continued his story.

"I'll raise the tail now."

I felt the control wheel move forward and his feet kicked the rudder gently. We deviated not one degree.

"I'll let her fly off the ground at ninety knots," he said, and by the time he'd finished speaking I felt the control column moving backwards.

I didn't even feel our wheels leave the ground. He applied a bit more right rudder and lowered the right wing to keep us from drifting off the runway heading. He used his left thumb to tell me to raise the landing gear. The hydraulic system groaned and then the two green lights were replaced by two red ones. As the airspeed passed through the 110 knot safety speed, he reduced the engine and prop settings to climb ratings. At 500 feet he commenced a rate one turn to port.

It was the most polished exhibition of flying I'd ever seen.

He shouted, "You've got it!" and I took control for the first time. The powerful aircraft, lightly loaded, felt like a spring colt as I did a few gentle turns, climbs, and descents on a wide square circuit. I barely had time to look back at Parky with raised eyebrows. This indeed was dual instruction with a minimum of wasted time.

Much too quickly for me, Moody got initial approach clearance from the tower and ordered, "Set up approach power and turn onto base leg. Make sure it's ninety degrees to the runway heading."

After I had sorted all this out to the best of my ability, he said, "I got it." We both checked carefully for other aircraft as he set up an approach with a descent of 500 feet per minute. He signaled me to lower the landing gear as he crabbed onto the runway heading, then asked for fifteen degrees of flap.

"Enough in this wind," he said. We passed over the threshold and before I was quite ready the main wheels kissed the runway. Moody had kicked off the drift a microsecond before we touched. A slight forward motion of the control wheel to stop any incipient bounce, and we were rolling along, still at a fast clip.

I started to say, "Very nice..." but Moody cut me off.

"Stay on your toes," he shouted, and I saw that he was still intently staring down the runway. He didn't turn his head.

"This is the tricky part. She'll swing right off if you aren't careful. I'll load the tail down and you dump the flaps. The rudders get blanked off, so you gotta be ready with the brakes and maybe even some throttle."

However, on this landing none of the correction action was necessary. The locked tail wheel thumped down and took over. I relaxed, but not for long.

Moody raised his hands and said, "You have control." I snapped to attention. This time my taxiing was improved. I found that if I stayed ahead of the responsive aircraft with just a touch of throttle and rudder, excessive brake was unnecessary. Back at the button of 28 I did a careful cockpit check, making sure to not overlook the elevator trim tab setting. This powerful airfoil was used on landing to help get the tail down. But if not properly reset at neutral before takeoff, the result could be control forces so powerful that no pilot could hold the control wheel forward. When this happened the Hudson zoomed up until it stalled. Men had died because the flight crew had forgotten to reset the elevator trim tab.

I opened the throttles and did my best to emulate Moody, and was able to stay on the runway in spite of the cross-wind. Around and around I went, and was just getting the feel of the aircraft nicely when, after my fourth landing, Moody signaled me out of my seat.

"Okay, Mac," he said with a slight grin, "you're ready to go solo." I couldn't believe it.

Now it was my turn to stand behind Parkinson. He was shakier than I had been. Moody gave him seven landings before he was satisfied. We taxied to the ramp.

"Watch that swing. Do four landings each," he said, then added, "good luck." He then proceeded to leave the aircraft. Suddenly I felt very lonely.

I did my four landings, which weren't bad, although I might have scared Parky a little. Then he did his four landings and he scared me silly. He was rough and far behind the airplane.

When we climbed out to good old Mother Earth we were both a bit wobbly. When we reported to Moody in his office he seemed satisfied. After all, we'd got his airplane back in one piece.

Our checkout continued the next day, this time in Hudson AE566. Again I was first and just after taking off Moody fastened a canvas curtain which cut me off from the outer world. It was the dreaded "hood." Now in the cramped cockpit I had only a half-dozen flight instruments to tell me what the Hudson was trying to do to me.

At my side sat a much different Moody. No more kindly suggestions on how to keep the aircraft docile. For a short time I flew the level courses he called out, working hard to hold my altitude within a few feet.

Then he said, "I have control," and began to do things which made the Hudson resemble an unbroken rodeo stallion. This exercise was called 'recovering from unusual positions.' Moody was finding some real beauts that I'd never dreamed existed. He'd rack the aircraft into sixty-degree banks with violent rates of climb or descent, then suddenly release the controls with a shout of "You've got it!"

I took it. the artificial horizon, directional gyro, turn and bank and airspeed were only references as I fought to get the Hudson back to normal level flight. In the gloom of the hood I was sure I was sweating buckets.

Then came the now-hateful words, "I've got it!" More torture. He did a couple of full stalls before giving the controls back to me. I still don't know how I avoided going into a spin or a death spiral.

Now he covered up the artificial horizon and the directional gyro, leaving me with the primary flight instruments of turn needle and ball, the airspeed and the ever-swinging magnetic compass. He called for rate one turns to a heading. Then rate one turns to a heading without the use of a timepiece. More turns while climbing or descending 500 feet per minute. These maneuvers were easy enough to do in the Link or a light aircraft, but very difficult in a heavy aircraft.

Moody made no comment as he put me through his tests. I assumed that meant I was passing. He gave me back the full instrument panel, then, without warning shut off the fuel to one engine. There was an instant and violent yaw which I corrected with rudder as the directional gyro tried to spin away. Keep the wings level!

Now it was urgent I identify the dead engine and take immediate action. The rudder pedals provided the vital information. I was using heavy right rudder.

Useful rule: heavy foot same side as good engine.

So Moody had cut the *port*.

Fast action called for as speed decays. Quickly reach down pedestal and use little handle to crank on plenty of rudder trim.

Leg pressure relieved. While right hand down, make quick flick over controls to make sure gear and flaps retracted.

Never dare to take eyes off flight instruments.

Six seconds gone.

More mixture control of good engine to rich, and increase prop revs and boost. Time now to retard throttle and prop on dead engine and set its mixture control to idle-cutoff.

Reach up for red button that will activate the feathering motor. Prop blades must be streamlined with air flow or Hudson won't fly on one engine.

Pause.

Pause to make sure I'm about to feather the proper engine. Remember stories of stupid reactions which caused horrible accidents.

Now hold proper red button down for three seconds.

One thousand and one.

One thousand and two.

One thousand and three.

Re-trim rudder as prop blades turn.

Fifteen seconds gone.

Juggle power to maintain single engine safety speed of 110 knots. Check course within five degrees. Check altitude within fifty feet.

Wipe forehead.

Moody calls for a couple of turns both ways to prove the Hudson won't drop out of the sky when turned into a dead engine.

Regain course and altitude.

"Whew!" I exclaim.

Sparse praise from Moody.

"Not bad. Put it all back together again."

Putting it all back together again was almost as difficult as taking it all apart.

Turn fuel back on by feel. Eyes glued to flight instruments. Throttle cracked. Ignition on. Hold that red button in until 1,000 revs show. Engine farts and then fires. Mixture full rich. Prop control fully forward. Watch course and re-trim rudder. Keep power low until cylinder heads and oil

© 2011-Donna McVicar Kazo

Lockheed Hudson

warm up. As the needles creep back into the green, increase to normal cruise power and re-trim.

We're back in business.

Now it was Parky's turn. He sweated his way through our airborne torture chamber until Moody was satisfied and indicated he wanted to go back to the airport. Parky complied, finishing up with an almost professional landing.

At the usual debriefing, Moody was kinder than usual. He told us he'd authorize the use of a Hudson for us to practice in as he had another couple of students to work on.

"Put up the hood and be as mean to the other guy as I was to you."

Parky and I looked at one another, and I thought I saw a gleam in his eyes. No mercy there! So I'd act the same.

Moody sort of smiled as he saw our byplay.

"When you get tired of instrument work, do some cross-country navigation. Use Ottawa and Smith's Falls, they're our favorite turning points."

"Yes, sir," we chorused, and for two days we took full use of our private aircraft. I couldn't help wondering what other outfit would trust a Hudson to such inexperienced students as we were. But maybe he was right. Each of us really tried to put our "friend" in as tight a position as possible. The navigation was a cinch for ex-AOS pilots.

Then it was time for the final checkout. I plotted a course to Smith's Falls using the false wind Moody had supplied. With Moody back in the right seat, after taking off and setting course, I got a pinpoint and figured out the correct wind. My Dalton whirled and I changed my course and worked out a new Estimated Time of Arrival. After hitting Smith's Falls on the nose I set course for Ottawa.

A few moments later Moody told me to rig the hood while he flew. Black in the gloom again I could feel him making turns while getting me well and truly lost. It was time to prove the radio range practice Parky and I had been doing had sunk in. ears must now work in close coordination with feet, hands and eyes. Same course and altitude limits. Tough.

More concentration. More sweat.

The possibility of another simulated engine failure without warning. Happy thought!

To open the scenario I had no idea where in hell I was. Which meant I had no idea where Dorval was.

Lost in the big, big sky.

I put my earphones on because now I would have to identify one of the four legs of an Adcock radio range which was sending the letter A—*dit-dah*—in two of its quadrants and the letter N—*dah-dit*—in the two intervening quadrants. Where the two letters overlapped the signal became a steady tone three degrees wide. That was the beam. The legs could be adjusted and one of them, called the approach leg, was directed at the runways of the associated airport, ideally, about three miles away.

At the transmitting station the four legs intersected and formed what was called a cone of silence. It could be identified by a buildup of signal strength, a short dead period when nothing was heard, followed by another buildup. After positively identifying the cone, a letdown using the approach leg could commence.

I turned on the radio range receiver, adjusted the volume control and soon heard the familiar 800 cycle tone. But hey! Something's wrong here! The identifier was sending *dah-dah-dah, dit-dah-dah*—O-W! Moody had pulled a dirty trick by setting up the receiver on Ottawa.

I cranked the handle around to Dorval's frequency of 248kc and carefully checked the identifier. There it was—*dit-dit-dah, dit-dah-dit-dit*—U-L.

I gave Moody a reproachful glance, but all I got in return was a slight smirk. All's fair in love and war and pilot checkouts!

I flew the compass heading of the bisector of the N quadrant until it started to fade. Now I knew which quadrant I was in, and in this case had to make a 180 degree turn. Once settled down it was time to turn ninety degrees until I intersected one of the legs, checked the steady tone of the on course and then another ninety degree turn to the left.

Hello! Here's a strong A!

Now I knew which leg I was on. I bracketed it down using a series of small course changes to allow for the wind. After I identified the cone of silence I turned and flew out on the west leg for three minutes. Then it was time for a procedure turn south of the leg, which got me back on the leg pointed toward the airport. Carefully bracketing the leg I let down to

1,200 feet over the cone. I made sure the gear was down, dropped half flap and reset the engine power to maintain a descent of 500 feet per minute at ninety knots.

Now as the tension built the hood seemed all-confining. It took a lot of concentration to stay in the center of the narrow approach beam. As 417 feet showed on the altimeter, which was just 300 feet above Dorval, Moody reached over and ripped down the hood. Dead ahead was the welcome sight of the whole 5,000 feet of runway 10. I'd passed the tough instrument and aircraft check successfully.

"You did okay. Don't bother to land. We've got no time to waste. Get out." Parkinson took my place and went through the whole difficult procedure again. He made a good job of his test. We were well satisfied as we walked away from our Hudson.

Later that day the grapevine reported that a pleasant young man known as "Jay" Bird from Mississippi had been washed out. Now we were five, and all we had left was the night-flying test.

The next evening Moody loaded a full house of pilots into his Hudson. In addition to Parkinson and me he had O'Neill and a couple of other would-be Captains named Pringle and Lange to check out at night.

For us two ex-AOS pilots the night flying was the easiest part of our captain's check, because the Air Observer Schools did a lot of their flying at night. They were training aircrew for Bomber Command who were forced to fly only under the cover of darkness after day bombing had proven suicidal.

O'Neill had no trouble, and Carl Lange, a saturnine pilot from Pennsylvania, also made the grade. But Pringle, a quiet man from Kansas, didn't.

Now we were four.

As we relaxed in my room at the Airport Inn, we planned the biggest graduation party Montreal would ever experience. Montreal girls get ready: *Montez vos gardes!*

We were quite certain that Ferry Command was the premier military flying organization in the world. And look! Here comes the pick of its pilots.

Maybe we were more than a little arrogant, but we were young, and we were positive that not many pilots could have survived the tough checkout we had just gone through.

It was after midnight when I fell into bed. Now all I had to worry about was doing my duty. Good would triumph over Evil. Freedom over Nazism. Us over Them.

What the hell, I might even survive the war.

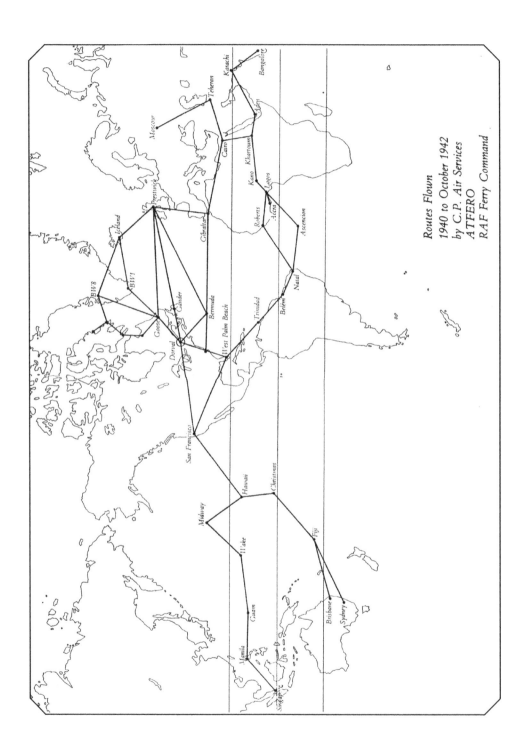

Routes Flown
1940 to October 1942
by C.P. Air Services
ATFERO
RAF Ferry Command

The Piccadilly Club

The Mount Royal Hotel was all I had dreamed it would be. I bounced up and down on the bed. The mattress was deep and soft, and wide enough so that I could actually turn over on it without falling off. There was a carpet on the floor. On one wall was a painting of ducks either taking off or landing, I never could decide which. I tuned in soothing music from my radio as I sat in the comfortable armchair reading the very latest edition of *The Montreal Star* under my reading lamp.

Best of all, I had a private bathroom. The towels were two inches thick, the bathtub three feet deep. Lots of hot water. A bathmat on the polished marble floor. Gone forever the rows of tin washbasins, public urinals and those horrible crappers without doors.

Yes, sir! This was the way a fully-fledged, red-blooded variable-pitch Ferry Command Captain should live.

A loud, strange noise jangled my reverie. For a moment I didn't recognize the sound of my own phone; it had been a long time since I'd had one.

A voice wanted to speak to Captain McVicar. Captain McVicar? Oh yeah, me. I recognized the Texas accent of Johnny O'Neill. Obviously he had some devilment in mind. I attacked before he did, using an affected drawl.

"Captain O'Neill, I presume? The famous American bird man and bullshit artist?" Somehow my friendly insult didn't come out exactly as planned.

O'Neill just laughed.

"Look who's talkin'. Meet you in five minutes for a drink in the Piccadilly Club."

"You bet."

In the intimate room of the exclusive club O'Neill's red thatch stood out like a burning haystack. The maitre d' politely introduced himself as Bob, at our service. I was impressed. No wonder the senior captains liked this place. The red leather armchairs were deep, soft and comfortable. Large old fashioned chandeliers cast a diffused coppery glow on the antique oak walls. The serving bar was far enough removed so that the drone of waiters' voices and the crashing of glasses were out of earshot. Altogether it was

Among the many different uniforms enjoying the beautiful Normandie Roof of Montreal's Mount Royal Hotel, New Year's Eve 1941 are Ferry Command pilots and their wives: Jack Ruggles, front left, across from Gracey Ruggles; next to him, Bud Merrill; unidentified woman; King Parker and Carol Parker. Others have not (yet) been identified.

very much like the Officers' Mess of an Air Force squadron; which, for Ferry Command, it was.

A pleasant-looking red-faced waiter was standing at the ready close to our highly polished table. We ordered VO and Coke. He told us to call him Tommy. We looked around, checking the stock. Bad news. No unattached girls.

A compactly built man with a winning smile joined our table. He turned out to be another good ol' Texas boy, Captain Don Teel. His bright blue eyes sparkled as he congratulated us on making captain. But his smile disappeared when O'Neill asked him how British Overseas Airways Return Ferry Service was performing. He shrugged his shoulders and reported he'd heard of no crashes lately.

He had been at Prestwick during the summer when the Return Ferry Service had crashed three Liberators, killing all on board. He and four radio officers were the sole survivors of forty Ferry Command flight personnel. One third of all our captains had been wiped out. He'd attended the mass funeral, then on his own had undertaken to write to the next of kin. We murmured what a great thing he'd done.

"What did our union, the Transoceanic Pilots Association, do about it?" O'Neill wanted to know.

"We didn't get what we really wanted," Teel replied slowly, "which was to use our own pilots on the Return Ferry Service, of course."

"How come?" I asked.

"Well, Air Chief Marshal Bowhill flew over to Prestwick right away and convinced most of us that he would personally guarantee that in future BOAC transatlantic pilots would be properly checked out."

"And the boys bought it?"

"Some quit on the spot and went to Miami and joined Pan Am Ferries. But quite a few others believed Sir Frederick who was quite a salesman that day. He had to be, because BOAC had started out with seven Liberators in the Return Ferry Service in April. By September they had four left. We knew our own men could do a hell of a lot better than that."

"I should hope so," I grumbled.

O'Neill got back in the act as he too grumbled, "Sixteen hours in a cold, noisy, uncomfortable bomb-bay riding behind pilots you don't trust. Oh my!"

"I suppose that's why we get the big bucks," Teel said with a tight grin.

That seemed to close the subject so O'Neill checked his watch.

"I wonder what's happened to Parky?"

I replied, "He'll be here sooner or later, so quit worrying. He told me he'd bring his brother-in-law who's just got his wings in the RCAF."

"I hope they've got some good black book numbers," O'Neill said fervently. "I feel like I must have made a mistake and signed up to be a monk in some damned monastery."

We both looked around again. There were plenty of attractive girls, but they all had escorts. After three weeks in solitary it seemed downright unfair. We had another round. Tommy thought things were a little slow tonight.

I looked up to see Parkinson's ugly face peering down at us. His voice boomed throughout the room.

"Hi, guys!" was his greeting, then he turned and with a grand sweep of his arm beckoned to some unseen companions.

There were two of them, and the first one didn't excite us. He was a tall blond youth in the blue uniform of the RCAF. The second, on the other hand, electrified us. She was stunning. Her jet black hair was set off by speckles of snow which had not yet melted. Her cheeks glowed with perfect health. Her eyes, of a strange hazel-blue color, were gabled by long lashes.

O'Neill and I jumped up for the introductions. The pilot's name was Kevin Kelly. I shook hands with him gravely. I had every intention of stealing his girl. Her name was Maureen, and she had a vibrant personality that quickly brought life to our table. How nice to meet you both. Are you really in Ferry Command? They're doing wonderful work. Good for you. Her brother was overseas with Coastal Command. Her father had been in the trenches in World War One. And in the Boer War too.

We responded in kind. Parky and O'Neill became expansive, with various stories of their adventures in the past. I came up with some thrilling bush pilot lines. Maureen was obviously enjoying the competition for her attention. We were all having a marvelous time. All except Kelly, that is. He sat and steamed into his Scotch.

I felt I had to make my move fast, and it had better be good. "Say Maureen," I blurted, "some people say that the picture on my pilot's license makes me look like Douglas Fairbanks, Junior. Would you like to see it?"

"Of course," this super girl answered, while my three male companions sneered. I'd beaten them all to the punch.

I looked across the table into her eyes.

"The light's bad over there, why don't you come over here?"

I was trying for the physical contact, the essential starting point of every courtship ritual. Maureen smiled mischievously as she jumped up and glided around the table. Then she lowered herself onto my chair's wide arm and *sat on my hand.*

The effect of this welcome and unexpected contact on me was sensational. A powerful flow of sexual empathy I could almost see surged between her soft behind and my bony hand.

She looked at my license.

"My, what a remarkable resemblance!"

"Aw, shucks," I simpered.

My three male companions sneered again, this time with more venom. Then we talked about movie actors we liked. Just the two of us. I sneaked a look at my competition. Parkinson was intent upon another target across the room. O'Neill was watching the scene with a half-smile. He'd given up.

But Kelly could stand it no longer. He stood up and took her arm.

"Come on, Maureen," he said firmly, "we're late already. Let's get going." She hesitated for just a moment. I felt my heart skip a beat. Maybe she would tell Kelly to leave without her. But no, she stood up like a good little girl. The temperature of my hand dropped about a hundred degrees.

"Good luck," she smiled, "maybe I'll be seeing you later." Kelly's scowl deepened.

We had just ordered another round when O'Neill beckoned to a thickset man with a creased face and a black moustache. He sat down and I recognized him as Captain Ralph Adams, originally from Kentucky. He'd been on the very first Hudson delivery to U.K. the winter before. He said he was waiting for Clyde Pangborn, a long-distance flyer who had made a record-setting journey in a single engine Bellanca from Japan to Wenatchee, Washington. I was proud to be seen with the veteran flyers.

Then Pangborn arrived, a mild man with deep flight wrinkles at the corners of his eyes and his shoulders rounded from countless hours behind the controls. That summer he and Bernt Balchen, a Norwegian air pioneer, had delivered a Catalina flying-boat to Singapore. I decided this was a good time to find our about these marvelous flying-boats with their two engines and thirty hours of endurance.

If I checked out in a Cat I'd be able to see parts of the world far removed from concrete runways. Pangborn had taken sixty-five hours to fly from San Diego through Hawaii, Midway, Wake, Guam and Manila to the Royal Australian Air Force base in Singapore. Then he and his crew had been brought back by Pan Am Clipper through Hong Kong.

The exotic names excited me. This was what being a ferry pilot was all about. Palm-lined beaches, tropical seas, well-sanded girls. Pangborn turned out to be very nonchalant about his Pacific adventures, probably because he'd described them countless times before. But never to such a rapt audience.

After drinking the rounds O'Neill and I had bought them, the two veterans excused themselves and left.

"Well," I said as they disappeared around the corner, "now we know a lot more about the history of Ferry Command."

Parky had an irreverent answer.

"Like it or not."

He paused before putting into words the thought that was uppermost in all our minds, then added, "I thought tonight was the night we were supposed to make history with Montreal women. Hell! Looks like we've struck out!"

"Sure does," O'Neill said sadly while I just stared into my empty glass.

Parkinson shrugged his shoulders.

"I guess we might as well call a taxi."

None of us really wanted commercial sex, but the pressure was intense and as we had no better solution, we decided to give it a go. There was nothing particularly memorable about our visit to Madame Gaby's place on Mountain Street. The girls were friendly and very expert.

O'Neill was a little upset when he saw the taxi driver enter with us, obviously about to enjoy the same relaxation we were. "It ain't fittin'," he grumbled. I sort of felt the same way, but I couldn't pinpoint the exact reason. Maybe we were closet snobs.

We spent the next week crewing up and were eager to get going to deliver our own Hudson. But on the seventh, the first Sunday in December, 1941, aircraft from four Japanese aircraft carriers bombed Pearl Harbor. This appalling disaster put most of the U.S. Navy's Pacific Fleet out of action. Luckily their aircraft carriers had been at sea, or they would have undoubtedly gone to the bottom as well.

The American bureaucrats and high military brass were in deep shock. They reacted in a very panicky manner by freezing all aircraft deliveries from the factories.

This meant that dozens, maybe hundreds of aircraft desperately needed in Europe lay idle all over the United States.

While we Ferry Command pilots laid idle around Montreal.

Christmas and New Year's came and went with nothing to celebrate. What news filtered through from the war fronts only worsened our already gloomy mood.

Hudsons enduring a Canadian winter

A Captain-Navigator

The slack period after Pearl Harbor, however, gave me an opportunity to qualify as a Captain-Navigator. This meant that when deliveries resumed I could do my own navigation and take an extra copilot.

The two weeks of intensive ground school study began with Flight Lieutenant Bill Longhurst in charge. He was a pleasant, intellectual Canadian who had joined the RAF before the war on a short-service commission. He had served with Coastal Command, whose pilots had to pass tough navigational examinations, the equivalent of a civil First Class Air Navigators Certificate. He was surprised when I showed up for the first class with copies of *Air Navigation, British Empire Edition*, and *The Complete Air Navigator* by D.C.T. Bennett.

"You must have been interested in navigation for a long time," he said as he leafed through my books.

"I suppose it goes with my hobby of ham radio, which helped me get my commercial radio operator's certificate."

He looked at me speculatively.

"Well, that's a lot better foundation than most of the Ferry Command pilots who want the Captain-Navigator rating have."

Deciding to lay out all of my brief experience as a navigator, I said, "I also used a surveyor's level to take astro shots when I was a pilot at No. 2 Air Observer School at Edmonton."

"You did?"

For a moment he seemed at a loss for words, perhaps doubting that anyone would try and take sights from the air without a sextant. Then he reverted to being an instructor.

"Well, when we get in a Hudson we'll find out in a hurry how good you are."

To this threat—or was it a promise? —I had no answer.

It seemed there were only a half dozen captains who cared enough about navigation to submit themselves to the grind.

Longhurst addressed our class.

"You have all passed plenty of examinations in dead reckoning navigation, meteorology, air regulations, radio, and so on, to get as far as you have. So we'll concentrate on astro navigation. This means star identification and plotting their resulting lies of position. We'll use the new AN tables which take out a lot of the pain of calculations while you're reducing a sight."

Four of us successfully passed the ground examinations and began our flight tests. On January 16, Longhurst took me aloft for an hour and forty-five minutes in a Hudson II to practice sun shots. We flew to Ottawa and back with me using the new Mark IX sextant. When he examined the lines of position I'd plotted on my chart he seemed satisfied.

"Maybe your surveyor's level did help you after all."

I tried to crack a joke.

"Yep, my heavenly body identification was spot on."

Inasmuch as the only heavenly body in sight was the sun he just stared at me, without answering. His eyes resembled those of a freshly caught cod. I had noticed that when an instructor cracked a joke, his students all applauded. On the other hand, when a lowly student tried...

Now came the much more difficult night navigation practical examination. This time the chosen course was to Millinocket, Maine, 248 statute miles distant. As the Hudson trued out at about 200mph, there was no time for error.

However, I got a practice flight, as that very night in Hudson III 9223, Longhurst took me and a couple of interested observers aloft for two hours and forty-five minutes.

My flight plan from Dorval to Millinocket was bound to be incorrect, because the wind aloft provided was false. However, the course must be flown, and at least Longhurst climbed to altitude over Dorval before setting course, just as I had done with my navigational students at the Air Observer School. He gave me the time over the cone of silence of the Dorval radio range and I began my air plot. Heavy curtains masked off the cockpit from navigator's position: and no peeking allowed!

I sat looking at my chart, fidgeting impatiently for about thirty minutes while the Hudson proceeded on its erroneous course. As we hummed along, from time to time I had been looking out at the black vault of the sky through the clear astrodome in the top of the fuselage. I'd identified the three stars which I wanted to use to make a good fix.

Now it was time to use my sextant to establish their altitude. I took three shots and used the average figure which was carefully noted against the time to the second. Those observations, with the help of the current Air Almanac, and the AN tables, enabled me to reduce my findings to lines of position which I plotted on my chart. From the resultant "cocked hat" I had to figure out our ground speed and the true wind.

Then I had to provide Longhurst with a new course and Estimated Time of Arrival at Millinocket.

He took my offering, which was written in large letters on a piece of paper, without comment, and stuck it on his instrument panel. Shortly after I felt the Hudson bank as he changed course. Time for more anxious waiting.

When my ETA arrived, Longhurst invited me up to the cockpit and pointed at a cluster of lights which stood out conspicuously against the black of the forest.

"That's Millinocket over there," he said, "You're about five miles off. Not bad for your first try."

On the way back to Dorval I plotted a series of radio bearings from the signals I'd selected of different range and broadcast stations. After we landed, Longhurst looked at my work.

"You're ready for the big test. We'll schedule it as soon as possible."

"Good," I replied, much relieved.

I was thinking of telling him that the short distance from Dorval to Millinocket didn't really give the navigator a fair chance, then decided to keep my big mouth shut. After I got my rating might be a better time to suggest improvements to the course.

But now the weather refused to cooperate, so it wasn't until January 21 that I got my final test. This time I was only about two miles from the elusive Maine target, and Longhurst seemed quite pleased. By now the radio work on the flight back had become routine.

After we'd landed at Dorval and were having a coffee in the restaurant, he said, "I'm giving you a 'Superior' rating."

"Gee, thanks," I replied.

He continued, "I'll tell crew assignments and the instruction department you're now a qualified Captain-Navigator. Have them endorse your competency card."

"I'll do that." Now was my chance.

"Don't you think the distance from Montreal to Millinocket is a little short for all the work you want us to check out?"

"Strange you should say that. I'm going to use longer courses from now on."

I knew he had kept his word when on February 2 I was assigned as pilot in command of Hudson 9223 to do a night navigational flight to Toronto. The return distance was 625 miles, which lessened the tension for my two RNZAF airmen. It was a measure of the cosmopolitan flavor of Ferry Command that on one night I'd carry two New Zealand men, on another two Americans, and on a third it could be a mixed bag of English, Canadian, or American.

Then the next night I did another navigational training flight in the same aircraft with diminutive and humorous American Captain Herb Huston, already a friend, and Ian Smith of BOAC. Huston navigated us to Blissville, New Brunswick, the radio range just east of Millinocket on Airway Green One, while Smith navigated us back. The return distance was 700 miles and our flight time was four hours and fifty minutes which gave them time enough to do a good job.

Back at Dorval I reported to Longhurst that when their ETAs ran out they'd both been within five miles of their target, which was a passing grade.

Merrill Phoenix

Another night Hudson flight put American senior captains Don Teel and Merrill Phoenix to the test. But we were forty miles southwest of Toronto when Phoenix said his ETA was up. When I turned in my report Longhurst scheduled him for another test.

Captain-Navigators had a very valuable option. I had always felt strongly that if the aircraft I was riding in somehow happened to get lost, I'd like to do it my way, just like in the song. Besides, I felt that after the takeoff, climb to cruise, and then setting course there wasn't really enough challenge to keep a good airman busy.

Two days later I rode with Captain Louis Bisson, in Liberator AL537, along with a bunch of fellow aircrew, to the airport at Detroit, Michigan. It was good to renew my friendship with Bisson, with whom I'd flown before out West. But more of this later.

The airport parking area was loaded with Hudsons from the factory, which made me wonder if maybe the Washington dam had burst. But only three other crews cranked up their Hudsons, so maybe it had only sprung a small leak. I got Hudson BW406 airborne, and aided by Scottish Radio Officer Donald Esler we got it safely back to Dorval.

Then with Radio Officers Bill Collins and George James I managed to deliver the same Hudson through some rather crappy weather to No. 31 Operational Training Unit at Debert, Nova Scotia. It was a remote, dismal place with much grouching going on, so once more I was glad to be in Ferry Command.

As a natural consequence of my doing so many navigational training flights, Bill Longhurst and I became quite friendly. Early one morning after a long session with the stars we had landed and were having our usual coffee in the restaurant.

"You must be a real nut for navigation to buy those two books," he said.

"Yeah, I suppose so."

"What impressed you the most in Weems' book?"

"I suppose it was the chapter concerning outstanding navigational flights. He summarizes the difficulties that the early pilots encountered, and starts with the Atlantic crossing of the N.C.4 in 1919. Their navigational problems were solved by the U.S. Navy who stationed ships every fifty miles across the Atlantic."

"Pretty tough to provide during wartime, I'm afraid," he laughed.

"Yeah. Then he tells of Hawker and Grieve's failed attempt in 1919, in spite of the fact that Grieve used astro. The next one, also in 1919, was the first nonstop flight of the Atlantic by Alcock and Brown. They followed the Great Circle course to Ireland in their Vickers-Vimy two engine bomber. Too bad they landed in a bog." I paused to sip my coffee. "The next long distance flight was in 1922 across the South Atlantic by Admiral Coutinho of the Portuguese Navy. He used the sea horizon for his sextant observations and specially prepared tables for reducing the observations to position. As a matter of act, his navigation was so good that he was able to pick up St. Paul Rock, a mere speck in the sea."

"No doubt you'll have to do the same soon."

"Thanks to you, I'm ready. Then he goes into the Dole Race from California to Hawaii in 1927, where the winning plane, the *Woolaroc*, navigated by Lieutenant Davis, used all four methods of navigation. All four! Then he mentions Lindbergh's New York to Paris flight where the 'Lone Eagle' used only pilotage and dead reckoning."

"I heard that after his Paris flight, Lindbergh decided to not attempt any more long distance flights without the aid of astro and radio. He said that not knowing where he was preyed on his mind."

"That's what Weems says too. The next notable flight was Post and Gatty around the world. Gatty was the navigator and used pilotage, dead reckoning and astro. Too bad he didn't use his radio."

"Maybe he thought he didn't need it."

"Maybe, but to me that's plain dumb. The next one is the flight of Mr. and Mrs. Lindbergh across the South Atlantic in 1933. Weems claims that this was the best example of efficient navigation to date. I'm sure Anne Lindbergh learning CW so she could operate the aircraft's radio was a big help."

"You're probably right."

"Of course I'm right," I snapped, annoyed that Longhurst didn't seem to be as keen about radio as I was. "It's too bad Weems doesn't mention the flights from Australia to the U.S.A., or the flights across the Pole. There were some epics there."

"I suppose he just ran out of space. Too bad. Now what about Don Bennett? I never got close to him because he was just leaving as I arrived."

"He was an Australian, but due to the Depression he had to leave there. He served in the RAF from 1929 until 1934. The year he left the Service he passed his First Class Navigator's license, becoming one of the first seven people in the world to do so. He also managed to collect the top civil 'B' pilot's flying license, a civil wireless operator's license, a flying instructor's certificate and ground engineer's 'A', 'C' and 'X' licenses."

"A bit like you, eh?"

"I wish I had his experience in the air! Someday after the war I might try for an Air Engineer license. Anyway, Bennett married a beautiful Swiss girl, then bounced around for some time before getting hired by Imperial Airways. He put in a lot of hours in 75-knot flying boats in Africa until in 1936 he gained command of one of the new Short Empire flying boats, G-ADUX, the *Cassiopeia*. He was still in his mid-twenties."

"Really? I hadn't realized that he was that young."

"His next feat was flying on the Mayo composite aircraft program to deliver the mail across the Atlantic. The plan went like this: Bennett and a radio operator in a small, heavily-overloaded four-engine float plane called *Mercury* would be bolted to the top of an Empire flying boat called *Maia*. Once in the air they would separate, and the *Maia* would glide down to a landing while *Mercury* would stagger on with its load of mail.

"Well, on July 20, 1938, this wild scheme was a complete success as the aircraft separated over Foynes, Ireland. Twenty hours and twenty minutes later he had covered the 2,930 miles to Montreal, and landed safely in the St. Lawrence River. Then, without a rest, he pressed on and landed in the Hudson River in New York City. The American press celebrated the event with big black newspaper headlines. He didn't smoke or drink, so I presume that's how he survived the festivities. When all the noise quieted down he flew the Atlantic back to England via Botwood and the Azores, finally landing at Southampton. I suppose he had to do it in relatively short hops because he didn't have *Maia* to lift him out of the water with enough gas to make a direct flight."

"I'll bet he never realized he would be pioneering the North Atlantic route in winter for Ferry Command so soon," Longhurst said reflectively.

"I suppose not." I scratched my head. Why would Bennett, any more than any other mere mortal, know the future?

"Then, on October 6, '38, he set a new long distance record, when with aid of *Maia* he flew *Mercury* from Dundee, Scotland to the Orange River in South Africa. He was in the air for an incredible forty-two and a half hours, while flying 6,045 miles. It's a real pity the blokes in England never gave him the proper recognition his feats deserve."

"That's life, I guess. I understand he was on flying boats with BOAC when war was declared and performed some hairy rescue work when France was overrun."

"That's right. His last landing with BOAC was at Poole, near Bournemouth on July 2nd, 1940. The Battle of Britain was about to begin, and in desperation Churchill had appointed the Canadian Lord Beaverbrook as Minister of Aircraft Production."

"I know the rest of the story—Beaverbrook hired Bennett to organize the ferrying of the badly needed warplanes across the North Atlantic in winter."

"Right, but maybe what you don't know is that a lot of civil and military experts, including our own Air Chief Marshal Bowhill, said it couldn't be done."

"Bowhill said that?" Longhurst was surprised.

"He sure did. But Bennett convinced Beaverbrook, then went to the Lockheed factory in California and made sure we had enough gas to do the trip. Then, as we were short of navigators, he led that first flight of seven Hudsons out of Gander on November 10th, '40. As you know, they all arrived safely in Ireland, and as they say, the rest is history."

Longhurst tried unsuccessfully to block a huge yawn before he was able to say, "And furthermore, I'm damned sure we're going to sleep safely and well when we finally hit the sack."

Hudsons getting delivery check, Gander, 1941

"No Speek English"

When an American pilot I'd taken a liking to teamed up with me, the relationship would have unexpected ramifications for both of us. His name was George Evans, from St. Louis, Missouri, a stocky, darkly handsome man with deep-set dark eyes, which told of distant Greek ancestry. He was also a crack pilot, and a genuine perfectionist. He was exceptionally smooth on the gauges and had the sensitive hands of a born flyer.

We would grab a "buckshee" Hudson—"buckshee" on the Canadian Prairies means temporarily idle—as often as we could, so as to polish up our instrument flying. We ran up and down the Dorval range until we joked that maybe we were wearing out the beam.

We were as tough on one another as Moody had been with us, as we were both convinced that our incessant practice of instrument flying training would pay off when we finally got on deliveries.

We were both more than pleased when, on January 8, Moody put us both through a tough ninety-day instrument check and we both passed with "Superior" ratings.

Things were so dead that I checked out in a locally built Bolingbroke No. 9072 with Flight Lieutenant Paddy Uprichard anxiously watching from the bomb-aimer's position.

Then, aided by Radio Officer Oliver, we delivered 9116 to Bombing and Gunnery School No. 4 at Fingal, Ontario. It was rumored that Bombing and Gunnery School pilots were serving a term towing drogues of flying obsolete bombers because they'd displeased some senior officer.

As I climbed into Hudson BW463, which would take me back to Dorval along with a couple of other ferry crews I was pleased I wasn't in the RCAF. Being in Ferry Command, I had a small but vital control over my career.

While I was scraping up what flying I could and trying to make myself into a more skilful pilot, my sex life was suffering. Suffering, hell! It was nonexistent.

In Montreal, as in most Canadian cities, it was almost impossible to pick up single girls while wearing civilian clothes. My being in Ferry Command didn't help, because the brass hadn't even thought about designing uniforms for their civilian flight crews.

A couple of Dutch naval pilots helped me solve my lack of that most important of life's ingredients. I'd met them at Dorval where they were getting checked out on Liberators they were going to take to the Dutch East Indies to fight the Japs.

Several times after flying, we'd belly up to the bar of the Pic and exchange flying stories. In the process I learned how to drink Bols their way, which was neat, chug-a-lug, followed by a lick of salt from the back of your hand.

I also watched enviously while they acquainted themselves with the flower of Montreal womanhood. They wore dark blue uniforms with gold stripes of rank on their sleeves, rather like the Royal Navy. After a few good belts they'd check the stock over, and when they spotted some lovely young things sitting by themselves, they'd march over to the girls' table.

There they would stand at strict attention until the girls looked up at them. Then they'd click their heels in the European manner and bow. As they bent over the table, they'd raise one of the girls' hands to their lips. Of course, this unique, very non-Canadian method of approach startled and pleased the girls.

Then one pilot would say, "No speek English," while the other would say, "Non savez Français." That took care of the Montreal girls, and while they were still in shock, the Dutchmen would say, "Dreenk?" while sliding into a vacant chair.

While I stood lonely and forlorn at the bar, my naval friends would order a round of drinks, and soon the four of them would be grinning and nodding away at each other like old friends.

Then, when the glasses became empty, the pilots would spring to their feet, positioning themselves behind the girls' chairs and say, "Room," in very military tones. The girls seemed mesmerized as they headed for the elevator like lambs to the slaughter. I'm sure my tongue was actually hanging out as my overactive imagination conjured up visions of those lucky couples in their bedrooms upstairs.

At the airport the next day, when I moaned about some people having all the luck, my Dutch friends were sympathetic to my plight. We talked the problem over and when I mentioned I still had my dark blue Air Observer School uniform—complete with two gold stripes and wings—in my room, we concocted a plot. I mentioned that there was probably some regulation about me not wearing the uniform now that I'd left the AOS, but they just laughed.

"Wars aren't won and sex isn't gained by people who follow regulations," Hans said sagely. "Honey catches the bees and uniforms catch women. If you want to get laid get in costume and show your wings. They all love a flyboy."

"Sure, why not?" I said, more to myself than to them.

The next night was a Saturday, ideal for our scheme. I put on my navy-blue AOS uniform and joined my two buddies at the Pic's stand-up bar. After a few Bols—now I knew what "Dutch Courage" meant!—we spotted three lovelies sitting by themselves.

We three musketeers marched over and I did the heel-clicking thing as smartly as any British Royal Guardsman. Maybe I was a bit sloppy on the hand-kissing, because in Western Canada we didn't get much practice.

I'd picked a sexy-looking blonde who owned a beautiful set of breasts to go with her soulful brown eyes. Soon we were sitting at the table, grinning at each other like a set of idiots. Step One successfully completed. My girl told me her name was Renée and didn't complain when I ordered her a drink.

We clinked glasses. Without a common language the atmosphere at the table was a little tense, but the drinks fixed that up. I realized that not having to talk was the key to the whole operation. When the drinks were consumed our leader pulled the "Room" ploy on his exciting redhead, and sure enough it worked. They drifted away towards the line of seven elevators arm in arm.

I wasted no time in making my move. "Room?" I said, trying not to leer. Renée hesitated for a moment as she regarded me quizzically and my heart dropped. Then she rose from her chair and joined me on our walk to the elevator.

Step Two completed.

After we got into my room, for a moment I didn't know what to do. Or rather, I knew what I wanted to do, but didn't know how to go about it. Renée was beginning to fidget. Bad news. Then I decided that the Dutch no-speaking approach had worked so far, so why not continue?

No talk meant lots of action, so I just grinned and pointed and said, "Bed." As Renée stared at me I could read her mind. Was this the way they behaved in Holland? What happened to foreplay? I didn't say a word in any language.

Then she shrugged her shoulders in a truly Gallic gesture. She removed her clothes and folded them neatly on a chair, then hopped into bed like a bird. Step Three completed.

My clothes fell in an untidy heap as I joined her. Very quickly I made the marvelous discovery that Montreal girls were indeed more adept in bed than the few Western girls I'd tangled with. We were soon doing very pleasurable things to each other I'd only read about. In the morning we had a glorious repeat, then breakfast of "oeufs et jambon" in bed.

Then she surprised me when she got out of bed and left our love nest to attend Mass. With no makeup, of course. I couldn't help wondering just what she said to the priest during her confession.

As she wrote her phone number in my little black book, I wondered if she knew all along that I was putting on an act. Was it possible that she wanted sex as badly as I? She was forbidden by the mores of the day from making the first move. Well, at least I'd solved that problem for her...

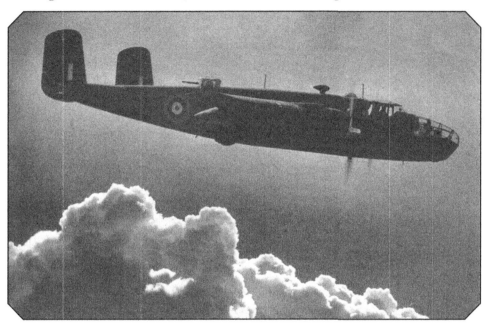

North American Aircraft B-25 Mitchell

At long last the men in Washington began to thaw out the Pearl Harbor aircraft freeze. The Hudsons, Venturas, and Liberators they hadn't appropriated for their own use slowly started to trickle through Dorval, but I wasn't senior enough to be assigned to ferry one overseas.

But then a brand-new American warplane appeared on our ramp. We called it the Mitchell while the USAAC called it the B-25C. It was a tricycle gear bomber, powered with Wright 1750 horsepower engines that pulled it through the air at speeds that were more than 110 miles per hour faster than our Hudsons. We marveled at the cranked wing which gave the big Hamilton Standard props their ground clearance. The cockpit was beautifully laid out with new fluorescent lights. It even had a new North American factory smell. Every pilot worthy of his profession ached to get his hands on it.

But what was it doing at Dorval? Rumors swirled around the Pic like snowflakes on a windy street corner. Finally it was established that the Dutch had ordered and paid for 162 of these fast bombers to carry on their war against the Japanese from the Dutch East Indies.

And furthermore, much more interesting to us, Winston Churchill had volunteered the services of Ferry Command to deliver them. We'd pick them up at Dorval or West Palm Beach, the big American base in southern Florida, then we'd take them through the Caribbean, into Brazil and down to Natal, and make the long hop across the South Atlantic to Freetown, Sierra Leone.

Then it would be a tedious, dangerous hot trek across Africa and through India to Bangalore. Then would come the jump across the Bay of Bengal to Sumatra, and finally to the military airport of Bandung, near Batavia, the capital of Java. Hearing these exotic names set my mouth watering again. I just had to get assigned to this operation.

Wally Siple was in charge, and nearly every time he stepped out of his office he was liable to bump into his faithful hound dog: me.

Meanwhile, senior Captains such as "Duke" Schiller and Andy Burke were checked out, crewed up and sent on their way to West Palm. And finally my turn arrived. But to formalize my position I was to hurry down to the Dutch Consulate to have my passport stamped. It didn't make sense. Here we were, ferrying desperately-needed aircraft to help them repel the Japs and all these "civil" servants could think of was putting their rubber stamp on our passports.

On the social side, I'd had a couple of dates with Maureen, and made several sincere passes, all of which she'd rebuffed. She said she felt a loyalty to Kevin Kelly, who was just starting his tour of thirty operational trips over Germany on a four-engine Halifax bomber with RAF No. 4 Group.

Newspapers tended to play down the truth about the horrible loss of flight crew in Bomber Command. After all, the night-flying bombers were carrying on the major share of the war against Germany. I'd temporarily given up on getting Maureen between the sheets, and had also decided to spare her feelings by not telling her that Kelly's chance of completing his tour alive was about one in six. Some people who should know whispered that the ratio was closer to one in ten.

There were even some squadrons, whose identifying numbers were mentioned in hushed tones, where *none* of their flight crew had survived to complete a full tour.

Arctic Challenge

I was on the ramp at Dorval airport one crisp winter morning, admiring the sleek lines of a new B-25 bomber, when I heard the snow crunching behind me.

Then, "Bonjour, Don, remember me?"

I turned. The man approaching was square-cut, wearing a parka and walking with quick movements. He carried his head at a slight tilt and wore a small smile. Captain Louis Bisson always reminded me of a hyperactive bluejay. He was one of Canada's most experienced Arctic pilots. Our first meeting had been in 1936 when I was practicing circuits and bumps in deHavilland Moth G-CYYG on skis at Edmonton's Blatchford Field.

I had spotted his ski-equipped Junkers F-13 in the air. There wasn't much traffic congestion at that time and another aircraft was a rarity. After we landed he told me that he was on his way to the Arctic, far to the north down the Mackenzie River. His unusual crewman was Bishop Gabriel Breynat. By using an aircraft the eminent Bishop hoped to capture native souls who still practiced heathen beliefs. He would take them under the wing of the Church of Rome before his arch-rivals of the Church of England could make their conversion.

The Junkers was made of corrugated metal and its engine was started by the explosion of a cartridge. What was even more remarkable was that the engine was water-cooled. That meant that every night Bisson and Breynat had to drain the engine and take the cans to bed with them in their tent so the oil and water wouldn't freeze. I admired their guts.

Bisson had joined Ferry Command before me, and as I wondered why he thought I should remember him I had a strange premonition connected with weather conditions. It was ten below at Dorval and 85 above under the palms on the beaches of Java. I wanted very much to make that flight. There was nothing on earth which could make me change my mind.

As this was Quebec province I made my effort at being bilingual.

"Hi Louis, comment ça va?"

Bisson spoke English and French equally well.

"Tres bon, Don. By the way, I see by the Crew Assignment board you're due to take a B-25 to Java."

I patted the camouflaged side of North American Aircraft's latest product fondly.

"That's right. It should be a helluva trip."

He hesitated for a moment, his face serious, then he continued.

"Don, you've always liked the challenge of the Arctic." It was a statement, not a question.

"Sure," I grunted. Hell, he knew I did, because we'd talked about the lure of the Arctic often enough.

"Powell has asked me to make an exploratory flight to Baffinland. He told me it's very urgent and top secret." Group Captain Griffin Powell, RAF, was Senior Air Staff Officer of Ferry Command, which made him our leader.

"Great, Louis, right up your alley. Nobody's ever flown up there."

"I've lined up two brand new Noorduyn Norsemen with new type skis. I need two because once the expedition gets up to Baffinland, the closest rescue aircraft will be more than two thousand miles away."

"True."

"So, in case something happens to one of our aircraft, the other one will survive."

"Our?" The bluejay was wasting no time. He slapped me on the shoulder.

"Yes, our. I want you to be the pilot of the second Norseman."

So that was it! Visions of Balinese dancing girls were replaced by vistas of bleak, cold, featureless Arctic tundra. I shook my head vigorously like a dog coming out of a river.

"No way!" I exclaimed. Bisson's face dropped. It was then that I realized that he had been really counting on me. This was a tough decision. He watched me without commenting while I convinced myself that Bali and the tropics would still be there when I got back from this once-in-a-lifetime opportunity. Here was a chance to fly where no other man had flown. Land where no other plane had ever put down. Make the impossible dream come true. And all of the other well-worn clichés.

I took a deep breath and stuck out my hand. "Sure, Louis, I'll be proud to be your wing man." For a long moment we kept our hands clasped. Our lives were now intertwined. He could save my life, or I his.

It was the 14th of February, 1942.

It was an unusual task for the RAF Ferry Command, which had been set up to deliver bombers and flying boats across oceans. But there was a good reason for it.

The American authorities had been appalled by the narrow margin of victory in the Battle of Britain. They had been even more worried when the German U-boats had installed what had become a target range in the North Atlantic. Many, many ships and their deck cargo of aircraft had gone to the bottom.

Signpost at Gander airfield, 1942

So USAAC General "Hap" Arnold and General Carl Spaatz commissioned Elliot Roosevelt, son of the President, to locate a far northern delivery route from North America to Europe. The distances between airstrips must be suitable for fighter aircraft, and in no case farther than 700 miles.

The original routing began in Presque Isle, Maine, then continued to Gander, Goose Bay, Fort Chimo, Frobisher Bay, Padloping Island, Greenland, Iceland, terminating in Scotland.

Canadian stations in the north were code-named "Crystal" and each had a staff of twenty men. Until landing strips were constructed, their main function was to provide weather reports.

Greenland was to have three bases, code-named "Bluie." Bluie West One was in the south of the ice island, up Narssarssuaq Fjord. Bluie West Eight was on the west side, well up Sondrestrom Fjord. Bluie East Two was on the east coast near the tiny Eskimo village of Angmagssalik.

Five-thousand-foot runways were to be constructed immediately. The incredibly difficult logistics problems at BW1 and BW8 were conquered by landing more than 1,000 men on the virgin rock at each proposed base. Machinery and equipment to carry out their mandate was also unloaded. They were supplied with enough food to last them from the fall of 1941 until the ice went out in the spring.

BE2 had a smaller cadre of 200 men and supplies necessary for their survival through the bitter winter. But included in their equipment were several antiaircraft guns. It was known that the Germans had also established bases somewhere on the east coast of Greenland.

The Crystal bases were located and the plans for their set up for the winter made by an American, US Army Air Force officer, Lieutenant-Colonel Charles J. Hubbard. He had a lifelong romance with the Arctic and had explored parts of Labrador before the Second World War.

Crystal One was on the Koksoak River just south of Ungava Bay near the trading post of Fort Chimo. It was staffed mainly by men of the United States Navy, led by Lieutenant Commander "Ike" Schlossbach, USN, who had much Arctic and Antarctic experience.

Crystal Two was first located on a small island near the mouth of Frobisher Bay on Baffinland. The site was less than ideal. The supply ships had arrived late in the '41 shipping season and had to unload in a hurry before winter ice locked them in. The commander of the base was Major John Crowell, USAAF, who had sailed as mate on the schooner *Gertrude L. Thebaud* when it had explored the bay some years previously.

Crystal Three was located on Padloping Island on the east coast of Baffinland, where the Davis Strait lapped at its feet. Colonel Hubbard, aided by an Eskimo pilot from Pangnirtung, the closest settlement, had set up this base. The US Corps of Engineers unloaded the vessel *Cormorant* and two smaller ships. The small fleet barely made it out of the roadstead before the winter ice would have clasped them so firmly it would have been July of the following year before they could escape. Captain James G. Dyer, USAAC, was left in command of the base.

All together the Crystal, the Greenland Bluie bases and the route from Iceland to Prestwick were code-named "The Crimson Route." It was only after the Americans had failed that Ferry Command got the assignment to make the first flights which would prove the route feasible. We were in his apartment when Bisson explained to me what had happened.

"Earlier this winter, Colonel Hubbard used two Norsemen on skis in his first attempt to fly up and inspect the Crystal sites. The aircraft were all right, but the Air Corps pilots weren't. One cracked up on an inlet on the south shore of Ungava Bay. That did it. The other Norseman pilot picked up the survivors and turned back."

I frowned. "Survivors! Gosh, what happened?"

"Hubbard told me they were good pilots, but neither of them had any Arctic experience, especially on river ice. You and I know how unreliable the magnetic compass is in the north, and that, combined with poor maps, was why they got lost."

"Tough luck. What maps there are, are pretty poor."

"Yes, that's true, of course. But Hubbard refused to abandon his pet project. Before the war he'd flown with Canadian bush pilots, the type whom he knew could do the job. So, he went to Washington and pulled some strings to get his pet project going again. The brass in Washington called the brass in Ottawa, who contacted Sir Frederick Bowhill, Ferry Command's big boss. Bowhill came to Powell, who came to me. I accepted the job and now I've come to you."

I found I had no answer to this.

Bisson stared at me as he finished this masterly sales spiel.

"It's an important job that must be done immediately to help the war effort. You and I, mon ami, we've got one very big responsibility."

"What do you want me to do?"

"Fly one Norseman, of course, that's your most important duty. But I also want you to look after the maps and our navigational equipment. We're both qualified astro navigators, so make sure to draw two new Mark IX sextants, two good watches, and all the necessary tables and air almanacs from Stores.

"I'll enjoy doing that. What about you?"

"I've got full authority to order anything we need. Woods Brothers, the outfitters in Ottawa, will manufacture special windproof clothing. Their sleeping bags, which are the best in the world, will have light flannel blankets inside and waterproof covers outside. They're also making two lightweight alpine climbers tents and protective cov ers for the wings and engines."

"Just like a real Arctic expedition."

"Don, this *is* a real Arctic expedition! We'll have a sun compass mounted in each aircraft to give us lines of position." He gave me a sly grin. We both knew we'd rarely see the sun through Arctic clouds and storms. I forced a grin back at him. Not many people had his experience in the North. Then I asked a very important question.

"Who else have you chosen for the crew?"

"Bill Baker will ride with you. He's a crackerjack maintenance engineer who did a great job for me when we were with Prairie Airways flying out of Moose Jaw, back in Saskatchewan. Lloyd Wheeler will be our radio man. He and the Colonel will ride with me."

"Sounds good." His smile changed to a frown.

"I've got another problem. The Americans want to combine our Crystal survey with one of their Greenland bases. The runways are completed, but no aircraft has landed on Greenland yet. I've got a Hudson assigned for the job. Who would you recommend for its Captain?"

This was totally unexpected. I thought of all the pilots I knew. There was bound to be a lot of real tough instrument flying involved. The Hudson captain would be landing in bad weather on one-way gravel strips, probably out of wind most of the time. If the weather socked in, alternate airports would be a hell of a long way away. Probably as much as 700 miles. This was no assignment for a hesitant pilot either. The Hudson was a tricky aircraft to fly. It took me a few minutes to make my decision.

"George Evans is our man. We've flown together a lot recently under the hood giving each other simulated single engine emergencies. He's the best instrument man I've ever flown with."

"Bon. Tell him to contact me."

Just as I knew he would, George Evans accepted the challenge. His crew was rounded out with one of Ferry Command's most experienced radio-navigators, a quiet man named Gerry Pollock. His flight engineer would be Gayle Swaney, who was a touch on the boisterous side, but long on experience in maintaining aircraft in the bush. Both were Canadians. Our team was complete and now we all plunged into a whirlwind of activity.

RAFFC flight crew L-R, Reeves, Fred Johnsen,
Captain Al Lilly, F.W. Baillie, Gayle Swaney

The Norseman needed additional range, enough fuel to make us as independent as possible of the few ground supplies. Baker designed a 110 gallon tank which would, when added to the normal 245 carried by the Norseman wings and belly, give us twelve hours endurance. The new tank would be mounted in the fuselage immediately behind the copilot's position.

Then he added a five-gallon drum of oil so the Pratt & Whitney R-1340 wouldn't starve for lubricant. A small hand-operated wobble pump transferred the oil in flight. We had oil dilution, which injected gas into the fuel system as we shut down. The lowered viscosity made for easier starts in the far-below temperatures we knew we would be experiencing. No more messy draining of the oil after every flight. No more difficult and dangerous blow-pots under a canvas shroud to heat the engine.

Bisson and a couple of scientists computed how much food we should carry in case of an emergency landing. They decided we should carry enough to support five men for three weeks. An active male requires about 4,000 calories a day in the south. In the Arctic he needs 6,000 calories a day.

Every item had to contain maximum nourishment for its weight and bulk. Bisson had a butcher shop drying buffalo meat to make old-style pemmican. He added bully beef, hardtack, dried soups, rolled oats, tea, salt, sugar, milk powder and blocks of chocolate.

Then a Primus stove for cooking the food. He wrapped our big wooden kitchen matches in waterproof containers. Wet matches meant no fire. No fire meant no edible food.

Each aircraft had a first-aid kit, flashlight and spare batteries, an axe, shovel, broom, snowshoes, skis, ski poles, crampons, amber sunglasses, a Coleman lantern and candles, a Very pistol and cartridges, a hand mirror to flash rescue planes, large knives and saws to make the snow blocks for igloos, a hand compass, fishing lines, hooks and sinkers, and a long chisel to chop holes in the ice to get at fish. And, probably the most important piece of all our equipment, a small gasoline-powered motor generator to recharge the aircraft's batteries.

We had to be self-sufficient, if we had to live off the country. So each aircraft carried a .22 rifle and an over-under .410 shotgun. The .22 was for small game, but, even at short range wouldn't knock down a caribou, the staple food of the North. But the .410 would do the job. Ptarmigan, Arctic hare, seal, walrus, musk ox, or even possibly a polar bear would help us survive.

The list seemed endless, but if just one item was overlooked we could be in serious trouble. Our emergency equipment had to be as complete as any old-time Arctic exploration expedition, because, of course, it was still just as cold and empty up there as it had been in the days of Admiral Byrd or Roald Amundsen.

We were already overloaded so the only items we cut back on to save weight were spare parts for the aircraft. All we carried were spare spark plugs, and bits for the exhaust. It was what could be called a calculated risk.

Our clothes were of the finest quality, with the closest weave possible. Every calorie of body heat had to be hoarded. The most efficient way of doing this is to wear several layers of clothing. The air trapped between the layers acts as additional insulation. For starters we wore a one-piece suit of heavy woolen underwear. A two-piece suit would crack in the middle and open our insulating cocoon to the deadly cold. Then a pair of quarter-inch-thick wool logger's trousers, held up by broad fireman's braces. A belt would cut off circulation.

For the upper body, two flannel shirts. Over this get-up we wore a pair of wind-breaking gabardine trousers. Our parkas were also made of gabardine filled with soft goose-down. The hoods were trimmed with wolverine, the only animal fur on which the human breath will not freeze. Our pants and parkas were even lined with silk to reduce the friction.

Feet, farthest from the heart, are very hard to keep warm. I used two pairs of heavy woolen socks. In spite of every precaution, feet will perspire and perspiration will freeze. So I carried two pairs of heavy felt insoles to absorb the moisture. Each night I'd remove one set and let it dry out, so that each day I was sure to start with dry feet.

A pair of moose hide mukluks (knee-high moccasins that I'd picked up from a Dogrib Indian squaw in northern Alberta) protected my socks. The mukluks were embroidered with multi-colored beads and strips of colored cloth, which made me a quite un-military-looking pilot.

Bisson, Arctic veteran that he was, also had a pair of mukluks. The rest of the crew had a variety of heavy boots, including some RCAF type fleece-lined flying boots. They were not very efficient insulators and awkward to walk in. The Indians and Eskimos were far ahead in warm, light footwear.

Sometimes I think that *hands* are harder to keep warm than feet, because the forefinger and the thumb must move freely to complete even a simple task. The RAF had carried out a lot of research on how to keep flight crews' hands warm at altitude and still leave them flexible. They'd settled on an underlayer of fine silk gloves closely covered with a layer of the finest leather. I'd tried them and didn't think they did the job. So I used buckskin gloves made by the Indians which gave me the warmth together with flexibility. When the cold became brutal I pulled heavy woolen mittens over it all.

When I went to Ferry Command Stores to sign for the two sextants, I also drew high-grade pocket watches with second hands. I would use the signals on 10,000kc from WWV, the official radio time station near Washington, D.C. to keep them accurate to the split second.

Hubbard had secured the latest maps from the US Navy and Air Corps and I had added the latest Canadian charts. But as maps go, they were a navigator's nightmare. The coastlines were well-defined, thanks to the mariners of long ago who were searching for the elusive Northwest Passage, but the interiors were another matter. Large expanses of blank white paper, marked "Unmapped." The elevations of high terrain or mountain peaks were very rarely indicated. Lakes, when drawn in at all, were usually labeled, "Position approximate."

I made up a little joke: solid blue lines represent rivers Eskimo Joe thinks are there, while dotted blue lines represent rivers Eskimo Joe's cousin thinks are there. Hubbard and Bisson were not amused.

On February 20, we picked up our Norsemen from the Noorduyn factory at Cartierville airport, a hop-skip-and-jump from Dorval. Ferry Command had borrowed them from the RCAF which had been using them for wireless trainers. Bisson's number was 2477, mine 2478. We each shot a few landings to get familiar once again with the uncomfortable slithery feel of skis on snow and icy patches.

Back at Dorval, Baker took over. In addition to the extra fuel and oil tanks, he oversaw the installation of the latest in high-powered aircraft radio equipment for both voice and Morse code on high and low frequency bands. A trailing antenna was fitted, very necessary for efficient operation on low frequencies. In addition, we got a brand-new direction-finding rotatable loop with a left-right indicator mounted on the instrument panel right in front of me. This was a really big improvement over previous installations which depended on the pilot's ears to detect what was called an "aural null."

I finally pried 2478 out of maintenance. In the air, with the aid of one of our best compass men, drift reader Bill Dixon, we carried out a very meticulous swing to compensate the B-16 magnetic compass. As we did so, I wished we had the superior English P-4 type compass we'd used on our Ansons.

At first our compass deviation card looked perfect. But after each landing we got puzzling readings. We went up on three separate flights and tried for over four hours and still weren't satisfied. The normal compass swing took only about thirty minutes. I would have liked to try again, but time was running out, so the corrections I'd made had to serve.

Bisson was far too busy to spend time swinging the compass in 2477, so he accepted the factory's figures on his deviation card. This was to cause serious repercussions for the expedition and all of us later.

Just as all seemed to be falling into place, spots erupted on the face of the Sun, which blotted out shortwave signals on Earth. I kept the thought to myself that perhaps the Sun Gods were angry at us because we mere mortals proposed to invade their beautiful, unspoiled white Arctic.

A Tough Trip to Goose Bay

The three aircraft of our exploratory expedition took off from Dorval on February 23, 1942. Due to the blackout we had no ongoing weather reports. Nevertheless we would try to make Goose Bay. But only Evans in his twin-engine Hudson, flying on top of the bad weather, made it that day.

Bisson and I were forced down at Seven Islands, a small fishing village on the north shore of the St. Lawrence River. The landing area was primitive, being just a widening of the direct road from the village to the seaplane base at Lac Rapide.

After we had landed our crew men jumped out and cut branches from the pines growing close to the narrow strip, and then Bisson and I taxied up on them before shutting down. The branches would prevent our skis from freezing to the snow. As I used my oil dilution for the first time, the fact that we were completely on our own for maintenance—or anything else—struck home.

Seven Islands was what could be called a "company town." Naturally we paid our respects to the Hudson's Bay Company's factor. He welcomed us and gave us some background on Fort Chimo, where he had previously been stationed.

The village of Seven Islands had no hotel, so he directed us to Madame Cloutier's boarding house. She laid a good table, and we slept well that night.

The next day we were up long before dawn, roaring up and down the strip attempting to take off. No go. The warm front whose low cloud had forced us down had struck again, making the snow on the strip soft and mushy. Our new wooden Bear-Paw skis were supposed to be the RCAF's answer to soft snow. They were broad in the front, tapering to a narrow rear, thus the nickname. But in sticky snow they behaved more like snow ploughs. Conventional straight, narrow skis would have served us much better. Back at Madame Cloutier's we sat around the big dining room table and gloomily stared at one another.

The next day we repeated our efforts to get our overloaded aircraft unstuck. Again no go.

On what turned out to be my last effort I tried too hard and slipped off the strip—there are no brakes on skis! The structure of 2478 was only slightly damaged, but I'd ripped a big hole in the fabric covering the belly. A jagged tree stump hidden beneath the snow had done me in.

Baker looked at the damage and said the bent aluminum ribs could be straightened easily. He was cheerful as he tackled the metal repair job before applying fabric. I was quite upset. An accident, even if it was a minor one, and we weren't even out of the Province of Quebec yet. Holy smoke!

"The two mechanics had dug a hole in the snow, where Baker lay on his back while he carried out the repairs."

The seals on my propeller had begun to leak, allowing a brown film of oil to form on the windshield. We didn't have the tools to remove the prop and replace the seals. I told Bisson I could look out the side window if the visibility got tough. He shrugged his shoulders and remarked that if I thought I could get away with it he had no objection.

Then while re-stowing some emergency equipment I slipped on the sloping, snowy floor of my Norseman. I came down hard on the sharp edge of a wooden box. The pain was intense. A visit to the local doctor confirmed that I had cracked a couple of ribs. Just like my aircraft, I thought cynically. All he could do was wind yards of adhesive tape around my chest to brace my ribs. Then he told me to take it easy. Sure.

Baker had received some assistance from mechanic Pete Midledge. He was stationed at the local base of Quebec Airways who flew a variety of aircraft including a deHavilland Rapide on their runs across the river and down the North Shore. The two mechanics had dug a hole in the snow, where Baker lay on his back (see photo) while he carried out the repairs. After he had applied a couple of coats of dope to tauten the new fabric on the belly Baker said 2478 was as good as new. I wished he could do the same for me.

The weather stayed warm for two more days and we did the same in Madame Cloutier's house. She had an old upright piano and I proceeded to prove that the money my father had spent on piano lessons when I was a student at St. John's College School in Winnipeg had indeed been a waste, as some of my friends remarked.

"Way Down Upon the Suwanee River" and "Comin' Through the Rye," if played often by an unskilled pianist will force captive listeners to don their parkas, grumbling to themselves as they take long walks.

So we were well behind schedule when a cold front barreled through and deposited a fresh covering of snow on February 28. The new snow was slick in the below-zero temperatures. Still without weather reports from Goose, Bisson got off first. It was a desperate takeoff as he staggered into the air at the very last moment. I could see him circling below the low overcast as he waited for me. I gritted my teeth as I shoved my throttle forward. The engine roared defiantly. This effort must be successful.

First an application of coarse rudder to kick the skis loose, with Baker outside pushing on the tail. Then slowly, oh, so slowly, as Baker scrambled aboard, the Norseman picked up speed. As the short runway disappeared behind me I think I would have aborted my takeoff if I hadn't seen Bisson make his. At the very last moment I hauled the control wheel back into my gut and snatched the aircraft off the snow. As we lurched into the air the skis came so close to the trees I could have counted the pine cones.

Above was the usual low, grey overcast dripping the usual snow showers. The visibility was very variable, so I got as close to Bisson as I dared, formatting on him just twenty short feet behind his starboard wing and ten feet above so I could see the yellow shape through my side window. The weather ahead was dark and ominous-looking, but at least we were in the air again.

I wondered if perhaps it would be wise to turn back and try when the weather improved but kept the thought to myself and stayed off my microphone. Bisson plugged on, staying just below the cloud. But now the land was rising, squeezing us between it and the rocks below. I hung in for as long as I could, but when we were down at about 100 feet I lost Bisson in another of those infernal snow showers. Yellow aeroplanes seen through a deposit of brown oil on the plexiglass of a windshield have a habit of vanishing. Forever.

My first impulse was to turn back, but I realized I couldn't do that. Bisson had trusted me to be his wing man, and good wing men just don't turn back. Besides, if I knew *my* Bisson, *he* would never turn back. During his Arctic flights under the same type of weather he had made it through somehow. This meant that I had to do the same.

The Mealy Mountains lying now across my course have occasional peaks as high as 2,500 feet, and were now buried in cloud. They appeared to be an insurmountable barrier. Better turn back. But wait—the ceiling lifted a bit and my map showed I was abeam the Natashquan River which emptied into the St. Lawrence. Its winding valley could be the way through the mountains to large areas of white on my map.

Just to make sure I got the message the white areas were labeled "Unmapped." Not very encouraging. But on the other hand I was sure that far on the other side of the mountains the broad Hamilton River ran from west to east, right past Goose Bay airport. Some early government survey party had surveyed the river. It would be a reliable guide to my goal.

But first I had to find it.

So I turned north. As I flew up the narrow valley the wings of the Norseman seemed to be scraping the towering cliffs on either side. The visibility became patchy and the turbulence got more violent as the compass spun aimlessly. Baker and I were thrown roughly against our safety belts as I dodged outcrops of rocks and clumps of trees. Finally we emerged from the mountain pass after almost an hour of violent maneuvering. It seemed more like ten hours to me.

But we weren't in the clear yet. First there was a long period while we bounced along, staring at endless stretches of rocks and pines, wondering just where in hell we were. At long last we were thrilled by the welcome sight of the turbulent waters of the mighty Hamilton River. It had cut a deep channel into the rocky terrain as it curved its way to the Atlantic Ocean. I dropped down below its high banks and flew downstream just above its black, foam-streaked water. As I followed its twists and turns the turbulence in the air was still violent. But the visibility was improving and were were a few more precious feet below the ragged cloud deck.

A direct flight from Seven Islands to Goose would cover just a shade under 300 nautical miles, so we should have taken about three hours. Not this flight. Five hours after shaking the snow of Seven Islands from our Bear-Paw skis we saw the white strips of the runways the Canadian government had slashed through Labrador's green pine forests. Mighty poor ground-speed!

I felt as if I had seen far more of Labrador than anyone in their right mind would like to. My head was aching and my stomach was complaining as I circled the airport looking for a windsock.

Where was Bisson? Had he made it? I'd spent almost two extra hours on my flight. Surely he must have been on the ground for a long time? But then I spotted his Norseman beginning to taxi towards the small buildings on the east side of the airport. Obviously he had landed just a few minutes ahead of me. This had an instant effect of restoring my confidence in my airmanship and navigation ability.

I landed and found the snow was slick as I taxied alongside Bisson's aircraft. We grinned at one another as we shook hands on the makeshift ramp, proud to be the first Ferry Command aircraft to land at what was bound to be a very important link in the transatlantic ferry program. There was no help on the ground from the contracter's men or the small RCAF detachment, so we secured our aircraft ourselves.

There were no quarters for transient aircrew either, so we lugged our duffel and sleeping bags into the McNamara Construction Company's bunkhouse. As usual in the North, the building was hotter than hell. It was so hot we didn't need our sleeping bags. But although the air was hot and crackly dry it was a lot more comfortable than a tent...or an igloo.

As we talked to W.H. "Bill" Durrell, the engineer in charge of construction, we found that Elliott Roosevelt had stopped in the area during his survey flights over the Crystal sites during the summer of '41. His Catalina flying-boat had landed at nearby Northwest River. The small settlement, in addition to being a Hudson's Bay Company trading post, boasted a unit of the Grenfell Mission, a charitable organization which administered to the medical needs of the inhabitants of Labrador. As far as Goose Bay airport was concerned Roosevelt felt that an airport must be built with no delay. But he also reported that he thought the Canadians couldn't do the job in time. He recommended to Washington that the Americans build the essential air base.

However, at the same time Canada was doing its own survey. It was apparent to Canadians as well as the Americans that Goose (no relation to Gander in Newfoundland!) would be a very important steppingstone for delivering war aircraft which could not make the long hop from Gander to Europe. Plus, Canadians had a lot of damn good engineers with plenty of experience in the bush. "Minister of Everything" C. D. Howe took the bit in his teeth and authorized the McNamara Construction Company to do the job. The Department of Transport would do the planning.

But it was already September, 1941, and the navigation season along the Labrador coast and up the narrow channels leading to Lake Melville ended in November. Then the ice would be too thick for even the icebreaker *McLean* to bash through.

Could the construction equipment and men to operate it be in place immediately if not sooner? Bill Durrell convinced Ottawa that he could set up three temporary runways on the snow and then lay three hard-surfaced runways which could accept heavy aircraft not later than the following summer.

Because of the urgency the activity was intense. Eight ships were chartered and loaded with men and equipment down south. There was a lot of anxiety but they all got through. Then two items vital to the project, a crane and a pile-driver, were delivered. Freight and men had been lightered ashore at some risk until the pile driver built a dock.

Everyone lived in tents while the continuous whine of the sawmill disturbed the peace. Lumber in many shapes and forms was essential. Giant bulldozers lurched through the bush, clearing roads and runways. The vital project, under the whip of Bill Durrell, progressed at a speed which might have impressed even Colonel Roosevelt.

By December 1, the DOT men had some of their antennas erected, their power plant running and their radio setup in operation. When atmospheric conditions permitted, their high frequency transmitter broadcast basic weather information. This allowed the Ferry Command forecasters to produce more accurate forecasts. Weather reports from Labrador, where most fronts first passed through to the northwest of Gander was like gold to the crystal-ball gazers.

We washed up and then, our appetites in high blower, entered the mess hall and sat on wooden benches at a trestle table covered with white oilcloth. It had been a long, stress-filled day so we proceeded to enthusiastically pitch into a typical northern construction worker's supper: high mounds of bread, big blocks of butter, soup, steak, potatoes, three kinds of overcooked, canned vegetables, four kinds of pie, three varieties of cake. Red-hot coffee as black as the proverbial ace of spades poured generously from a blue enamel pot. Coffee so strong that the local joke claimed a tea spoon would stand vertically in my big white porcelain mug. It really did—almost.

That night we found that the first civil aircraft to land at the Goose Bay airport had been a Quebecaire ski-equipped twin Beechcraft on December 3. The first RCAF aircraft to make it through had arrived on December 9. Then more and more aircraft kept funneling in supplies and men to construct the base. But we were the first people to pass through to actually use the facility for the purpose it had been constructed.

The Back of His Hand

Now Hubbard came down with a case of the frets. In addition to his explorer's credentials, he was an Establishment American, Harvard football captain, light colonel at thirty-one, organized achiever Grade One. This was his second crack at getting through to his pet Crystal stations, and it wasn't starting off very well. Downright inauspiciously, in fact.

What bothered him most was that the weather reports were not getting out in time to be useful. Ominously, Crystal One hadn't been heard from for several weeks. The synoptic and hourly reports from Two and Three were spasmodic and always late. The weather reports from Greenland had been missing from the charts of the weather forecasters for days at a time. Hubbard had good reason to worry, and naturally we also felt the pressure.

There is an editor's saying that the only use for yesterday's newspapers is to wrap fish. You can't even do that with yesterday's weather reports.

We held a council of war. We must push on, so we decided that the Hudson, even without weather reports from Bluie West One, would wait until the next high pressure system from the west moved through Goose. Sixteen hours later, when it should be affecting Greenland, Evans would take a shot at BW1. It was crude, elementary forecasting, but it was all we had.

The two Norsemen, even without any ongoing weather forecast, would head north the next morning, hoping to make it to Crystal One. If the weather permitted, we would land at the weather station. If it forced us down, why then we'd see just how good our emergency preparations were.

Early the next morning, as a yellow sun momentarily peeked from under a layer of grey cloud, Bisson and I had no trouble lifting off the hard-packed snow of the well-rolled runway. Ceiling about 5,000 feet; wind calm, visibility good, outlining ridges of low black mountains and Lake Melville to the east. But far to the northwest the clouds were ominously dark. More snow showers, without a doubt.

We were well below the clouds after we had climbed to a comfortable height, I'd formated on Bisson, then waited for him to set course. When he did so, I stared at my B-16 magnetic compass. I couldn't believe my eyes.

It was reading a surprising *ten* degrees, so, allowing for 30 degrees west variation we were flying on a track of 340 degrees true. I knew the proper track from Goose to Crystal One was 320 degrees true, or 350 degrees magnetic. After all, I'd measured it often enough.

Unbelievably, we were starting off on our hazardous mission flying *twenty degrees* off the proper course. I picked up my mike and respectfully suggested that our proper compass heading should be 350 degrees, seeing there was no wind to speak of.

There was a rather long silence while we droned on. Then Bisson got on the air to inform me that his compass reading was okay, and furthermore, Colonel Hubbard had said that he had flown in the Arctic for many years, and furthermore, knew this part of Labrador *like the back of his hand*.

I looked over at Baker and shrugged my shoulders. A wing man's duty is to follow his leader, so I just said, "Roger." Baker didn't say a word.

Our maps were useless and for one of the longest four-hour periods of my life we flew through the usual series of snow showers over poorly marked terrain, which consisted of ice patches, rocks, and scrub pine. I stayed on Bisson's wingtip, not wanting to lose him again. Nothing on the ground added up as we continued to drone on.

At some point, Bisson and the Colonel must have realized they were lost. The ceiling was getting lower and the light was failing, the visibility getting poorer by the minute, when Bisson finally came to the only possible decision.

Land immediately. He picked his spot and quickly spiraled down with me clinging like a leech. I saw a tail of snow as he bounced across the rough ice of a small lake. I quickly followed suit, once again marveling at how a Norseman could take such a pounding. I had to grit my teeth to avoid biting my tongue.

We were down with no damage, except possibly to Hubbard's pride.

The Bear-Paw skis grated on the crystallized snow as I taxied close alongside my leader, more relieved than I wanted to admit. With our engines idling, we both began to dilute our engine oil in the approved manner. I hadn't a clue as to where we were.

As the seconds ticked by I said to Baker, "I guess the good Colonel must have remembered looking at the back of someone else's hand."

"Yeah," he said glumly, "or maybe he looked at his left hand instead of his right."

I grinned.

Finally satisfied our oil was thin enough for a cold morning's start, he grunted, "That's it." Then he moved the mixture control into idle cutoff and the prop shuddered to a stop. We both climbed out without regrets. Fate was fate, we were down safely, and tomorrow was another day.

We all crunched around in the snow to prepare for the night. First we fitted the canvas wing covers and engine tents. Next we chopped holes in the ice for our rope tiedowns. The ice would soon freeze them as solid as if they were blocks of concrete on a ramp. Aircraft have first priority in the Arctic.

Then we erected our two tents, securing their peaks to the wings of each Norseman. We used freshly-cut snow blocks to hold down the bottom edges and snowshoes stuck in the snow as anchors. While we were doing all this the wind began to rise with a series of gusty whines. It looked as if we were going to have an unscheduled rest period.

Both of the tents had canvas floors and Bisson decided that one of them would be our living quarters with our sleeping bags. The other would be the location to store our emergency supplies and act as our cooking and eating place.

Baker and I, as junior members of our expedition, were "elected" cooks. We began to unpack our emergency rations and cooking utensils. We were happy to be inside and out of the wind, which made our Coleman pressure lantern sway gently in the peak of our tent as it shed a homelike white light.

Meanwhile, Bisson, Hubbard and Wheeler busied themselves outside, their bodies hunched well down in their parkas. They were using axes and coarsely-bladed saws as they cut additional snow blocks for a windbreak. Already snow pellets were hurtling by like bullets. We could hear them hitting the canvas walls of our tent. It looked as if the coming blizzard would be a rough one. I knew we were lucky to be on the ground.

Inside the tent, we cooks had decided to stick to standard Arctic emergency fare. First, tin cups of heavily sugared black tea. This was accompanied by hardtack and bully beef seasoned by melted Oxo beef cubes heated in an enamel bowl over our Primus stove. The mixture was nourishing, but it looked gruesome and tasted not much better than it looked.

I suppose Baker and I hoped we'd get a complaint. Just as in a duck hunters' camp, if one of the members not tagged with cooking duties complained, he'd become the new cook. But Bisson and his crew were too wily for us. "Yum yum," they said as they spooned our mess down. For dessert we served the sandwiches left from the lunch the construction company's cook had packed for us back at Goose. First class all the way, they said, yum yum.

So with full bellies and a warm shelter we rolled into our sleeping bags, snug and secure. For the time being, life in the Arctic was a picnic.

The storm got stronger as it howled throughout the night and well into the next day. A real Arctic blizzard. We lay low and conserved our energy. When we poked our noses out of our tents the blowing snow cut visibility to just about zero, which was more than a few degrees above what the thermometer was reading.

Finally, late in the following night, I got a time check from WWV. Then, as the clouds rolled away, I used my new Mark IX sextant. In spite of freezing fingers I was able to take a series of sights on the brightly twinkling stars I needed for a fix.

When I plotted the results on my chart, it seemed we actually had landed at 58.213N 64.26W. This was a cool 130 miles *east* of Crystal One.

As a joke, I named the site of our first forced landing Crystal Zero, because we seemed to be going backwards.

The other crew members didn't seem to think it was all that funny.

"For the time being, life in the Arctic was a picnic."
Author emerging from tent; Bill Baker on right.

First to Baffinland

The next morning the ceiling wasn't very high but the visibility was fair. This was good enough for Bisson and Hubbard to decide we should take off. Breaking camp, stowing our tents and food and preparing the aircraft took over an hour.

When I got in the cockpit I noticed the altimeter was indicating 2,200 feet above sea level. Both our engines started easily, but on our takeoff run the skis, the aircraft and the crews took a hammering hard to believe as we skipped from one hard ridge of snow to another. Even with flap it seemed like forever before I could lift the skis free.

As Bisson set course I noted that once again he was heading too far to the north. But I kept my mouth shut. Junior pilots soon learn their place.

When we headed out the ceiling slowly lowered, taking the visibility with it. Soon Bisson began to wander around over the rugged ground, obviously searching for a place to land. Finally he decided to land on the soft snow of a river and I followed him down. Later we identified our blue squiggle as the Koroksuakh Brook, which flowed into the lordly George River, which, in its turn, emptied into Ungava Bay.

We had been in the air an hour and a half and had progressed less than a hundred miles.

We set up our tents and made camp once more, late in the afternoon, this time with a lot less trouble. I supposed that practice does indeed make perfect...

In spite of the poor light I took our .410 and managed to pick off a couple of rock ptarmigans which added a gamey flavor to our stew. After we'd cleaned our tin plates clean I announced that we were now at Crystal Minus One. I thought the joke was pretty hilarious but neither Bisson or Hubbard appeared to be the least bit amused.

The next morning we woke to a long-overdue break. The weather was clear, the sky a shining blue. We broke camp and got off with no trouble. We then flew over the carcass of the USAAC Norseman which had crashed, ending Hubbard's first air effort. It was sitting on the ice near the mouth of a small river which led into Ungava Bay.

The previous night, in our tent, Hubbard had tried to convince Bisson to land so they could inspect the wreckage. I was glad when my leader refused. If we landed there was nothing to be gained for our expedition, and every landing in the wilderness is heavy with risk.

As we flew on, even with good visibility we still had trouble pinpointing due to our poor maps. We followed the south shore of Ungava Bay and finally found the mouth of the Koksoak River where it emptied into the broad bay. Then we turned south and followed it upstream until we saw the cheery red roof of the Hudson's Bay Company's factor's building on the east shore.

We landed with extreme care on the ice in front of the Post. Although it turned out to be fairly smooth we had to be alert for hidden cracks. The Koksoak River at Fort Chimo features a thirty-foot tide, which turns the whole shore into a giant bowl of ice cubes.

We were greeted by a crowd of friendly Eskimos who informed us that the American base which we knew of as Crystal One was a few miles upstream on the west side of the river. While we were standing there arranging for more gas, a short stocky man arrived and introduced himself as Commander Schlossbach, USN. After some palaver back and forth he admitted that the reason no weather reports had been sent out was that he'd had a mutiny.

"A mutiny?" Hubbard said incredulously.

"Yes, I call it a mutiny. This base is manned by United States Naval personnel," the Commander said somewhat reluctantly. "Some of my men, the wild ones who thought they were going to be posted to the Pacific, got so angry they burned our radio shack to the ground."

Hubbard was industriously taking notes. He seemed relieved that nobody had been killed. He looked up from his notebook.

"We'll send you up all the radio equipment and building material you'll need to get back on the air." For the first time Schlossbach smiled. I too felt better. We'd accomplished the first very important part of our mission.

Baker had been busy organizing the wobble-pumping of gas from drums into the aircraft. We were somewhat taken aback when we found that each Norseman had only sixty gallons of fuel left when it landed. This was sufficient for two more hours of flight. This amount is ample for flights down South. But having just two hours' reserve is mighty lean in the Arctic where filling stations are few and far between.

Our warm-ups, followed by three long ski takeoffs and then eight and a half hours flying had sucked up most of our supply. The long-range fuel and oil tanks that Baker had worked so hard to install had already proven their worth.

I took Schlossbach and the Hudson's Bay factor and his wife, Mr. and Mrs. Stewart Nicholls, up for a survey flight. We decided that the runway should be sited near the military camp on the west bank, and so it was. After landing, Mrs. Nicholls produced a lovely supper and that night we slept in the HBC house. I felt as if I were going to die from the heat. My body was already acclimatizing itself to the cold.

It had taken us ten days to get just this far, mainly due to our forced landings after flying Bisson's compass courses. So we were well behind schedule. After breakfast the next morning we were standing on the ice beside our aircraft when Bisson took me aside and went into his bluejay act.

He cocked his head and his words astonished me.

"Don, it's obvious my compass is useless. How would you like to lead us on the next leg?" Wow—leader! I scratched my chin. We would be crossing the Hudson Strait, which meant open water. It would be a very tough leg. Still, it would be a pleasure not having to follow that elusive yellow Norseman on a course to nowhere.

Of course I had already plotted how I'd fly the hop in case I lost him once again.

"Sure, Louis, if you say so." Bisson looked over at Hubbard with a smile. It was obvious that they'd agreed that something had to be done about the lousy compass in their Norseman.

I paused to collect my thoughts.

"You realize that as we fly down Ungava Bay the land on the east shore is too low and too poorly mapped for good pinpointing."

"Oui. So?" The head was still cocked over inquisitively.

"So I'll lay off a direct course for Cape Hope's Advance. Thanks to the old marine navigators the capes are well mapped. From there I'll fly directly across the Straits to the only settlement on the south coast of Baffinland. That's Lake Harbour where we can get a fix after we see their buildings with their red roofs. Then we can set course directly across the mountains to Crystal Two."

Bisson grinned as he slapped me on the back.

"Bon, Leader. Sounds good. Let's get going."

After getting airborne we leveled off well below a deck of altostratus and bounced along on my chosen course. Beneath us the white wastes slowly unrolled like an endless carpet. Land or sea, who could tell?

Baker remarked that Bisson was tucked in beside us. More than two hours elapsed before I positively identified Cape Hope's Advance. I wondered whose hope that godforsaken bit of rock could possibly have advanced.

The Arctic is dotted with names like that, names that hark of the hopes and hardships of the adventurers seeking the Northwest Passage. There are bays named Resolute, Repulse and Deception, an island named Resolution, a cove named Despair. They are hard, chill, windswept names, entirely apt.

We were out of the sight of land, well over Hudson Strait when the engine of the Norseman began to act up. I was sure that it was missing on a cylinder or two, although all the temperatures and pressures were normal.

Ask any pilot what happens when he or she begins to fly over open sea in an aircraft with just one engine. You'll be told that the engine goes into "Automatic Rough."

There is a reason, of course. The danger below makes the pilot's hearing much more acute. So every previously innocuous little rattle, knock, exhaust bypass or roughness is intensified. Thus the mixture setting which has never been seen on any pedestal, known as "Automatic Rough." The disturbing malady mysteriously disappears when the water below changes to friendly, solid land.

I looked down. The sea was a cold blue-green, speckled with grey ice-pans bobbing in the wind. If our engine ever quit here we were dead. Dead. Our lifespans would be measured in minutes in that cruel, frigid water.

Baker's brown eyes were thoughtful as he gazed out of his side window. Maybe he was wondering if that worn exhaust clamp he'd tightened up just before takeoff was vibrating loose? I didn't ask.

Eventually the mountains of Baffinland revealed their black, rugged profile in the far distance. I'd been continually descending to stay below the cloud deck and they disappeared into cloud at about 1,000 feet above us. Our maps did not even approximately indicate the height of land in the interior. So we would have to try to sneak across through a series of valleys. A most dangerous business.

Murphy's Law has a regional corollary reserved for the Arctic. If the weather closes in behind you it will do so at the worst possible moment. We had passed over Lake Harbour and flown for about twenty minutes when it happened to us.

Ahead, the clouds met the mountains, and I turned back. I was watching Bisson out of the corner of my eye. Could we get back to Lake Harbour? No. The weather had closed behind us. We were trapped. Bisson dived for the ground, while I cut my throttle and followed. It was hard to keep him in sight, and his wings were almost vertical as he spiraled down towards a lake deep in the valley. Would he make it?

Finally I saw a big plume of snow. He'd made it! I swung around sharply, my wings now almost vertical as I too dove for safety. Just off the ice I straightened out to land in his tracks. They were the only thing that gave me the least hint of depth perception in that blinding whiteness.

With a long bounce we were down with a shower of snow flying over the cockpit windows. I discovered this lake had a deep coating of powdery snow when I had to use almost full throttle to taxi to shore where Bisson had already stopped.

As usual, diluting the engine took some time. After shutting it down I felt really cold. My body seemed to be deeply chilled, yet I was wringing wet. I scrambled out, put on my snowshoes and started to unload our tents and emergency equipment before I froze up.

Ten minutes later the whole valley went zero-zero. A real Arctic white-out. Visibility and depth perception zip. It had been a narrow squeak. Only Bisson's snap decision to land immediately had saved our lives. And now, according to my screwball accounting system, we were at Crystal Minus Two. I kept my mouth shut. Somehow my corny joke didn't seem funny at all.

© 2015 Donna McVicar Kazo,
after L.R. Williams

*"Bisson dived for the ground,
while I cut my throttle and followed."*

I Crash a Norseman

W e were the first land aircraft to arrive in Baffinland. Great place if you like white. On the ground the snow was up to our armpits. Overhead, the visibility was a thick, opaque rimless zero. White men in a whiteout, that was us.

We wanted no more dangerous forced landings now that we were this far on the mission, but we had to continue, even without any weather information. About noon with the visibility slowly improving we broke camp, then taxied up and down the narrow valley in order to compact the soft snow. This time the Bear-Paw skis proved their worth. I got off after a long run and circled; then Bisson took the same long run before formating on my right wing tip.

As I looked out of the cockpit window I was impressed with the grandeur of the black mountains which contrasted impressively against their garlands of snow. We were far north of the tree line. Only moss and lichens existed under the white blanket. It took only a little over an hour of flight over the mountains.

I felt a great sense of relief when I glimpsed the frozen waters of Frobisher Bay. Then it was time to search for the small dot of an island which held Crystal Two. The islands in the bay were barren rock and all of the same shape. After a long careful scanning, I spied the low-slung buildings of the camp. And, just for us, a short runway heading with the lie of the land, northwest, southeast. But also, just for us, was a prominent rock ledge close to the northwest end.

Now Bisson took over. It was his decision whether to use the short strip or to land on the bay ice. There was unlimited space in the bay, of course, but even from our height the surface looked rough, scarred by windblown ice ridges. Also there was the real danger of falling through possible hidden pressure cracks.

I was glad when Bisson chose to land on the short strip. After he had taxied clear I followed him in. The surface was smooth but short. Major Crowell had done a good job considering the space and equipment he had to work with. When we climbed out, he and all his men were ecstatic that finally someone had made it to his base.

That night we slept under a hard roof once again. And once again the interior was terribly overheated, the humidity almost zero, typical of the Arctic.

In the morning, Hubbard came into his own on what might be considered US Government property. Records showed that the weather observations had been taken religiously, coded up and broadcast. But he found they were supposed to be picked up by Greenland for relay to Washington and then on to the weather forecasters. All this was taking much too much time.

When and if received—and that was a big if—the reports were stale. Solution? Cut out Greenland and make Dorval the main distribution center. Hubbard was busily scribbling away as Crowell told of his problems.

One small but aggravating problem was the contents of the base's library. Undoubtedly it was one of the finest available on Arctic history and survival in existence. But somehow when a person can look outside and see the real thing, Arctic lore isn't all that fascinating. Some good murder mysteries and a few hot sex stories were sent up on the next ship.

The next day the local weather was good, so we took off, in spite of the radio blackout, which meant no Met. reports from our destination of Crystal Three. While Baker took a turn at flying I was sketching in geographical details on the blank spots on my map, of which there were plenty.

Then, about an hour out, we started to fly over some scattered to broken cloud. It seemed to be moving from east to west, which was unusual. We kept going, hoping the undercast would break up. It didn't. Instead it thickened up. We turned back, but we had waited too long, and the solid cloud below us now stretched from horizon to horizon. We were caught on top, a very bad scene.

Bisson and I talked our problem over. His compass would not guide him back to Crystal Two, even if we knew where we were, which we didn't. So I volunteered to descend through the cloud and get contact and a pinpoint so we could set course back to Crystal Two. According to my flight plan we should be over the center of Cumberland Sound.

So I throttled back and down I went.

The undercast was thicker than I expected and contained plenty of rime ice—the tough granular stuff. I looked over at Baker, who looked very worried. But as we were committed, I continued my descent, hoping we would be able to climb back up with the load of ice we had accumulated.

When we finally popped out of the bottom of the cloud I made a terrifying discovery. Instead of being over Cumberland Sound I was over *land. Land!* There were mountain peaks sticking up into the cloud nearby. So it was just plain dumb luck that I hadn't let down into a "stuffed cloud."

After some intensive map-reading I established my position. Then, with wide-open throttle we slowly and painfully began the long climb. For some time I wondered if we were going to make it, but finally the sky began to lighten and we finally staggered back on top. The widespread deck of cloud was smooth and inviting, but we'd just proven how dangerous it could be.

Baker and I searched all around until we finally found Bisson with his unreliable compass circling aimlessly. We joined up and I led him back to Crystal Two.

After we landed he said I'd saved his life once more.

Our three and a half hour flight turned out to have been a dangerous exercise in futility, but for all I knew a lot of exploratory flights ended in that manner.

The next day dawned clear. The visibility must have been a hundred miles. Time to try again. Baker and I tried to knock off the rime ice which still stuck tenaciously to 2478. We couldn't reach the top of the wing, so we used a piece of half-inch rope to saw away at the miserable stuff. Finally we were sure the wing and the tail were reasonably smooth. Baker carried out his usual preflight inspection, then we wobbled fuel from the base's 45-gallon drums. Full to the brim, as usual.

There was just a light breeze from the northwest as Bisson started his takeoff run. Although he seemed to be accelerating quite slowly, he skimmed over the menacing rock ledge at the end of the runway safely.

One away.

I kicked rudder to free my skis and began my takeoff run. The snow was sticky and my acceleration painfully slow. Even with the engine roaring away at maximum recommended takeoff power, the rock ledge loomed closer and closer. It was decision time.

As the airspeed needle at long last crawled up to minimum flying speed I hauled back on my wheel. My action was a bit coarse, but I was sure the Norseman's low wing loading would let me get away with it, especially with the big flaps set for maximum lift. Bob Noorduyn had designed the ailerons to come down a certain amount with the flaps to give even more lift. But this also meant some loss of aileron control. Finally the skis broke loose and for a couple of seconds we hung on the prop.

I thought we had it made. But then the left wing started to drop. I quickly applied full right aileron and kicked on some right rudder. The wing slowly began to come up, when I heard a sudden loud bang and found the control wheel rotating freely in my hands. Now we were drifting off the strip with the left wing almost dragging.

I closed the throttle and pulled the wheel back into my gut. Without power we simply fell out of the air. There was a thirty-five-foot drop from the runway to the lower beach. The thought flashed through my mind that we were in for a heavy impact, and could be crunched and trapped in the wreck while it burned.

Was this the end?

But just one thing saved our lives. The Norseman fell into a twenty-foot layer of soft snow, which cushioned the crash. We were flung violently against our seat belts, but were not hurt. With the engine silent there was no noise except for the crackle of hot metal being cooled by the snow.

As we pushed our doors open against the bank of snow I grabbed the fire extinguisher, while Baker clutched his camera. Maybe I had always subconsciously wanted to be a fireman. Maybe Baker had always wanted to photograph an aircraft accident. Although, probably not his own! There was no fire in any case, which was damn lucky for us.

Bisson returned immediately. Only his skill kept his overloaded Norseman from running out of runway. He and the Colonel raced over with Wheeler following. They seemed to be more shaken up than Baker and I.

The author at left, talking to unidentified man, deals with the aftermath of the Norseman crash, as an Inuit man looks on.
Photo by Bill Baker

Bisson, Hubbard, and I trudged back to the main camp building to plan our next move. Baker, muttering something rude about airplanes which let you down, began prying into the innards of our Norseman.

An hour or so later he joined us, pale and visibly upset. He reported that a pulley bracket right behind our heads, carrying the flying control cables to the ailerons, had snapped. That explained the loud noise we had heard. It also explained why the lack of tension on the cables had allowed the wheel to rotate freely in my hands. He suspected a cold weld at the factory.

He was even more upset when he told us that the long-range fuel tank in the cabin had moved forward a full three inches by the impact. It would have come loose altogether had he not personally taken extra care while installing it. If the aluminum tank had split, raw gas would have soaked us and the hot engine. It would have been "*whoomp*" and goodbye.

A McVicar/Baker roast.

It came to my mind, how fitting were the first two letters of the aviator's phonetic alphabet: ABLE BAKER.

Much later, at the inquest, the Board of Inquiry decided that I was blameless. This was a matter of pride with me after my first accident, as it would be with any professional pilot. Later the RCAF reclaimed their Norseman and barged the bits back to the factory for rebuild.

"The Norseman fell into a twenty-foot layer of soft snow, which cushioned the crash." Photo by Bill Baker

In the comfort and safety of the base communications room, we all concurred that the pulley bracket could have failed at much worse places. At any of the Crystal Minus landings, for instance.

Or, horrible to contemplate, *in the air.*

After our impromptu investigation was completed, Hubbard announced that in the Arctic he always carried a bottle of Hudson's Bay's overproof rum: the 140 proof stuff. Strictly for medicinal use, of course. As he uncorked the 40-ounce bottle he informed Baker and me that we had qualified. My flight engineer and I naturally saw no reason to argue with this decision. The Colonel poured us each a stiff one with very little water in standard blue enamel cups. We said "Cheers" and with no delay began our cure. It didn't take long for us to relax and begin to grin at everybody.

But perhaps the good Colonel's prescription was too strong. Either that, or we were in much deeper shock than we realized, because very quickly we got drunkenly out of hand. Baker took one of the expedition's guns and I took the other and we started a mock duel. Well, it wasn't completely mock because we were using live ammunition!

I had the shotgun and managed to shoot the roof off the local wooden outhouse. As we fired random shots into the air, terrified Eskimos scattered in all directions. Our drunken shouts echoed from the naked rocks. We were real menaces.

But Mother Nature had her cure. Soon the sub-zero temperatures wore away our feeling of euphoria. Our keepers were able to disarm us with no arguments. Then we tumbled into our iron bunks, and soon were fast asleep. We detected no aftereffects, so the medical profession might consider the merits of our "Crystal Cure" for shock.

We woke up to find that no one held our shoot-out against us. One of the American radio operators even told me the episode had relieved the monotony of the long winter.

RAFFC crew: L-R, D. Mackay, W.C. Ross,
Capt. L. Bisson, Sgt. Griffiths, A.M. King

Arctic Exploration

It was time for another council of war. We all agreed that when the radio blackout lifted, the Hudson should be ordered to join us immediately. But where could it land? The strip on the island was obviously too short. That meant we would have to use the bay ice.

We all donned snowshoes and trudged for what seemed like endless miles. Our feeble efforts to compact the snow failed. Then Major Crowell's engineers rigged up a roller made of 45-gallon drums. They were filled with water which was allowed to freeze around a 4" by 4" wooden axle. The base's small Caterpillar tractor pulled this makeshift contraption up and down the bay along the line of our projected runway. But it wasn't heavy enough to do the job either.

Yet another council of war. We'd have to forget about the Hudson coming to Crystal Two. There was no hope of another ski-equipped aircraft coming up from the south before breakup. Reluctant conclusion: We'd have to rely on our remaining Norseman to continue the survey.

Bisson asked me to figure out the all-up weight of 2477 with Baker and me added to his normal load. When I came up with the somewhat frightening all-up weight figure he studied it for a long time.

Then he made his decision: he would try. We would stick together and pile into his Norseman and fly over the mountains to Crystal Three. Baker and I were very relieved. The thought of spending some months isolated on an island in Frobisher Bay waiting for a rescue aircraft wasn't very appealing.

Let's call our escape Step One.

Step Two of the new plan would take place after we landed at Crystal Three. We reasoned the radio blackout couldn't last much longer, so the Hudson could be summoned to land there. From their Arctic experience, both Bisson and Hubbard were certain that the ice around Padloping Island, where Crystal Three was located, would be thick enough to support a heavy aircraft.

So, let's get the show on the road!

But the weather hadn't heard of our ambitious plans, as it turned sour again. Blowing snow and low cloud made sure we weren't going anywhere for a while. I realized we had now been away from Dorval a whole three weeks with no report able to reach them as to how we were making out. I imagined they'd be frantic in the Ops room at Headquarters. Or, with all of their other distractions, at least a little curious as to our well-being.

How to get through?

I'd had experience with radio blackouts in the Arctic before. I remembered that the Royal Canadian Corps of Signals had shifted to very low frequencies in the Northwest Territories when the high frequencies were washed out. Interesting.

I thought back some more. Marine stations used low frequencies all the time to communicate with ships. The Department of Transport maintained marine radio stations all the year round in Hudson's Bay and Hudson Strait. They gave bearings and weather information to ships bound from Europe to Churchill, Manitoba, and return.

Was it possible that we could contact one of these DOT chain of stations which was just 100 miles south of us on Resolution Island? It certainly was worth a try.

So we removed the radio from 2478, which, because it had been designed as a radio trainer, covered the marine frequencies. Wheeler and I strung up a long piece of wire as high as we could for an antenna. We used our emergency motor generator and the aircraft's battery to supply the necessary twelve-volt current. We set up the equipment in our sleeping quarters so we wouldn't interfere with the base radio station, which was equipped with only high frequency transmitters and receivers.

The first night we cranked up our generator while I put on my earphones. As I tuned around I could hear nothing but the crackle of the Northern Lights. Very disappointing. Then I remembered the DOT operators wouldn't be maintaining a continuous 24-hour watch during the winter when there were no ships in the Arctic. But they would be sending out synoptic weather reports on a regular schedule. Churchill collected all the data and put it on the landline to the south. So be patient.

I sat there for several hours resolutely tuning over the empty band. I was just about to pack it in when I tuned across a weak signal sending Morse code. Eureka! I used the variable frequency control of my transmitter to zero-beat the unknown signal. The motor generator whined as I pumped away on the aircraft's hand Morse key.

I was sending *B-K*, *B-K*, which signified I wanted to break in. For a long time it seemed I was doomed to fail. I'd almost given up when the DOT station finished his weather traffic. I held my breath as he wished his friend in Churchill *7-3* and sent *V-A* which means, "end of transmission."

Had I failed? Then he sent *Q-R-Z* which means, "Who is calling me?" I let out a long breath of relief.

This is a 2014 photo of the inhospitable but once strategically-important Padloping Island, taken from a jet aircraft travelling from England to California, © Doc Searls, used with permission.

The station I'd raised was on Nottingham Island at the top of Hudson's Bay, almost 500 miles to the west. He seemed to be astonished as he copied my message to RAF HQ at Dorval.

Finally he acknowledged and we exchanged our 73s. Then I could hear him relaying our sad tale to Churchill, which was out of my range. I sat back and grinned at Wheeler. Dorval would soon know where we were, and would no doubt inform Washington, although there wasn't a thing in the world any part of those huge organizations could do to help us.

Both Bisson and Hubbard were pleased and impressed when I told them what we had accomplished.

On March 13, the weather finally took a turn for the better. Time to move on. As we taxied out I was in the copilot's seat and Bisson remarked that we were now *over*-overloaded, if such a thing was possible. I just nodded.

The wind was light and northerly as we all stared down the strip towards our nemesis the rock ledge. Bisson opened the throttle quickly to the recommended maximum manifold pressure of 36 inches. I noted that there was still lots of throttle movement available on the power pedestal.

For the moment, the Norseman refused to move. Then Bisson kicked the rudder pedals hard and the skis broke loose. Slowly, slowly, almost painfully we started to move. As the engine roared we ate up the short strip. Then suddenly we were so far down the strip that we would crash into the rock if Bisson tried to abort the takeoff; and we still didn't have flying speed.

We weren't going to make it.

I had just survived a short, painful course on crash takeoffs. Without much thought my left hand snaked out and fire-walled the throttle. Right to the limits of travel. The engine let out an angry howl of protest. Its normal

The still-forbidding and desolate Cumberland Peninsula, taken from a jet plane
© *2014 by Doc Searls, used with permission.*

output was 600 horsepower, but now in the cold, dense air with the manifold pressure needle far above 36 inches, it was putting out more than 700.

Bisson didn't say anything as he quickly reacted. He snatched the Norseman off the snow right on the edge of a stall. We staggered into the air and cleared the rock by a few inches.

Crowell told me later that he had never heard an aircraft engine give out such a tortured scream. But it kept on running even with all its temperatures and pressures in the red.

We climbed carefully and painfully down the bay before setting course across the mountains of the Hall Peninsula. I decided that I'd write Pratt & Whitney a letter someday telling them they had a great engine.

Bisson was still pale, and I suppose I was too. He turned to me and said, "Don, that's the second time you saved my life."

"Mine too," I answered, not having a better rejoinder to such an unexpected compliment. As my heartbeat returned to normal I concentrated on filling in those blank spots on my map.

Bisson flew smoothly on as he turned on course over the scattered mountains of the Hall Peninsula. We both checked our pinpoints to adjust for the unreliable magnetic compass. The air smoothed out as we crossed the Cumberland Sound, a wide and lonely indentation of the ocean into southern Baffinland.

As we flew over the Cumberland Peninsula the air became rougher. Then we began to fly over black snow-crowned unidentified peaks, some reaching towards the sky with tops as high as 7,000 feet. Deep chasms separated the many ranges. I hoped I wouldn't get to know those dreadful gorges better in days to come.

An errant thought— the noise of our engine was without a doubt disturbing the everlasting silence of the Arctic. Was our intrusion causing seals, walruses, ravens, foxes and other wildlife to look up at this strange creature? Were they wondering if this bizarre new bird was going to swoop down and attack them?

After we passed the height of the land, still in that rare marvelous visibility we could see the eastern coast of the island was even more deeply indented than the west coast. After we spotted the low mountain on Padloping Island we cautiously began our letdown.

We then flew low over the tarpaper and wood buildings of the farthest east Crystal weather station. Maybe it was a victory zoom for us, or maybe we wanted to give the men some relief from their monotony.

Now for the landing. Bisson flew low over the ice of the inlet in front of the lonely-looking settlement. We were pleasantly surprised to find it wind-scoured and looking as smooth as a billiard table.

After we had landed without incident, we found that was the case, which was very good news indeed. As soon as we skidded to a stop a group of men clad in various scraps of Arctic gear came running out to greet us. They were all grinning widely, obviously very pleased to greet the first aircraft ever to land there. I climbed down, grinning just as widely as we shook hands all around. Across the Davis Strait was Greenland. We were getting on with our job.

Inside the base's dining area, over steaming cups of real American coffee, we found that the personnel were in good shape. They had plenty of supplies, but were unsure if the weather reports they worked so hard to garner were getting through. Once again, Hubbard was busily scribbling away. This Crystal Three station was his very own baby and he had helped unload the supplies on the barren, rocky coast just last year.

Worrying about my friend George Evans and his Hudson crew, I found out from a resident fishing nut that the ice in the bay averaged more than seven feet thick. Good. Plenty strong enough for the Hudson.

Of course, I visited the radio shack and made friends with the radio men, finding out that several were hams. That night, just before I dropped off to sleep, their chief told me that a few high frequency signals were starting to sift through. So the blackout was beginning to lift. About time, I thought. I fell into a deep, happy slumber. My part of the Norseman effort on the survey was complete.

Or so I believed.

The next morning, Hubbard and the base commander, Captain Dyer, checked the contours of the land of Padloping Island. They were hoping to find a level portion where a landing strip could be located. Nothing doing. Too rough. We all began to examine our sketchy maps. There was a chance of more suitable sites further north along the coast. It looked as if the Norseman survey wasn't quite over, after all.

In the meantime, radio conditions picked up rapidly. Bisson was excited as he grabbed my arm and blurted, "We've found the Hudson!"

"No kidding," I replied, pleased and relieved.

After all, many terrible things could have happened over there in desolate Greenland, and I was the one who had recommended Evans.

"Where is it?"

"Just across the Strait at Bluie West Eight. We've ordered Evans to come right over. He should be here in a few hours."

"Great!"

Long before the Hudson's estimated time of arrival every man not on duty was outside listening. In the somber silence of the far North we heard the aircraft long before we saw it. Then the speck to the east rapidly grew larger until the bomber roared over our heads. It was camouflaged in the RAF manner, painted with haphazard wide stripes of what was called earth brown and dark green. The roundel on its side stood out like a bullseye.

I thought that while the camouflage might make it harder to spot over in England, it sure made it stand out like a beacon against the white of the Arctic.

Evans shot us up in famous Service style, then turned around and landed without a bump. He let his aircraft roll for almost a mile without braking to avoid a ground-loop on the slick surface.

It was the very first wheeled aircraft to arrive in Baffinland.

Evans slowly taxied back, slid to a stop and shut off his engines. The sudden silence was unnerving for a moment until the three crew members hopped out. Pollock and Swaney hadn't changed, but Evans had grown a black, luxuriant beard. This was unusual because the experts said that in the cold of the Arctic your breath would freeze in the hair with pretty horrible results.

We shook hands in the usual pilot-to-pilot offhand style. Then I hinted that I was glad to see him and the aircraft in one piece. But I couldn't help mentioning that Santa Claus had a *white* beard. He just laughed as he ran his fingers through the tangle of face foliage.

He said, "You got it pretty tough, but the only time I get cold is when I walk from the Met. office to my aircraft."

"Too true," I replied glumly as I thought of those long days and nights in our tents. Slowly we all began to troop into the base building to hear his report. As we walked along, I gave him another needle.

"It took the RAF Ferry Command to show the Yanks how to use their own bases."

He had a quick answer.

"Sure, but part of it was with an American pilot flying an American aircraft." I decided we'd tied on that exchange.

We all stripped off our heavy clothes as Evans began his report. After leaving Goose in the good weather of a cell of high pressure, he'd run into a cloud deck. Rather than return to Goose, he had kept going up Narssarssuaq Fjord. At Bluie West One they had been astounded to see his Hudson land on their 3,000 foot steel pierced-plank runway.

The temporary landing strip had been laid directly over blasted and bulldozed bare rock. To make things more interesting it had an eight degree upslope from sea level towards a dead glacier looming over the station.

"I was the first aircraft to land there," he said, his voice proud.

There was a low chorus of "Good" with even Colonel Hubbard joining in. Evans' voice became even more serious as he gave us the gen.

"Land uphill and make it good the first time, because there's no room to go around."

Jeeze, I thought to myself. He continued with more good stuff.

"You've got to take off downhill and don't worry about the wind. Once you're over the fjord, turn left and climb like hell."

"I presume the engineers will do all they can to lengthen the runway," Hubbard said.

"Sure, they'd better, or else!" Evans left that warning hanging in the air for a second or so before continuing, "after I landed I found I was the most popular man in Greenland."

"Why was that?"

"Because I had brought the Christmas mail which had been stacked up at Goose."

We all laughed and then Bisson asked, "Why did you go to Bluie West Eight?"

For a moment Evans hesitated. I realized he might have been ordered to stay at BW1. then he said, "Well, I felt pretty isolated in the blackout, so I took matters into my own hands and delivered the Christmas mail up there too."

Bisson and Hubbard both nodded, and the Colonel said, "You showed the proper initiative."

Evans looked a bit relieved as he continued, "The strip at BW8 is longer and has much better approaches than BW1. After I landed I looked at the map and figured that BW8 was the best place to start a search in case you guys got into trouble, so I stayed put."

After a private discussion, Hubbard and Bisson had decided they would board the Hudson to complete the Greenland part of the survey. They hadn't confided in me, and actually I hadn't really thought that far ahead when Bisson in his own way let me know of this decision.

We walked outside, away from the others, and I saw his head cock over. He was wearing that old bluejay smile as he made his pitch.

"Don, I know how worried you must be about losing 2478."

This was more of a statement than a question. He was absolutely correct in his assumption, so I just nodded.

"It really wasn't your fault. Your first accident. We all know that. But I'm afraid some people in Dorval might not look at it that way."

This was a new angle. "I suppose so," I said slowly.

Bisson paused to let the facts as he saw them, sink in, then said, "So, just to show my confidence in you, I'm going to let you take 2477 back."

"Oh," I said noncommittally. As I looked over his head at the distant mountain peaks I still felt a strange sort of shakiness in my bones. Maybe the cure for the shakes was to get back in the air in charge of an aircraft as soon as possible. I'd heard that's what the military believed, anyway.

Bisson decided to sweeten the pot.

"I'll give you both Baker and Wheeler, that should help."

I guess I would have taken the trip solo to re-establish my precious reputation. So I took a deep breath.

"Sure. And thanks a lot, Louie."

Bisson now said, "Oh by the way…" Instantly I was alert. For me, an "oh by the way" statement instantly brought bad news.

"Yes?"

"The Colonel and I would like you to fly up the east coast and see if you can find a suitable landing area, seeing that this isn't suitable." He waved his arm at the black mountains which covered the island.

I had already accepted the fact the rest of the Norseman survey flight was now my responsibility, so it took no effort to say, "Sure, Louis, I'll do that little thing."

My ex-leader shook my hand and wished me luck, then climbed into the Hudson. Without wasting a second, Evans cranked up the two engines and roared off in a huge cloud of snow. As it disappeared across the Strait, for a moment I did feel a touch of loneliness and a lot of worry. Ahead of me and my crew were more than 3,000 miles of hazardous flight with no comforting safety Norseman on *my* wing.

Farthest North

I had begun to plan my flight north, but the very next day two Eskimos appeared in their dog-sled with an appeal for help. They had made the hazardous journey across the mountain passes of the Cumberland Peninsula. Their village of Pangnirtung was gripped by an influenza epidemic. What could the white men do to help?

Captain Dyer and I decided the only way we could find out what help we could give was to go and see for ourselves. A rare spell of nice weather allowed us to make the flight across the peninsula in good visibility.

As we flew on we inspected the fjords which made deep gashes through the mountains. It had taken the Eskimos over two weeks to make their trip. It took us exactly two hours. The sea-ice in front of the little cluster of buildings was rough, but we were on an errand of mercy. We made a couple of bounces which shook my teeth before we grated to a stop.

As I got out, I fixed a glare on Baker.

"You stay on board and don't, for Christ's sakes, let the engine die."

"You bet. I don't want to spend the rest of the war here," he replied with a grin.

It was a tough walk across the piled-up ice. Sort of an obstacle course. In the small cabin which served as a hospital the stench was powerful. Many sad brown eyes stared at me hopefully. The Health Department nurse said there were more patients confined to their igloos. She had been on her feet day and night, and she threw her hands up in despair as she admitted there were no more drugs in stock.

The Hudson's Bay Company's factor and the Royal Canadian Mounted Police officer joined her in saying the whole settlement would be wiped out if some serum wasn't delivered quickly—long before the next ship was due.

Dyer and I agreed that only air transport would get the lifesaving special serum here in time. I decided to exercise authority way over my head, and told them that down south at Ferry Command Headquarters I'd make damn sure some of the serum would be delivered right away. Maybe it could be parachuted.

Even as I spoke I realized it was a pretty far-out idea. But at least everyone looked more cheerful with some thin strand of hope to cling to.

We all shook hands and I marched out with a heavy load on my conscience, determined to find some way to help.

The engine lifted us off easily. But maybe it was because we were light. Or maybe it was because of the prayers of the inhabitants of Pangnirtung. I thought wryly they had a lot of faith in the first aircraft they had ever seen.

On the flight over I had done some canyon-crawling, so now on the way back I climbed to 11,000 feet to get an idea of the lay of the land. The scene was both spectacular and frightening. The mountains appeared to have been torn willy-nilly out of the bowels of the earth in jagged and uncompromising lumps. The Canadian Rockies looked smooth compared to the peaks and precipitous valleys below. It was as inhospitable a stretch of country as I hoped I'd never have to walk out of.

To the north was a small replica of Greenland's ice cap, called the Penny Highlands. The white expanse of ice had spawned numerous glaciers, just like its big brother across the Strait. On the coast near where they flowed into the sea, there seemed to be some flat land. Grist for my exploratory flight.

A wide expanse of cirrus cloud to the west was giving warning of bad weather to come. After we landed at Padloping, or Crystal Three as we now called it, I could see layers of altostratus. For sure we were in for some bad weather.

So we tied the Norseman down with extra care. We chopped holes in the ice about three feet apart, then threaded rope through them which we tied to the wings and tail. The holes soon filled up with water which quickly froze solid. We had tight, strong tiedowns. Let the Arctic winds blow.

As the clouds drifted lower they darkened. Soon they were sliding down the precipitous sides of the mountains. By nightfall it was snowing, with a vicious wind whipping through the base's antennas. We were back in the clutches of the dreaded whiteout. But this time we didn't care. Inside the warm building, Captain Dyer's men treated us like honored guests. I slept well that night. The man who advised people to take life one day at a time must have had the Arctic in mind.

The next day we staggered through the whiteout a couple of hundred feet to try ice fishing. We chopped holes in the ice then baited our hooks with bits of bacon and began to jig. In short order, we caught two cod and an Arctic char. When we jerked them out of the 28-degree water they froze instantly in the 35-below-zero air. The cook filleted them and broiled them. I've never tasted anything as delicious, not even in the best restaurants of Montreal, San Francisco, or even New Orleans.

After two days, on March 16, the weather improved enough for us to fly out. We broomed the snow off the Norseman, none the worse for its exposure to the storm. The engine rumbled happily into life at my first touch on the starter switch. Thank God for oil dilution, plus—this was an important plus!—we always removed the battery and took it to bed with us.

In the Arctic, happiness, make that *survival*, is a hot battery.

After taking off I decided to fly at about 400 feet above the sea to get a close look at the terrain. At first the land sloped sharply down from the mountain peaks to the sea. Nothing suitable here. Flat land was as scarce as women on Padloping's beach.

But as we flew farther north, the land leveled out with an occasional promontory. This was more interesting, and I kept flying until the mountains met the sea once more, at 69 degrees, 13 minutes North latitude. It was by far the farthest-north penetration by aircraft in eastern Canada to date, other than those of early explorers who brought them aboard ships.

There was a strange tingling in my testicles as I realized how far we were from any help. Maybe that was what people meant when they said pilots flew "by the seat of their pants." For once I let discretion prevail over valor and turned south. It seemed as if a great weight lifted from someplace.

On the way north I had spotted an area which looked suitable for an airport at a place called Kivitoo on Kangeeak Point. Now I landed there on the snow, which turned out to be quite firm. The place was about 68 degrees North, so isolated that there were no Eskimo villages within hundreds of miles.

Leaving the engine running, as usual, I walked around and then dug through the snow. The surface below was smooth rock with a moss covering. To the west, the first mountains were a dozen miles distant. I decided that this was where the new Crystal Three should be located.

We bounced our way into the air and headed back to what had now become home: bleak Padloping Island! Another storm chased us down the coast. After landing, we once again took extra tiedown precautions. This new disturbance lasted two days.

So, I caught up on my sleep and confirmed my claim to being the new Canadian cribbage champion. Me and every other Canuck. All Canadians consider themselves to be the national best player. Never mind if you happen to lose a game or two, or even get skunked. Under the unofficial Canadian rules, one's championship status is automatically restored at the stroke of midnight.

Captain Dyer remarked that there had been a marked increase in his men's morale after our aircraft had landed. We had given them something to do other than peel potatoes and count clouds. At the same time he mentioned that they had joined up before Pearl Harbor and most of them wanted to get out of Padloping and into combat.

During a break in the bad weather on March 17th, I almost destroyed all our hard work. Bein' as it was St. Paddy's Day, begorra, I decided to celebrate by firing a green cartridge from our Very pistol. It went up in grand style. But I'd misjudged the wind and it drifted down almost onto the fabric-covered wing of our Norseman. Baker, Wheeler, and most of the Americans glared at me until I wished I could disappear like one of those ice-worms in the famous song.

On March 19, the storm broke and the snow stopped. Crystal Two reported good flying conditions there. En route weather conditions were unknown, as usual, but it was time to head back. It was essential to remain below any clouds.

Intensive study of my rudimentary charts seemed to indicate that Padle Fjord would be the best route to the height of land of the spine of the Cumberland Mountains. From there it might be possible to creep down Kingnait Fjord to Cumberland Sound.

I took off and gave the camp a bit of a thrill with a farewell buzz job. A flat cloud deck was garlanding the mountains ahead. Not so good. But it was an unpleasant fact that the weather was unlikely to be more than marginally flyable over the whole flight route.

Well then, press on!

As we flew up the fjord under the grey cloud deck, the sheer black rock of the sides of the narrow fjord began to close in on our wingtips. In the immensity of the mountains our little aircraft seemed no more than a bug in a giant insect press. The riverbed below me was slowly but steadily rising as it approached the height of land. Then, bit by bit the cloud deck began to close off the fjord ahead. Decision time! I could climb on top, or turn back.

Both were unpalatable alternatives.

But wait: Tessiquidudjak Lake, just below my skis, was long and narrow, its surface polished as smooth as a mirror. Maybe that damn cloud deck would lift in a few minutes or so. I threw out a roll of colored toilet paper to check the wind and give myself some depth perception, then began my approach. We touched down smoothly, but there was a bit of a crosswind and as we slowed down we spun around slowly like a kid's toy top.

The black mountains rose vertically, like prison walls. If we were unlucky enough to get stuck on this lake we'd be in real trouble. Crystal Minus Three here we are! With the engine just ticking over we waited. And waited. Would the diurnal heating I was counting on lift the ceiling? At long last, a crack of blue showed beneath the dark grey cloud deck.

Time to go!

I opened the throttle, slithering around while making a wide 360-degree turn to pick up speed on the narrow lake. We lifted off and climbed toward our escape route. Once more the rocks seemed to want to crush us. No way to turn back now, even if I wanted to.

And then our yellow Norseman slipped through the tiny opening safely into the blue sky beyond. As I hunched over the flight controls, I figured that the ceiling was maybe fifty feet, and we had less clearance than that on each wingtip. The mountains began to fall away, and I wiped the sweat from my palms and the control wheel. Whew! That had been close.

I looked over at Baker. The muscles around his jaw were just beginning to relax. Wheeler was staring straight ahead. Maybe he wasn't too pleased that his Captain had left him in my tender clutches, but if so, he never complained.

My new highway in the sky was Kingnait Fjord which emptied into Cumberland Sound. Visibility was now unlimited, which I truly appreciated because my magnetic compass, never reliable, was behaving like a metronome. Maybe there's a huge iron deposit up there, who knows?

Once across the Sound, the mountains of Hall Peninsula looked as flat as Saskatchewan prairie compared to the peaks we had just flown over. I had decided to hit Frobisher Bay well down towards Davis Strait. When we were over the ice a turn to starboard would put us on course for the tiny island's landing strip.

As we approached the bay, we ran out of clear air, catching me between cloud layers. Not at all what I wanted. But again I was lucky. After diving through a hole in the undercast there was Crystal Two just where we'd left it.

It had a new airport marker: my yellow Norseman, also just as we'd left it. (*See photo*) Sure felt good to slide without incident onto the short strip.

Major Crowell said that the situation at Crystal One was unchanged. No radio contact, which meant no weather reports. But, if it would cheer us up, the Hudson had finished the Greenland survey and was waiting for us at Goose Bay. This was sort of reassuring. We hadn't been forgotten after all.

After we had secured the aircraft I went to visit a young Eskimo in his igloo in the local village. I had knocked down his snow palace during my brief post-crackup binge, and we'd become friends the next day when I apologized. He'd just laughed and shown me how quickly he could build an igloo made of snow blocks shaped by his walrus-bone saw: in less than two hours.

He could speak quite a bit of English, so, aided by many hand gestures, we were able to communicate quite well. He had green eyes, almost the same color as my own. Light eyes are unusual in Eskimos, and greatly prized. In his case, I suspected a Scottish Hudson's Bay ancestor. His nickname was Terrienniak, the Eskimo name for the white Arctic fox. He was just over five feet tall, and very muscular.

Inuit man in kayak, 1929, Point Burwell in what is now Nunavut. Photo credit R.S. Finnie

For uncounted centuries the hostile environment had forced the Eskimos to live an extremely uncomfortable and dangerous life. Even after the arrival of white men they still stalked seal, walrus, and musk ox, but their main food has always been fish, which they net and dry for themselves and their dogs.

Each family has its own sleigh called a kamitouk, which had ice-covered runners. The Baffin Islanders use thirty or forty husky dogs on individual leashes to pull their kamitouk. The driver commands them with loud shouts, backed up with a sealskin whip about fifty feet long. His efficiency at cracking this weapon over an individual dog's head would put an old-time Missouri muleskinner to shame.

Not mentioned in the travel folder is that fact that the fish diet makes the dogs slightly jet-propelled. This explains why passengers are often seen running alongside the sled, out of the slipstream. Or should that read, "fart-stream"?

Eskimos have always preferred to travel during the everlasting night of winter when everything is frozen. They have their own method of navigation by the stars and their sense of direction is uncanny. The lore is passed from father to son. They make long trips from one hunting ground to another, and when the weather turns bad they build an igloo and wait it out. If the journey takes longer than planned and they run out of dried fish, they always have emergency rations at hand: they eat their dogs.

When Terrienniak was seventeen years old, his father had been killed by a polar bear. Despite his youth it was the lad's duty to supply food for his mother and sister. One day on a hunt he had suffered a terrible accident. He had been stabbing a seal which had suddenly moved, causing his sharp walrus-bone spear to cut a hole in his mukluk. His foot had frozen instantly. Such an accident would normally have ended in his death, but the Americans at Crystal Two were able to treat him with modern drugs.

So, although he had lost part of his foot, he was still able to hunt. In the old days, he, his mother and his sister would all have starved to death because survival was so difficult that one hunter could kill only enough food to supply his own family.

The Eskimos call themselves "Inuit" which means "The People" and are open and friendly. Each morning, without fail, they greeted me by shaking hands, at the same time grinning from ear to ear as they wished me good luck. That kind of spirit is catching. It even started to wear off on me, who needs three cups of coffee in the morning before I'm approachable.

After supper that night I started to worry about tomorrow's problems. I was determined to push on through. Maybe I'd be lucky with the weather and be able to find Crystal One with no trouble.

And maybe I wouldn't.

It was likely that the usual low ceilings and variable visibility in the eternal snow showers would hide the place. I knew from previous experience how hard it was to find the mouth of the Koksoak River, the key to finding Fort Chimo.

I laid out my maps and started to lay off courses and measure distances. I decided to fly down Frobisher Bay, slowly climbing, and when I had sufficient altitude to clear the mountains I'd turn to starboard. Once across the rugged peninsula, Saddleback Island, a prominent landmark, would be a good point from which to set course. Then it would be a straight shot across the dreaded Hudson Strait until I could see our old friend, Cape Hope's Advance.

Then I'd set a southerly course along the west coast of Ungava Bay. But this shore was poorly mapped, and if I missed a landmark we might be spending the night at Crystal Minus Four, not a pleasant thought.

I sat back and studied my chart. There was lots to think about. In addition to the lack of reliable pinpoints there was the extreme magnetic variation which would change rapidly as the flight progressed; an unreliable aircraft's magnetic compass; little likelihood of seeing the sun so I could use my sun compass.

We were in a pickle. However, the Norseman had a good direction-finding loop and an expert radio operator in Lloyd Wheeler to operate it. What I'd give for a radio beacon at Crystal One!

I rubbed my head in frustration, and maybe that caused my brain to produce a unique plan. It went like this: the Hudson was at Goose. It had a low-frequency transmitter capable of putting a healthy 100 watts into its trailing antenna.

And, Hudsons can fly, right? So, supposing I told Evans to fly to Fort Chimo and circle there with his low-frequency antenna pumping out a signal? He had a crack navigator and a good magnetic compass. He also had two engines and twelve hours of fuel. Let him find that elusive place called Chimo and then act as our airborne radio beacon. As far as I knew the scheme had never been attempted before, but I couldn't think of any logical reason why it wouldn't work.

Now for the operational planning. I'd take off at 08:00 sharp. That would enable me to land and refuel at Chimo with a fair chance to reach Goose before darkness. My flight plan to Chimo would be four hours, putting me in at high noon.

I wanted the Hudson to be in position at least half an hour before my estimated time of arrival. He would take about two and a half hours to make his flight from Goose to Chimo. That called for his departure at 09:00. But let's give him a half-hour cushion while he searched for Chimo. So make his takeoff 08:30.

I thanked God the blackout was over as I entered the radio shack and began to talk to Goose. We had a good solid contact. Evans got the idea immediately and confirmed his takeoff time. I told him to get his radio operator, Gerry Pollock, to tune his transmitter to 600 kilocycles and key it every couple of minutes—and be damned sure he got it tuned up for maximum output. I figured that if we were both at 500 feet above ground we'd be able to hear him about fifty or sixty miles out. Higher would be better, of course.

The next morning we got off dead on time and everything went according to plan. The engine slipped into "Automatic Rough" over the Hudson Straits, but that was only to be expected. Then Cape Hope's Advance loomed out of a snow shower and we all breathed a sigh of relief. Now if the engine quit we had a fighting chance of survival.

We were about 75 miles out, abeam of Leaf Lakes, or rather where Leaf Lakes would have been had I been able to see them, when Wheeler shouted, "I've got it!"

I clamped my earphones against my head and listened. The signal was weak and fluttery but undeniably it was there. My scheme had worked and Evans had come through. Marconi couldn't have done it better. In about fifteen minutes the tone was strong enough for a useful bearing and I altered course to port. A full *twenty* degrees— God! But fie on thee, Crystal Minus Four.

Half an hour later we sighted the red roof of the Hudson's Bay Company's building, with our Hudson circling above. It sure looked like home.

We'd had headwinds, so our flight had taken four hours and forty-five minutes and we still had a long way to go. I wasted no time as I hopped out of the plane and Baker hustled up the friendly Eskimos who rolled up drums and began to wobble in the fuel we needed for the next leg.

We strode up to the factor's house hoping for a quick meal. But Mrs. Nicholls would have none of that. She'd been waiting for us to come back and had a roast goose and apple pie on standby. It took a little longer than I'd figured to do justice to her home cooking, but we couldn't hurt her feelings.

Meanwhile, overhead the Hudson was droning around restlessly. Finally we excused ourselves from the table and ran to the Norseman.

"From one Goose to another," I cracked, and Baker and Wheeler grinned.

After takeoff I formated on the Hudson. Or tried to. Our cruising speed was pretty close to his minimum control speed. We were both having control problems in the air below the cloud deck, which was turbulent and loaded with snow showers.

Evans' voice rattled my earphones.

"Did you enjoy your dinner?"

"Sure did."

"Great," he came back sarcastically, "my engines enjoyed all the gas they've been eating while we waited for you."

"Tough, friend," I replied coldly, thinking of how much a margin of safety he had compared to us.

"Well, let's get the show on the road. I'll get on top and let you know how thick the clouds are." Before I could answer the Hudson disappeared in the grey overcast. Baker and I looked at each other.

"I sure hope he doesn't leave us behind," my trusty flight engineer said.

"No fear, Evans is a good man," I replied, masking my apprehension that I too feared we might never see the Hudson again. Soon Evans was back on the air.

"The cloud isn't very thick, and it's smooth and lovely and sunny on top, so come on up. No problem." No problem for him, but plenty for me.

It seemed I'd been climbing through ice-filled clouds a lot recently. But if I didn't try again I could lose my guide. And my unreliable magnetic compass was always in my mind. I looked over at Baker, who was watching me intently.

"Want to chance it, Bill?"   He took a deep breath, hesitated, then nodded.

"Sure, why not."

I opened the throttle to take-off power and let the aircraft accelerate until the wings began to vibrate. Then I pulled the control wheel back into my gut. We shot up like a rocket for just about 500 feet into the grey cloud. Then the speed decayed and the rime ice started to get to us. We were just on the stall when at last we broke through into Evans' blue sky. I throttled back to cruise power. For what seemed the millionth time we'd barely scraped through.

We could see the Hudson far ahead. "Come on back, George, come hold my hand. I'm lonely." He laughed as he turned around.

"You bet!"

Soon he was making passes like a frolicking puppy around our clumsy Norseman. His turbulent wake was causing me to struggle with our flight controls.

"Cut it out, George," I grated, "you're nothing but a damned showoff. Set course for Goose."

"Sorry," he said, although he didn't sound sorry. But he did settle down.

"Course for Goose 172 degrees magnetic," he soon reported.

"One-seventy-two magnetic," I repeated, leaning forward to set the numbers on the aircraft's directional gyro. The magnetic compass read *twenty-two* whole degrees different.

We managed to keep the Hudson in sight until just after the sun set. By then we had Goose Bay in sight and the flare pots they had set along the active runway made the night landing a breeze. The Colonel and Bisson were out on the tarmac to congratulate us. We were just as happy to see them as they were to see us and the Hudson.

That night Hubbard slept in Presque Isle while Bisson and his crew slept in Montreal. But we Norseman crew weren't jealous after what we'd been through. To sleep in the construction company's bunkhouse at Goose Bay was fine with us. I hugged my pillow, relieved that our dangerous exploratory flight was over.

However, next morning it seemed that our adventure wasn't quite over, after all. Dorval airport reported that they were fresh out of snow, and there was none in the weather forecast, either.

And all we had were skis.

It would have taken weeks to get a set of wheels from the factory. I decided to land on the grass of the infield. I'd done that before out West without cracking up. Both Baker and Wheeler declared they were game, so we took off and set course for the bright lights. Downhill all the way, we picked up an unusual tail wind. The flight time was an exceptionally quick six hours and twenty minutes. Damn good.

We flew over Montreal.

"Dorval tower, Norseman 2477 is on skis. Have you got any reports on

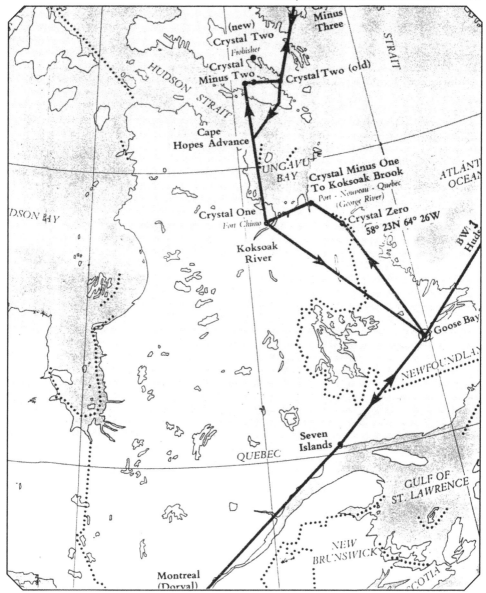

Exploratory Norseman flights, February-March 1942

the condition of the grass in the infield?" I asked very sincerely.

"You want to land on the grass?"

"That's right."

"Don't be silly."

"I'm not being silly. Get me a field report."

Long pause. Then, "Well, we don't have an official one, but a truck got stuck in the mud this morning."

"Good enough. Landing clearance, please."

"Cleared to land at your own discretion."

Where had I heard that one before?

Baker and Wheeler had moved all our survival and emergency equipment to the rear of the fuselage and tied themselves on top of it. That put the center of gravity as back as could be. It would be an ignominious end to our brave adventure if our skis stuck and we flipped over on landing.

Making sure we were directly into the wind with no drift, I brought her in with tail well down, full flaps, right on the stall. Almost a tail-first landing. When I felt the skis touch I cut the power. There was a huge cloud of mud, grass and dirty water. Then the tail wanted to come up as the skis tried to dig in. I blew it down with a quick, heavy blast of engine power, holding the wheel right back in my belly.

We were safely down, but if we stalled out here we'd be up to our knees in mud when we disembarked. So I kept up the momentum with almost full throttle as we blasted our way through in a cloud of muddy water to the edge of the parking tarmac.

Home again! I shut off the engine, but there were no cheering crowds to greet us. Maybe they were all too busy laughing.

I screamed at the tower, and after a while a Ferry Command station wagon appeared. Baker and Wheeler and I said au revoir to one another and patted 2477 farewell.

It had been some kind of airplane.

The Briefing

Early the next day after I had splashed mud all over Dorval, I was ordered to report to Headquarters. Group Captain Powell would like to see me. Short leave period...

Bisson and Evans were there ahead of me, waiting in the outer office and looking somewhat apprehensive. I thought that I was the one who should be looking apprehensive. I was actually wondering if I was going to have the crashed Norseman charged against my pay. It would have to be a very long war before I got in the clear.

But when we were ushered into his office, the wide smile on "Taffy" Powell's face told us that we were all in the clear. He shook all our hands and congratulated us as he said, "Bloody good show. We feel that considering the conditions you had to contend with the expedition was lucky to escape with only one accident."

I gave a sigh of relief and Bisson and Evans looked pleased. But Powell wasn't finished with us yet.

"Come with me," he said, "I've got a surprise for you." He led us down the hall until suddenly we found ourselves in the office of Air Chief Marshal Sir Frederick Bowhill, top man in Ferry Command. It was the first time I'd seen him close up, so I examined him carefully. His face had the weather-beaten look of a longtime sailor, or aviator, both of which he'd been. His piercing blue eyes under bushy eyebrows added to the old sea dog impression. He wore a broad smile as he rose from his chair to shake hands with us.

I'd never seen so many rings of rank in my life. They started at his wrist and climbed almost to his elbow. A wide band was topped by three narrow rings, which meant that his RAF rank was equivalent to that of an American four-star general. His pilot's wings soared over three rows of colorful and impressive ribbons. They included a GBE, which meant that he was a Knight Grand Cross of The Most Excellent Order of the British Empire, a KCB, indicating he was a Knight Commander of The Most Honorable Order of The Bath. His DSO was the Distinguished Service Order, awarded only for gallantry in the field. They made a very impressive array.

Before coming to us he had been Commander-in-Chief of Coastal Command for four years. It was a well-known fact that due to his sailor's prescience he had been able to work out the German battleship *Bismarck*'s actual position in the Bay of Biscay while the Royal Navy was busily steaming in the opposite direction. The course on which he had set his Catalina PBY had resulted in the discovery of the massive super battleship and its eventual destruction by aircraft from the *Ark Royal* and RN surface ships.

In spite of this impressive military background he seemed genuinely interested in three civilian pilots bare of any decoration as he leaned back and invited us to tell him all about our adventures.

There was an awkward moment of silence. It seemed that we weren't prepared for this impromptu interrogation, even if it was meant in a kindly

manner. Evans and I seemed to have lost our tongues.

Finally Bisson said, "It really wasn't so much, sir. We were just doing our duty."

Now there was a longer moment of silence. Powell to the rescue!

"Obviously these men are being very modest, but believe me, sir, they've suffered quite an assortment of hardships." He knew that we wouldn't disobey a direct order, so he turned to Evans and said, "Captain Evans, why don't you tell us how you came to be piloting the first aircraft to land in Greenland."

Air Chief Marshal Sir Frederick Bowhill GBE, KCB, CMG, DSO

That broke the ice.

Evans then told his story about bringing the much-delayed Christmas mail for the troops, and how he'd handled his Hudson on the sharply-slanting pierced-plank runway of Bluie West One.

Then Bisson recounted how he had learned the hard way how to endure in the Arctic completely independent of outside help and how this had allowed us to survive in tents after we had been forced down.

I explained how difficult it was to fly on skis under different snow conditions and how a broken aileron bracket had caused my crash.

Bowhill was obviously impressed. He congratulated us again on our successful completion of a difficult task. Then he told us a little more of his personal history, and how in the First World War he'd survived more than a few crashes of flimsy flying machines constructed of just fabric and wood. We listened intently, making the appropriate noises at the right times.

The interview ended with another round of handshakes and mutual good luck wishes, after which Powell marched us back down the long corridor to his office.

I wondered what new challenges Fate had in store for me.

Powell called in his assistant, a pilot who had been on the first Flying

Fortress deliveries. Wing Commander Don Ross, our Senior Air Staff Officer, to give him his official title, sat us down. Powell's face was serious as he wasted no words.

"Your friend Colonel Hubbard has made his report to Washington, and the Americans have taken a very good view of the work of Ferry Command in the north to date. They would like to see us continue to prove out the Crimson Route East. We in our turn have agreed to attempt to deliver aircraft via Goose, Greenland and Iceland to Prestwick. As this route has never yet been flown I must tell you that the powers-that-be consider this matter to be very urgent and of the utmost importance."

He paused to let us digest this startling news. We sat speechless, like a row of toy soldiers, each wondering what was coming next. We soon found out. Powell fixed us with a steady stare.

"You three men have been chosen to prove this new far northern route is feasible." We were stunned. From our work in the North we knew the secret route had not yet even been scouted, let alone used to actually deliver aircraft fresh from the factories.

I wondered if the bad jam-up of aircraft at Gander because of the usual westerly wind had made the sense of urgency even more intense. Obviously, an alternative air delivery route avoiding the German U-boats would be of immense, even immeasurable value to the war effort. Powell decided that the few minutes he had given us was enough time for us to make up our minds.

"Well?"

Bisson, as leader, answered first.

"Oui, yes indeed, I'd love to take part."

Evans wasn't so flowery. He just said, "Sure."

I hit somewhere in between.

"Yes sir, count me in."

Powell looked pleased, then Bisson inquired, "What have you planned, sir?" Powell rubbed his hands.

"McVicar and Evans will each take a Canso, the Canadian name for an amphibious Catalina flying boat, as you no doubt know."

He saw my startled look and read my mind. "It might be slow and cold, but it's got the range you need and Coastal Command is in desperate need of more flying boats." Both Evans and I stared at him without replying. He continued our briefing.

"You probably will have trouble getting any weather information from your Greenland or Iceland destinations, and it's a long way back. You know all about the American installations in Greenland, and we'll provide you with a list of the American radio frequencies and their code books. If you can't communicate with them for some reason or other you're on your own.

We also want to know why their weather reports are not getting through. Any questions?"

"What about Iceland?" I asked.

"The RAF have a Coastal Command squadron stationed there, but radio communication to the Americans in Greenland seems very spotty. Any further questions?" He glared at me.

Evans and I just nodded glumly. We'd just been through the problem of getting one part of the Allied war effort to talk to the other part. This time we'd have to do it in a slow amphibian designed to operate in a moderate climate. A sort of consolation prize was that if we were forced down at sea we could float around until somebody came to our rescue.

After a short pause Evans took the initiative.

"I'll do my best," he said, and I added, "Me too."

Powell glanced at us keenly, satisfied with our laconic response, then continued, "Captain Bisson, you will be given a Liberator and your orders are to follow the Cansos over, acting as a mother ship. Once you have all arrived at Prestwick you will immediately bring our flight crew personnel back. The quicker these deliveries are completed and the crews returned the more we will impress the powers-that-be in Washington and London."

With that we were dismissed. Just one of his problems. A very busy man.

I'd been too tired the night before to think of sex, but now I had the strength, the desire, and the time to get caught up. I got out my little black book.

Six calls later it was apparent that people who leave town to visit the Arctic lose their priority. Maureen couldn't be reached, but that didn't bother me too much. My pressure was so high and my need so intense that I knew I couldn't handle a long seduction scene. The other girls were just "busy." I didn't really want to know what that cryptic word meant. But there was one bright spot. After a masterly sales job on Renée she said that just for me she'd cancel the date she already had made for tomorrow night.

Later, while lying in bed I looked down. It really would be only twenty-four hours, but it seemed like forever before I could count on Renée to get rid of that impressive but annoying "tent."

Sexual/Aircraft Competency

There was a delay in securing our two Cansos, so I took the opportunity to add some types to my aircraft competency card. On March 24, Hunter Moody checked me out in Handley-Page Hampden AN148. It was a twin-engine light bomber being built in Canada from a prewar English design, already considered obsolete for operations.

It had one good feature I thought other aircraft designers should copy: its dinghy was stored in the port engine nacelle from which it could be released either by a hand lever in the cockpit, or by an automatic immersion switch which would allow it to float free. Aircraft that carried their dinghies in the fuselage presented a big hazard. After a ditching, the problem of getting the rubber boat out of the door was too much for many crews, who perished in the frigid waters of the Atlantic.

The pilot sat in lonely grandeur because the English apparently didn't believe in copilots. The English also apparently didn't believe in tail-wheel locks either, so the Hampden had a tail-wheel shimmy which wouldn't go away. Maybe a grass runway would solve the problem, but Dorval was fresh out of grass runways.

The Handley-Page Hampden, "a twin-engine light bomber being built in Canada from a prewar English design, already considered obsolete for operations."

An interphone was supposed to keep the pilot in touch with the gunner/radio man who lived behind the bomb-bay. When the wet cell battery which powered this pathetic contraption froze up—which it did with monotonous regularity—communications over the span of the bomb-bay was via a note on a clothesline arrangement.

To top it off, the pilot had no control over the fuel supply. So, if "Sparks" got the chop, the aircraft could be forced down by fuel starvation with plenty of fuel still in the wing tanks. Ah, those English designers!

The next day R/O Spry and I started to ferry AN148 to Halifax. But the weather turned duff and I had to return after two hours of hazardous flight. On this, one of my first delivery flights, even if it was only local, I'd had to dodge far too many clouds over the rugged mountains which lay west of Millinocket, Maine.

The Hampden's radio was an ancient Marconi layout with controls situated back in the radio operator's station. It was certainly not designed so that a pilot could fly the North American radio range system. When I returned and checked into Field Operations I got an unpleasant surprise. A dull clod called Squadron Leader Wakeman who had dispatched various flights that morning was very snarly. In fact, he came as close as damn is to swearing, to accusing me of cowardice.

Naturally this upset me mightily and I had to be physically restrained from vaulting over the crew assignment counter and hammering the clown. While all this was going on George Evans arrived. He also had found the Hampden not fit for real instrument flying in North America. Dealing with two strong-minded Ferry Command Captains, even if they were quite junior, had the effect of calming Wakeman down, although he was still grumbling when Evans and I took off for the Mount Royal Hotel.

Powell or someone else in authority must have realized that Wakeman was a dud, because he was soon transferred to some post where his arbitrary, bureaucratic manner couldn't screw up our flight operations.

That afternoon Al Leeward took four pilots over to St. Hubert airport in a Hudson. Each of us would pick up a Hampden from the factory where they were built or overhauled. I climbed into P5336 and carried out a test flight, then ferried it over to Dorval where a RCAF pilot would pick it up and deliver it to one of their stations.

Al Leeward

My abort of the Hampden delivery to Halifax had two good results. One was that in spite of my best (worst?) efforts I failed to kill Spry and myself in the horrible weather. The other, almost as important, was that I was able to meet Renée again that night. After only a couple of drinks she seemed as eager as I to get into bed. What a welcome, if unexpected, development that was! I hurried her into an elevator which seemed to move far too slowly. Maybe we knocked down a couple of old folks as we spurted out of the elevator and raced down the hall, and then through the door which led to pure bliss.

Now that all my plans were falling into place I decided to prolong the delights of anticipation. While we were undressing I told her a corny joke.

"I'm suffering from that dread Hawaiian disease called 'lackanookie,'" I said with a straight face.

"What do you mean?" She seemed alarmed.

"'Nookie' is what the Americans call making love. When you're not getting any you suffer. Get it?" She laughed and gave the reply I was hoping for. "We'll soon fix that," she said as she slid between the sheets. Of course I wasted no time in joining her. She proceeded quickly to skillfully provide the only known cure for this widespread malady. And sure enough at the same time she solved my "tent" problem.

As I lay back in complete relaxation I realized that each time we made love my command of the English language was improving at a rate which would have made the Berlitz language school jealous. Renée must have noticed, but for reasons of her own she did not bring up the subject. Then, after a short rest period, she performed some further pleasurable maneuvers which she assured me would prevent recurrence of any "tents" for a long time to come. I felt that what she was trying to do was impossible, but somehow never bothered to stop her from trying.

"For me (the Ventura) was just a blown-up Hudson fitted with the much more powerful R-2800 engines."

The next day I took the opportunity to have my Ferry Command pilot competency certificate endorsed for a Lockheed Ventura. Bill Longhurst took Evans and me around the circuit for a half hour of dual each in AE708 before turning us loose. I really didn't like the big awkward beast. For me it was just a blown-up Hudson fitted with the much more powerful R-2800 engines. That night I took four RCAF pilots on a four hour long navigation flight over North Bay and Toronto.

Then at long last Al Leeward gave me my long-awaited checkout in North American B-25 112-440. He gave me only an hour dual but in that short time I came to like the aircraft. The only thing that bothered me a little was the Mitchell's 150mph single engine safety speed. But it was a dream to fly.

Just to finish out the day in style, I took four navigation students in Hudson BW477 on a five hour flight to Moncton, New Brunswick, and back.

Powell now kept his promise to Evans and me and authorized the beginning of our four-engine checkout. We'd already passed the ground school course. Normally a Captain would have ten or more twin-engine deliveries under his belt before he could aspire to four engines.

There was some grumbling from the odd senior captain, but we told them that one Norseman flight into the Arctic equaled ten normal deliveries. The grumbling got louder, but we paid no attention as Captain Al Leeward gave us each five landings and an hour of air work in Liberator B24D serial No. 11108. Things were at such a rush that they hadn't got around to erasing the USAAC numbers on many of our aircraft and replacing them with RAF numbers.

The big, adjustable seat was comfortable, which was more than could be said for British warplanes. The instrument panel was well laid out, with the same remark applying. Once I got used to the heavy controls I learned to like the ugly black monster. Of course, having four engines might have had a lot to do with my affection. Leeward said we were doing fine and he'd finish up our four-engine check when we got back from our Canso delivery.

It had been a very busy week. I'd had no trouble conquering a wide variety of new aircraft types. A crusty, very experienced aircraft instructor had given me rare praise as to my ability.

My sex instructor Renée had told me that I had been an excellent pupil, and that after graduating from her courses cum laude, I had become a very competent lover.

I wasn't sure which achievement was the more important.

The Crimson Route East

My Canso turned out to be No. FP533. Captain Hunter Moody took George Evans and me out to the ramp the moment it arrived from the Consolidated factory in San Diego. It was a big beast, with a wingspan almost that of a Liberator.

Its two engines were mounted high in the wing to keep them as far from the water as possible. No flaps, but giant ailerons which I would find very hard to move. The hull was the best feature, beautifully streamlined, with a pronounced step to assist in getting into a planing attitude while taking off from the water. The three massive wheels stole valuable space in the fuselage when they rotated up to hide in the hull.

After our walk-around inspection we climbed up a rickety metal ladder and entered the fuselage through one of the two Plexiglas aft gun "blisters." The rear compartment contained four fold-up canvas bunks and was positively commodious compared to other aircraft I'd flown. The electric hot plate and compact food pantry would supply meals on our long, long flights.

Bill Baker's legs hung down from his flight engineer's position in the tower that connected the hull to the wing. He was surrounded by engine gauges and controls. We would split the engine starting duties, with him in control of the mixture, fuel cocks, hot air for the carburetors, fuel pumps and the inertial starter switches. Up front I had the throttles, magneto switches and the prop controls and feathering buttons.

Communication could be by interphone, but we preferred to use a selection of small lights mounted on my control column and his panel. When I wanted something done, such as changing from rich to lean mixture, I would turn that light on. When he complied, Baker would signal by turning the light off.

The rear compartment was separated from the navigator's compartment by a watertight bulkhead with a small, lockable door. As I opened the door and stepped over the threshold the amenities provided for the navigator—which I intended to be—excited me.

On the port side there was an extra large plotting table where even the largest air plotting charts could be laid out without awkward folding. There was even a bookshelf for nautical tables, AN tables and other navigator's necessities. There was a spacious drawer for maps and charts beneath the plotting table. I noticed with approval a special compartment set into the table with a transparent cover to house the aircraft's official timepiece. Overhead was a hatch that could be swung down to avoid parallax when taking astro shots. There must have been plenty of input from US Navy navigators on this design.

The radio equipment occupied the starboard side. There were two powerful Bendix TA-2J Liaison transmitters with two companion Bendix RH1-B receivers. The direction finding loop mounted on the outside of the fuselage was controlled by a single Bendix MN-2 radio compass receiver. The two pilots, the bombardier in the nose, the flight engineer, the cooking quarters, the port and starboard blister stations and the tunnel gunner's station connected by a Type 3617 interphone system.

After climbing into the port pilot's seat, I noticed that the props were only a foot or so from my head. Moody climbed into the starboard seat and grinned as he told me I'd better wear both phones and ear plugs, because the fuselage had no insulation and the noise was terrific.

Our seats were massive and uncomfortable, and the control column which held both our wheels could have been used to steer a battleship. Consolidated Aircraft had been powerfully influenced by their main customer, the United States Navy. The throttles and propeller controls hung from the top of the cockpit enclosure, along with the elevator and aileron trim tabs.

I looked back at the long expanse of the wing, thankful to see black rubber inflatable boots on the leading edges which would give some protection against ice buildup. At the very end of the wings, two large floats, almost the size of small canoes, hung down. In the water they would prevent the Cat from capsizing. In the air, when retracted, they would form part of the wing. The stout struts on each side of the fuselage made sure it and the wing didn't part company.

Forward in the nose there was a hatch where the anchoring rope could be handled. The so-called "bombardier" controlled a single .30in caliber machine gun. There was provision for one .30in machine gun in each blister position. The Cat wasn't over-armed.

The engines fired up with no trouble and the tricycle gear made taxiing easy. After only five landings each, plus an hour of air work each, including single-engine procedures, Moody was satisfied we could handle the big amphibian safely and soon we were taxiing back in.

Other than finding the controls heavy I thought it flew like a big Piper Cub. The airspeed was a rather unimpressive 115 knots, but it had lots of range and good single-engine performance at normal gross weights. We never flew at normal gross weights, of course.

As I had taken the astro course I talked Powell into letting me act as my own navigator. He responded by assigning me two copilots, neither of whom spoke much English. They were escapees from Czechoslovakia when Hitler's hordes had overrun their homeland. Their names were Hubacek and Baillik, and both held the rank of sergeant. Neither of them had seen the inside of a Canso before, nor were they likely to do so again. They were fighter pilots and would remain in England.

They had no instrument or multi-engine experience, so I figured the automatic pilot would do a better job. They were keen to help me fly, but I thought differently. I told both of them, and I thought they understood, that they were NOT, repeat NOT, to touch any aircraft control.

I did my own compass swing, an operation which I felt should always be done in the air with the landing gear retracted and all radio and electrical circuits operational. Radio man Eric Rush joined our crew and calibrated the direction-finding loop while I compensated the ship's magnetic compass. He was a slightly plump radio graduate of the Canadian Department of Transport who had a pleasant expression and a quiet manner. In fact, he often looked as if he were fast asleep, but I was to find that no message addressed to our aircraft ever escaped his sensitive ears.

With the many necessary preparations finally completed, our three aircraft got away on the 5th of April. I had a fast but turbulent flight. We banged through an active cold front which deposited a dose of clear ice all over the wings and fuselage. For a while I had to increase power to stay in the air, but after flying a single engine aircraft with absolutely no de-icing equipment, I had a lot of confidence in the Canso.

After we landed at Goose we found that once again we were on our own. That night in the construction company's bunkhouse we made our plans. Our first decision was that we'd make the slightly longer flight to BW8 rather than use BW1. Both Bisson and Evans didn't like the winding, narrow approach up the fjord to BW1. We decided on a night takeoff so that we'd arrive at noon, when any ground fog should have burned off.

Dorval advised that they'd got a rare weather report from Greenland. Unfortunately, it was not favorable, so we took a 24-hour delay. After the tension of getting prepared and enduring the recent miserable rough flight we were glad to enjoy a short break.

The next morning Bill and I did a run-up to make sure everything was working properly. Bad news. One of our two voltage-control regulators, a small unit consisting of relays and coils, was kaput. There was no way I'd consider leaving with just one generator charging. If it quit we could quickly run the ship's batteries flat. Bill looked at the defective unit and admitted he didn't have the facilities to repair it. It would probably take Dorval several days to send a serviceable unit.

It looked as if we were stuck right at the beginning of our great adventure. Then we spotted a US Navy Catalina which had wandered into Goose on some sort of a sightseeing trip for the brass. We were sure its two voltage regulators would be in first class shape. Bill and I agreed it wasn't worth the effort to ask for one of them—we both knew the answer. Northbound, two were necessary, but southbound they could get by on one.

When nobody was watching we removed our unserviceable unit and made a quick trip to the electrical panel of the ship with the big white star on its side. A deft flick of a screwdriver, a change of units and a quick trip back to our Cat. We now had two serviceable generators. As we shook hands, Bill and I swore each other to secrecy. We were now partners in crime.

Late in the afternoon the Dorval Met. people came up with a very general forecast: Goose not so hot, en route probably solid cloud for 75 per cent of the flight. But BW8 would not be under the influence of any low pressure system, so it could be in the clear.

We decided to go.

The night was extra dark under a heavy, low overcast as Evans got away first, and his navigation lights soon disappeared. Now it was my turn. I knew the safety height to clear the mountains within twenty-five miles of the base was not less than 3,000 feet. Even with a gross take-off overload weight of 34,000 pounds, very high for a wheel operation, I felt we should be able to climb through 3,000 feet with time to spare.

The flares along the packed snow of runway 27 were flickering in the blackness of the forest as I took a deep breath and opened the throttles. After a long, long run I eased the nose wheel off. Then the main wheels reluctantly left the surface and I got a positive angle of climb.

I groped down below the instrument panel and found the landing gear control level. It was a vertical handle which turned through an arc of about sixty degrees. I heard the groan of the hydraulic system as it started to lift the big wheels. My eyes were glued to the instrument panel as we were now in the thick cloud. To save the engines I reduced the boost and props from the takeoff settings and prepared for a slow but steady rate of climb.

Then I realized we weren't climbing. We were just getting through the air. I started to sweat. Unseen hills were getting dangerously close. Why weren't we climbing? I put back on takeoff power despite Baker's cry of dismay as he saw the temperatures of his engines shooting up into the red danger zone.

Why the hell not?

The landing-gear position indicators are dim little discs of plastic located away over on the copilot's side of the cockpit. I checked them and to my astonishment saw a smudge of green, which meant the gear was still extended. The resistance of the massive wheels to the slipstream was the reason we weren't climbing. I reached down and checked the landing gear control lever. It told me that my friendly Czech copilot had decided to be helpful. For some unknown reason, he'd turned the unmarked lever so that the gear had gone back down after I'd retracted it.

I felt like smacking him in the chops, but I was far too busy for that pleasure. I put the lever in the up position, and once more the hydraulics complained as the main wheels lifted to their recesses in the hull. Then came the welcome bang of the nose-gear doors clanging shut. The indicating light went red and very slowly we started to climb.

Baker shouted that the engines were burning up, so I pulled back to normal climb power and let the airspeed build up just a bit. At the same time I started a turn to port to avoid the mountains hidden in the cloudy darkness. I wondered if I'd waited too long, and felt my body tensing against the possible crash. But as the minutes inched by like snails the needle of the altimeter slowly crept past 3,000 feet.

I drew in another deep breath. It seemed we had lucked out.

I set course for Greenland, engaged the automatic pilot and looked across at my copilot. He seemed blissfully unaware of what he'd just put me through. I decided to hold my temper. After all, he'd tried to do his best. He would soon be in a Hurricane or Spitfire intent on killing Germans where his life expectancy could probably be measured in weeks. But I made sure on future takeoffs he would sit with his arms folded.

Dorval meteorology had been right. We were soon in solid cloud complete with rime ice. I shone the Aldis lamp on the leading edge of the wing. The telltale white line was slowly building up but I didn't turn on the boots. Accepted procedure was to wait until an inch or so accumulated and crack it off. The props were a different matter; with ice buildup power could be lost. I turned on the alcohol which fed the anti-icing fluid to the individual blades. Soon I could hear the soft ice being thrown off by centrifugal force beating on the top of the fuselage right behind my head.

In spite of its de-icing devices the heavily laden Cat ran right out of climb at 11,000 feet, still in cloud. No astro tonight, so I set a dead reckoning course which would place us well clear of the icecap, deep in the Davis Strait.

Rush couldn't raise BW8 on the American frequencies. Then back on Ferry Command's North Atlantic frequency he contacted Dorval and Gander, neither of whom had anything of value for us. We plugged on, hour after hour. Ever so gradually the eastern sky lightened. Just as the sun came up we popped out of the cloud bank.

No land in sight on either side. It was awfully lonely as I altered course to starboard. It took some time before the impressive, shining icecap showed low on the horizon. For an inhospitable two-mile-thick ice cube it looked very welcome.

*Typical of "the jaggedly indented" west coast of Greenland, Kekertarmiut
Island is south of Sondrestrom Fjord (now known as Kangerlussuaq).
Photo © 2007 Doc Searls, used with permission*

As we flew over the jaggedly indented coast I worked to pinpoint our
position. Not an easy job, as all fjords look alike. Then I sighted what I at
first thought was our own shadow proceeding up the fjord I'd identified as
Sondestrom. Then I looked again.

It wasn't our shadow, it was the other Canso.

The approach up wide Sondrestrom Fjord was easy at our height and I
followed Evans until we were both on BW8's 5,000-foot-long gravel runway. We had just parked and finished diluting our engines when Bisson's
Lib appeared and crunched down in a cloud of flying dust and stones.

When we trudged up a slope and entered the USAAC Ops room, I looked
around. Lots of maps and radio equipment.

Then I asked the vital question, "Did you receive our flight plans?"

"Why no, we didn't know you were coming," the operations officer replied. He seemed somewhat offended we'd landed without his permission.
I gritted my teeth. A weather report, a bearing, or just a signal report would
have been very welcome during the long night. But there was no point in
antagonizing our allies.

Then a huge bear of a man joined us, his face creased with a friendly smile. I'd finally met one of my heroes, Bernt Balchen, the great Arctic explorer. His big hand crushed mine.

"Welcome. I'm the commanding officer here. Anything you want, just holler."

"I hope you get your communications straightened out with Goose and Gander," I replied, rather surprised to see that he wore only the twin bars of rank of a captain in the USAAC. With his background I thought he should have been a full chicken colonel. Later when the subject of rank came up he said it meant little to him. He was Norwegian born and just wanted to serve his adopted country.

When Balchen heard of our difficulties he said, "I'm sorry you couldn't raise us last night. I thought we'd got the radio frequency thing sorted out after your Hudson landed here. I guess we'll have to get Washington on the ball."

"Good," Bisson said, "Now how about Iceland?"

"We don't get much from that place." This was bad news indeed. It meant that we were going to have to make another blind flight into an area notorious for its stinking bad weather.

We decided that once again a night takeoff would be necessary so we could crawl into Iceland at high noon. I managed to put the chilling thought of flying over the icecap at night out of my mind.

The Canso started with no trouble, and after a tense takeoff to the west between two lines of flickering flares we retracted the wheels and began a slow climb. The unseen, jagged mountains were too close to the fjord to risk a turn and a takeoff to the east was out of the question.

It seemed like forever before I gained enough altitude to safely turn east. Then the painfully slow climb continued to what I considered the safe altitude of 14,000 feet. My chart indicated that 12,000 feet would clear the icecap, but the man who had created that chart wasn't sitting in a cold Catalina. We had just leveled off when things started to go the way of the Greenland bases: *Blooie*.

First the heaters gave up the ghost. They weren't much help at the best of times, but they did take some of the chill off the cabin. Their name was "Southwind" but we thought the name "Northwind" would be more appropriate. The outside air temperature was now minus 40 degrees; Fahrenheit or Celsius, it didn't matter. The wind whistled through the cracks around the poorly sealed cockpit. I was thankful for my heavy Norseman clothing, which had proven itself. The Czechs weren't so well off. They had only the standard RAF issue flying suits and boots. I told them to keep moving around in the navigator's compartment to keep from freezing.

Then the Northern Lights began to stage a ghostly dance across the sky. To most people the purple and orange streamers and banners would have been a pleasing and spectacular sight. I'd often enjoyed watching them back in Edmonton. But to a navigator they were just another headache. At best he would have trouble seeing his stars through the ever-changing bands of light. At worse he'd lose any chance for astro.

It soon turned out that the question of astro was academic. I had put my two copilots back in the cockpit, making sure the automatic pilot had full control. I had my sextant in my bare hands, which was necessary to set the controls before I shot my stars. But the navigator's hatch was frosted over. When I opened it the icy blast paralyzed my fingers and my eyes ran with frosty tears.

With a curse that was almost a groan I shut the hatch and buried my hands in my armpits. I stood in the companionway watching one of my copilots trying to scrape the ice off the outside of the windshield while his buddy scraped away at the frost on the inside.

I was dismayed. No astro. How bad could things get? We were now on a dead-reckoning course using a very doubtful wind component over a most hostile land.

Just as I was reflecting the flight had had its full share of troubles, the sickly smell of burning electrical insulation began to permeate the frigid air. Thick black smoke was pouring out of the radio operator's side of the compartment. I was struck by real fear while Baker joined me in a hunt for the source. The swirling air stream made our task very difficult. Finally we pinned the source down to the wing float relay box. Baker removed the cover and we both recoiled from the ominous glow inside. Both relay windings were red hot. It seemed their contacts had welded shut.

Baker shut off the aircraft's main electrical bus line, which had the same effect as if he had pulled a master circuit breaker. This threw us into darkness, but stopped the fire. We got out our flashlights whose beams proved to be dim. The extreme cold had reduced their battery power, but we had enough light to see to disconnect the defective unit. Then we connected the main bus back on the line.

Nothing happened. The direct short had not only discharged our batteries, it had also seriously damaged our whole electric system.

What to do now?

We had one last line of defense. It was our auxiliary power generator which was powered by a small petrol engine, just like a lawn mower. It was supposed to start when a small length of cord was pulled with vigor. But ours would not. It was being just as balky as its grass-cutting cousin. At an altitude of almost three miles we couldn't even get a cough out of the damn thing.

We all took turns yanking on the cord and one of the Czechs passed out from the exertion. He apparently had a heart condition that he had successfully hidden from the medical examiners. While we admired his spirit he was a heavy load to carry aft to a bunk.

The aircraft wasn't equipped with oxygen, so it wasn't long before we were all exhausted. I told everyone to quit trying. We would just have to fly on in total darkness alleviated only by our weakening flashlights. We now had no lights, no radio, and no heat. We were almost frozen, and I was unsure of our position.

If we'd had any sense we should have been petrified with fright. Instead we just pressed on. Things were bound to get better, right?

Wrong.

The Gods of Flight weren't through with us. Suddenly we were subjected to an intense display of St. Elmo's fire, a phenomenon caused by an excess of static electricity. Purple, orange and white balls formed on the windshield before rolling over our heads towards the wing. Then the propellers became circular sheets of variable colors.

Abruptly two small spheres of intense blue formed inside the cockpit. My copilots and I managed to dodge them, and after they had roamed aimlessly around the cockpit they headed back through the fuselage and disappeared into the tower. Soon we could hear Baker's furious oaths as he forced them out of his small windows.

St. Elmo's fire is considered by experts to be harmless. But I doubt that any of those "experts" had ever been in the same circumstances we were in that night. The display did us no real physical damage, true enough, but it scared us out of our wits. Aboard an already crippled aircraft weird ghostly balls of fire were doing everything but clanking chains. To me, that could certainly be called harmful.

As we plowed on, the eastern horizon lightened to a vivid pink and angry grey. I figured we were now safely past the icecap and decided to start my letdown early to avoid cracking into one of Iceland's mountains while still in cloud. I wanted to have visual reference a safe distance from the island.

The air was a confused, turbulent mass of many layers of clouds. After what seemed to be an eternity I started to glimpse the icy seas of the Denmark Strait. Even at 300 feet, where I wanted to level off, a big iceberg could have knocked us out of the air. But I needed all the forward visibility I could get, so I continued down to just about 100 feet.

Visibility varied between a mile and zip. However, the black sea's long trails of white spume showed we had a quartering tail wind. As we bounced along with everyone looking out anxiously I was glad I had let down early.

The first sign we were near land was a cloud of seagulls. Then we spotted a fishing trawler which was pitching and tossing wildly in the open sea. So much for the reassurance of being in a flying boat. If we'd landed on the water under these conditions our hull wouldn't have lasted ten minutes.

I reached up and pulled the throttle back a bit to reduce our speed to ninety knots. Then I altered course to starboard where I had a gut feeling Reykjavik lay. It was just a sailor's hunch, and I felt more like the captain of a surface vessel as I tasted the salt spray flying over the windshield.

I was the first to catch sight of land. The dark smudge on the horizon proved to be the southwesternmost part of the island. We hedgehopped to the Reykjavik airport, avoiding the high land and trying to dodge the worst snow showers.

When I saw the runways I made a tight circle with no radio contact and was rewarded with a green flare. Someone in the tower was on their toes. Even Coastal Command wasn't flying in this weather, so I came straight in and landed.

The tower must have notified the RAF base when they spotted our roundels, because a ground man appeared and waved us to a parking spot. I gave the signal for Baker to shut off the two marvelous Pratt & Whitney engines. They hadn't even coughed during the eight and a half hour flight from Goose to BW8, nor during our recent eight hour dreadful trip from Greenland to Iceland.

I was unloading my bags through the blister when I noticed a delegation had arrived to greet us. Only fair, I thought. After all, this was the first aircraft flight ever over the icecap from west Greenland to Iceland.

Maybe somehow someone had told somebody we were coming sometime.

The Army general stuck out his hand. "Hello, I'm sure glad to see some Americans."

After my recent flight I wasn't feeling particularly diplomatic. "Americans, hell. We're Canadians." Wrong thing to say. Without another word he dropped my hand in mid-shake and strode away, followed by his retinue. As I stared at their departing backs I realized I'd goofed.

But all was not lost. A small group of US Navy officers in their blue uniforms had seen us come in. One of them came over and introduced himself.

"Don't worry about the brown jobs," he said, "we love Cats and we'll look after you."

"Hey, great," I said, and quickly introduced Baker who produced a long, long list of snags. The engineering officer didn't seem the least bit fazed, so it was obvious that they must have an extensive stock of spares, plus good mechanics. That was the American way.

There were about a dozen amphibious Cats scattered around the airport. I found out that they were an American Navy squadron sent by President Roosevelt to help us on anti-sub patrols, even if some of his advisors thought they would be more useful in the Pacific.

We removed our flight gear, showered up and were soon being royally entertained in the American Officers' Club. When I finally got around to reporting to the RAF people they were a bit miffed, but after all they had no spare parts for our Cats. Nor had they any knowledge of Evans' Cat or our Liberator.

But just as I hung up Bisson slid under the overcast and landed. When he joined us and learned Evans was missing, the panic really started. The ground radio ops became hoarse with futile calls while the tower fired rockets through the overcast, hoping to attract the attention of the missing aircraft.

I kept my worries to myself. Evans and I had flown on instruments a lot together and I admired his ability. But most of his experience had been gained in the States and Canada flying between closely spaced radio range stations. Here was a very different kettle of fish. If he hadn't crashed he would still have plenty of fuel, but where in hell was he?

Three long hours after I'd landed he showed up out of the snow and fog. His Cat arrived from the east, of all things. I ran out to greet him. His whole crew were quiet and grim. They'd had a radio failure. I found out later that Evans had not let down soon enough. Propelled by the un-fore-casted tail wind, his first sight of land as he broke cloud was a mountain. Only a violent turn had saved their lives. Completely lost, he'd followed the rugged northern and eastern coast all the way around the island until he'd stumbled into Reykjavik.

It had been a tough flight—for both of us. Evans declared that if he never saw another Cat for the rest of his life it would be okay with him. I was almost in agreement.

The next morning, thanks to the good old US Navy, both our Cats were back in first-class shape. We took off in what Iceland thought of as very fine weather: a 500 foot ceiling and two mile visibility; variable in showers, of course.

There were a couple of fronts on the way to Scotland, and I foolishly tried to climb over one to avoid the icing. The Met. people had said I could top it at 13,000 feet and I finally gave up at 17,000 feet. This was really high for a Cat, and I made good time as we let down in a hurry. After the day before, however, this flight was more like a holiday outing. I got contact near Stornoway for my first view of my father's rugged homeland.

After we landed at Prestwick our three crews were given a right royal welcome. Ferry Command had pulled it off. Invitations to live it up in the bar of the stately Orangefield Hotel that night came from all sides.

However, that was put on hold when Bisson decided to begin our return B-24 flight that very night. Evans and I agreed. A quick turnaround would convince those legendary powers-that-be that our new route was feasible.

We decided to flight plan direct from Prestwick to BW8, avoiding Iceland and its perpetual bad weather, not to mention its short runways. I would act as copilot on the Greenland leg and Evans would navigate. We would exchange duties on the BW8-to-Goose leg.

One promise I'd be pleased to keep was that after leaving BW8 we'd make a detour over Baffin Island. When we passed over Pangnirtung and their invalids we'd parachute the vital serum we'd brought from the medical people of Montreal's famous Royal Victoria Hospital.

After refueling at Goose we'd immediately fly to Dorval where three Hudsons were waiting for us. When we delivered them via the Crimson Route promptly, the viability of the new far northern delivery route would be proven.

This was all very patriotic. But it meant that if we left immediately we'd have to forego the party celebrating our pioneer "round the houses" delivery flight our Prestwick people were cooking up.

This was unfortunate, because with my name I could do no wrong in Bonnie Scotland. I told my new friends to save the booze, and boasted that I'd be back in just one week with a Hudson strapped to my ass. Then we'd really tie one on. They didn't believe me, of course, not only because I was a new boy, but because normal crew turnaround time had been running a month or more.

So I bet Wing Commander Jimmy Jeffs a pound note I'd do it. The onlookers were impressed with such an expensive, if not quite properly frugal Scottish proof of my sincerity.

Crew of Marco Polo*: L-R, F/Lt. H.J. Farley, F/E A. Wright, F/O A. Colato, R/O C.P. Meagher, First Officer E.E. Abbott, Captain George P. Evans, OBE*

Proving the Route

hile the Met. people were preparing a weather folder for our return Lib flight, I sat in the dining room of the Orangefield drinking tea. The stuff they called coffee could have been used to poison rats. The meager, paper-rationed four-sheet copy of a daily London newspaper told something of how badly the war was going for us.

The Battle of the Atlantic, which Churchill always had said was his biggest worry, was going the way Hitler and his Admiral Karl Doenitz hoped. If the British government's published figures concerning tonnage being sunk were even close to being correct, food would soon have to be rationed even more severely. And if many more of those tankers swallowed U-boat torpedoes and blew up in the night, the Bomber Command's offensive against Germany could soon grind to a halt.

"Not very good, is it?" Jeffs asked. His normally cheerful face mirrored his concern. Although I agreed, I made an effort to cheer him up.

"The Yanks are coming. They're already churning out bombers by the hundreds which will beef up Bomber and Coastal Commands."

"Do you really believe that bumph?"

"Certainly. Roosevelt promised 'em by the thousands, and he's got a habit of coming through. They're building new aircraft factories all over the States. And let's not forget our new delivery route will allow the bombers they're building at such a mad rate to get here a lot quicker."

"I certainly hope you're right," he sighed with a weak smile. Any smidgeon of good news was very welcome.

I put down my cup and wandered across the road where the meteorological centre was housed in a converted country mansion. Once passed by the security guard, I approached a forecaster who was bent over his synoptic chart of the North Atlantic. As I peered at the wide sheet, he rather furtively erased a report he'd just finished penciling in. I presumed this was super secret stuff, not for the eyes of mere aircrew. I wondered if the report was from one of our convoys of weather ships. Or maybe it was from a German aircraft or U-boat. I'd heard rumors that we'd broken the Germans' code.

It never occurred to me that the German boffins might have done the same thing to our secret codes. It turned out later that this unpalatable development had never occurred to the officers in charge of intelligence for the Royal Navy either. How many tonnes of Allied shipping went to the bottom because of this blindness would never be known.

The artist who had plotted the lines of equal isobaric pressure on this weather chart had produced a masterpiece which resembled a big black spider's web. Its center was about 500 miles due east of Bluie West One. The isobar lines were tightly packed, which indicated the low was very intense. From the center, a red line indicating a warm front and a blue line indicating a cold front wandered across the complex picture. An area of high pressure was just sketched in over central Greenland.

There was a total lack of reports from Greenland stations, and I presumed that was why the high so important to us was just lightly indicated. Data on the wide expanse west of Greenland was scarce. There were only two reporting stations. One was Churchill, and I felt a thrill of pride as I saw the second was none other than Crystal Two.

I had been the first arrival for the weather briefing Bisson had requested earlier in the day. Now he and Evans joined me, and the forecaster began his spiel. His black horn-rimmed glasses made him look much like a schoolteacher as he used a wooden lecture wand to point out the important features on his chart. With such a scholarly demeanor I was not surprised by his Oxford accent.

"Actually, you've got a quite good setup for your Greenland flight. We believe that Bluie West Eight will remain clear in the grip of this stationary high. If you fly a great circle track north of this low you'll get a good tailwind component."

Bisson reached forward and used his forefinger to trace our projected flight track.

"We'll be flying right over Iceland. We can get a radio fix there, but we'll need astro later. What height will be needed to top the clouds?"

It seemed to be a tough question. After an uncomfortable pause, the forecaster replied slowly, "This is a very complex system, but you should be clear of all cloud above 20,000 feet. In cloud we're calling for just light icing."

The aircrew who flew the North Atlantic knew from bitter experience that the chances of topping all cloud at 20,000 feet were quite rare. Yet in the briefings the forecasters kept insisting it was possible. Bisson continued with his next critical question.

"What can we use for alternate airports in case Bluie West One goes flat?"

With a rueful shake of his head the Met. man replied, "Well, I'm afraid Iceland won't be much help. The ceiling there probably won't go above about two hundred feet. The visibility will vary from a mile to half a mile."

I felt our collective eyes shifting from that plague spot to southern Greenland. The Met. man had also done so, and now proclaimed, "We haven't had any reports for quite some time from Bluie West One. All I can tell you is that the flow will be up the fjord from the Davis Strait."

An easterly flow up the narrow fjord usually meant the airport was fogged in. Bisson turned and looked at me.

"What do you think, Don?"

All eyes focused on me and I felt a momentary flash of sympathy with the weather forecasters of the world. But something had to be done, so I stuck my neck out.

"It seems to me if that if the high is stationary over Bluie West Eight we won't need an alternate." The Met. man looked quite startled at this heretical statement from a flight crew member. But when I saw Evans slowly nodding his agreement I felt a lot better. This was a survey flight, after all.

But Bisson was still doubtful. In the final analysis it was always the Captain's decision. He hedged around a bit.

"If the Group Captain hadn't told me so emphatically that this new route is so important to the war effort I think I'd wait." Nobody said a word. After a moment his lips firmed and he made the crucial decision.

"We'd better go while we can. Maybe that low will move faster than they think and Prestwick will close in on us if we wait." There was a murmur of agreement.

Bisson turned to Evans and said, "I'll go straight up to 20,000 feet right after we take off. Plot a great circle course which will put us north of the low and give us tail winds. Check me with your flight plan as soon as it's completed."

As we turned to leave, we thanked the forecaster who was watching us intently. I saw his eyes fix on the big high he'd drawn over our destination, and for a moment thought he was going to say something. But he just shrugged his shoulders very slightly as he wished us good luck.

Bisson and I left Evans with the weather folder, his flight chart, his protractor and his circular computer, while we went out to check out our Liberator. It was a standard B-24D, serial No. 11906, with its guns removed. Scottish Aviation had laid a new floor made of plywood covered with mattresses and blankets in the bomb bay. The rubber tubes of an auxiliary oxygen system dangled from the top of the bomb bay. The setup was much like that used by the BOAC Return Ferry Service Libs. I felt a touch of claustrophobia as I inspected the windowless metal box, very glad to be part of the flight crew up front where I could see out.

Evans came up with a fast six-and-a-half hour flight plan for the 1,458 nautical mile flight. We had fuel for twelve hours, so Goose Bay could be a long shot if we really got into trouble.

© *2011 Donna McVicar Kazo*

B-24 Liberator

We loaded our passengers. There were now a dozen of them, including the inevitable hitch-hikers. Bisson made a smooth takeoff and I performed my copilot's duties with no trouble. All the engine pressures and temperatures remained in the green. I retracted the landing gear and bled up the flaps on Bisson's signals. With power reduced to climb settings, a gentle turn put us on our chosen course. We seemed to be off to a good start.

Our takeoff was at the ungodly time of two o'clock in the morning, because we wanted a daylight landing in Greenland for obvious reasons. There was only one factor which could affect our performance. We had been on duty for twenty hours without a break. We were facing a tough flight into a single strip airport in a difficult location. Being young and keen, I wasn't worried. I supposed that these factors were normal for any exploratory flight.

This Lib had the new turbo superchargers fitted to its engines to give them sea level power at altitude. Instead of relying on internal gearing, as in the type I'd been more used to, the turbos got their power from the exhaust stream. I'd been quite startled the first time I'd seen the high-speed, gleaming-red-hot turbines in the bottom of the engine nacelles. The engineers assured me there was no danger of fire. I had to assume those engineers knew what they were talking about. After all, those turbines were also fitted to the Boeing Flying Fortress which was designed to do its damage from way up there at 25,000 feet.

After a normal takeoff, as we climbed away we made the unwelcome discovery that the automatic pilot was unserviceable. I would be its replacement. Captains must save themselves for important decisions.

As we passed through 10,000 feet we donned our oxygen masks. Mine cut into my face, especially the bridge of my nose. Maybe the designers had used a flat-nosed monkey as a model. The constriction was hateful and the smell of the rubber made me feel a little ill. But, as I watched the little red ball bobbing up and down in its glass cylinder, whether I liked it or not, the oxygen was keeping me alive.

When we popped out of the undercast the change was dramatic. All around us in the black velvet sky the stars twinkled their cheery message.

"We'll take you wherever you want to go," they seemed to be saying. For the first time I was sure we'd make it.

Yesterday Prestwick, today Greenland, tomorrow the Pic. Oh boy!

I leveled off at 20,000 feet and set up cruise power, according to the book. But Bisson had an annoying habit of resetting the power to lower numbers. He then expected the Lib and me to maintain an altitude and airspeed just below our capabilities. Of course I knew why. He was hoarding our fuel like a miser against some as-yet-unknown catastrophe.

So I wasn't really surprised when he reached forward and cut the boost back a whole inch on the four engines. I felt the Lib falling off the step as the airspeed dropped back. This wasn't hoarding fuel, this was wasting it. I grabbed the four throttles and put the power back up, daring him to override me. Perhaps my eyes above my oxygen mask were fiercer than I realized, because he just sat, arms folded, not saying anything.

Ahead we briefly could see some dark shadows, and suddenly we flew into some snow-filled clouds. So much for topping them all at 20,000 feet. I looked out at the leading edge of the wing. Good. No ice. But no astro either. Then, without warning a commotion erupted in the cockpit. Baker had appeared and was tugging urgently on Bisson's sleeve.

"Louis, big trouble. Number Two engine's on fire!" he shouted. His voice was hoarse with fright and I felt a giant hand clutch my heart.

Bisson didn't panic. He told Evans to go aft and check from the small window behind the bomb bay. I put the thought of being cooked alive out of my mind by concentrating on holding our course and altitude.

When Evans reported back his face was tense with worry. His voice stuttered a bit. "Yes, there's a big red glow near Number Two. Sparks are streaming from the nacelle."

We all looked at the engine instruments. No sign of anything wrong.

Bisson now made the decision which he had to do as Captain. Shut the thing off before it burns into the wing. He pulled the power back on the suspect engine, then reached up and punched its feathering button. As the engine chattered to a stop I turned off its fuel supply, then reached down and pulled out the fire extinguisher which was situated near my right foot.

Now Bisson made another decision. He gestured with his right thumb over his shoulder without saying a word. I began a careful turn back towards Prestwick. As I did so, radio man Rush sent a priority message that we were coming back.

We were only in the cloud for a few minutes, and when we came out of the white sheath Baker reported the red glow had almost faded away, and that the sparks were no longer streaming back.

Bisson looked at me with the palms of his hands up as he shrugged his shoulders. The message was clear: Was there really a fire out there? In turn, I shrugged my shoulders and pointed my forefinger like a gun over the nose. We were committed to returning to Prestwick. Our fast return plan through Greenland and Goose to Dorval was blown all to hell.

But, so far...we weren't.

The weather at Prestwick had remained good and Bisson took over and made the landing just as dawn was breaking. We all tumbled out to make our individual inspections of the feathered engine. As we looked up at the wing we could see no sign of burnt metal, or even black soot or smoke trails. But right next to the Number Two engine nacelle I could see a big red formation identifying light, not fitted to earlier models of the Lib. I had my suspicions, but I didn't say anything. After all, I was part of the crew.

Maybe it was just as well, because I found out later that the control for the light was on the instrument panel. But it wasn't marked. Furthermore, it was mixed in with the engine starter switches, the engine primer switches, and the engine fuel booster pump switches. In their haste to carry out modifications on the run the engineers had also failed to label some of these switches as well. How this miserable formation switch got knocked on we never learned. It could have been me with my clumsy flying gloves. Or just as easily, it could have been some other clot.

In any case, the frightening red glow had been a false alarm. But the combination of it and the glowing turbine wheel in the snow flakes had convinced several experienced men that a real risk of fire existed.

I decided that Bisson had made the right decision. Fire in the air, or just a threat of fire in the air, is something no one in their right mind fools around with. I was reasonably sure that Group Captain Powell would rather have us back a day late, than having to solve yet another mystery of an aircraft gone missing. Still, it was annoying to be shot down in full flight, so to speak. Annoying, hell! It was just plain stupid.

The mechanics from Scottish Aviation towed our Lib across the runway to their hangar. There, they'd flush off the carbon dioxide from the engine which I'd sprayed around so liberally. They would also fix the automatic pilot, and do a good inspection and check for other snags.

After we caught up on our sleep, Bisson decided that perhaps a stop in Iceland would be a good idea after all. If we took off from there for BW8 and it went "Blooie" we could count on using Goose for an alternate. Or, if we conserved our fuel, we might make it all the way back to Dorval.

On April 13 we made our second attempt. After takeoff and into the climb Number Two engine's indicators were right up there with its mates. After a calm daylight flight of four hours and fifteen minutes, which was mostly between layers of cloud, Bisson slipped nicely into Reykjavik's short 4,200-foot runway.

As we taxied in, I couldn't help wondering why BOAC didn't use the

Iceland route. Perhaps because they had nineteen hours of fuel they were dedicated to trying for the direct Prestwick-to-Montreal flight which averaged a bum-and-brain-numbing sixteen hours.

We stopped at Iceland only long enough to refuel and discover that the Met. people had nothing new in the way of BW8 weather. They gave us the happy news that the big area of high pressure seemed to be lingering on. Good enough.

This time our takeoff was more than a bit hairy as we took a long roll and barely skimmed over some of the buildings which closely surround Reykjavik airport. Then, as we flew on across the Denmark Strait the clouds began to slowly dissipate.

Highs are great stuff to fly in. I even spotted the elusive Bluie East Two at Angmagssalik on Greenland's east coast. Best of all, we could see Sondrestrom Fjord from the center of the icecap. This made BW8 a cinch to find, which was just as well as once again we weren't able to establish radio communication and the sun was beginning to set.

On landing we kicked up a great cloud of dust on the gravel runway. Then we taxied up to the ramp where we found the inhabitants were pleased to see us again. They hadn't yet had a visit from an American aircraft, so the RAF Ferry Command had once again broken their deadly round of daily monotony.

After we had refueled, Bisson was anxious to press on, but I convinced him that we must keep our promise to drop the serum to those suffering souls at Pangnirtung. After some hesitation he agreed. He knew as well as anybody that we needed daylight to make the parachute drop. But that meant we had to stay overnight, and that night the temperature, under the influence of our old friend, the Arctic High, dropped far below zero.

In the morning, in spite of the fact we'd used our oil-dilution system, our engines were stiff, reluctant to turn over. Our friendly high had turned into an enemy. We needed every bit of help from Bernt Balchen's men, their ground power unit, and their Herman Nelson heaters to get going. At long last all four engines were turning over, coughing out great clouds of blue smoke from their rough-running cylinders.

As we taxied up to the runway they started to smooth out. But on run-up we had trouble getting the turbochargers to come on stream properly. The additional power they provided, even at sea-level where we were, was essential for takeoff. Everything else checked out okay, so, with Evans in the copilot seat and me in the jump seat, Bisson lined up for takeoff on the gravel strip. The air was crisp and cold and the exhausts of our engines formed four long streams of steam-like vapor behind us in the calm air.

Bisson began to open the throttles, then released the brakes. As we began to move Evans followed the throttles with his left hand behind Bisson's right, the normal procedure. We were picking up speed nicely when out of the blue Number Four engine gave a big surge and the prop seemed to be running out of control. The intense cold had somehow affected the guts of the turbo!

From my jump seat just aft of the control pedestal I could see Bisson's feet move as he applied rudder to counteract the unexpected swing. But as the airspeed was still building up nicely, I thought all was well. Then all of a sudden he began to close all four throttles. I was horrified. We had used up nearly all of the runway and just ahead I could see big boulders left over from construction. These ominous looming obstacles were getting larger by the second. It was apparent to me that there was just no way we could stop in time.

It was fly or crash.

I reached forward and strongly pushed the throttles back to the wide-open position. Bisson realized his mistake and released his hold on them while Evans kept them wide open. The engines roared.

Then Bisson used both hands on the control wheel to haul it back into his gut, just as he'd done with the Norseman at Crystal Two. We lurched into the air and cleared the boulders with absolutely nothing to spare.

Evans retracted the gear and bled the flaps up. Then he reduced the engine power to normal climb settings. The engines ran as smooth as silk. The emergency was over. When he looked back at me I wondered if my face was as pale as his. Bisson was silent, sitting stiffly in his seat as he stared straight ahead.

Once safely up at cruising altitude over the bobbing icebergs of the Davis Strait with Baffinland in sight, Bisson relaxed. He said with feeling that was the third time I'd saved his life. I didn't quite know how to handle this unexpected compliment, so I just nodded. But at the same time I couldn't help thinking that someday I also could owe my life to a sharp copilot.

The sky was cloudless and visibility at our altitude was hundreds of miles. We flew over Crystal Three just to show that we hadn't forgotten them. Somehow the climb over the jagged mountains of the Cumberland Peninsula with four engines wasn't nearly as frightening as with just one.

Bisson buzzed the few buildings of Pangnirtung, then we came back more slowly at about 500 feet, ready for the drop. I was dropmaster, standing near the rear side hatch with a rope tied around my waist. When Bisson thought we were in the right position he shouted over the intercom. I threw out the precious package with a sincere prayer that the parachute shrouds wouldn't tangle with the horizontal stabilizer. They didn't, and I saw the white silk of the parachute as we flew on.

When Bisson made a 180 to check, we were all thrilled to see a smiling Inuit reaching towards heaven with the well-padded package in his hands.

Back at 9,000 feet, a good height for economical cruising without nasty oxygen masks, I handed Bisson his first course with the estimate time of our arrival at Goose. I found being a straight navigator was an enjoyable experience. As we passed over the Hudson Strait I was somewhat amused to discover that those cold waters didn't frighten me a bit. Four engines: that's the only way to go.

I took another drift sight, and then told Bisson to alter course a few degrees, just as any crack navigator would. My landfall on the Button Islands, Canadian mainland's northeast extremity, was right on the button, so I settled back in my chair and relaxed.

I saw Rush change our radio equipment from the USAAC voice frequency to Ferry Command's North Atlantic CW frequency of 6500kc. Shortly after, he grinned as he told me that Goose Bay had just joined the net. As a navigator I was happy to hand him our ETA at Goose, because I doubted if the Americans had got their communication problems with our outfit sorted out yet.

We landed after a seven-hour flight and raced over to the mess shack for a hot meal. There was a lot of activity on the base, and much had changed even during the few days since our last visit. On April 6, our chief meteorologist, P.D. McTaggart-Cowan, affectionately known as "McFog," and who reined supreme at Gander, had dispatched one of his key weathermen, Don McClelland, to provide on-the-spot forecasts. Accompanying him were a skeleton staff of decipherers and plotters. Operations would be taken care of by Flight Lieutenant Tim McGrath. Their magic chariot had been a Canso. Tough way to travel...

On the ramp stood a civilian airliner far removed from its normal intercity routes. It was a Douglas DC-3 in the markings of Northeast Airlines. They were about to make the first flight with supplies from Presque Isle, Maine, over to BW1 on a contract given to them by the American military. Evans and I talked to the pilots and wished them the best of luck. We figured they'd need lots of it as they navigated the torturous fjord from the sea to the single strip.

There was also a C-47, the military equivalent of the DC-3, on the ramp. It had brought up a squad of US Army Corps of Engineers. I listened to their chatter in the mess shack. Goose must have hard-surfaced runways instead of gravel as soon as possible. An icebreaker could open up Melville Sound weeks ahead of the normal breakup. Gotta figure on a big concrete parking ramp south of the runways. Let's make it big enough to hold at least a hundred in-transit bombers. Nobody can work outside here, so we need a hangar—maybe two. Barracks and cook houses. A hell of a lot of fuel storage tanks. Good, powerful radio transmitters and receivers. Better weather facilities. Much, much more of everything.

The Yanks were on the move. The conversations I overheard make me think.

"Louis," I said, "do you think our recent flights have anything to do with what these guys are planning?"

"Oui, of course, Don. Colonel Hubbard told me before we started out on our Norseman and Canso flights that if we were successful the Americans would go all-out to develop the Crimson Route."

"Looks like they weren't kidding."

"No, mon ami. For sure they weren't kidding, as you call it. Washington has finally come to realize the U-boat sinkings are seriously crippling the Allied war effort. They're planning to deliver most of their twin-engine bombers this way, because of the short distance between bases. There's talk they might even use the route to deliver twin-engine fighters like the P-38."

"Well, summer's coming," I said.

That seemed to cover the situation, so we turned our attention to our immediate problems with the weather. Things didn't look so hot. There would be en-route turbulence and a heavy headwind. There was more than a chance of moderate ice. Dorval's conditions would be, in a word, lousy. The best we could hope for was a ragged 300 foot ceiling. The visibility could be down to a mile or less in rain and fog. We didn't delay our takeoff for a minute. The homeward bound syndrome had taken over.

The last leg of our operation was long. It was a rough and turbulent four hours and forty-five minutes complete with a dose of ice, just as the forecaster had promised. At the end, Bisson executed a perfect radio range approach and greased the black monster on the runway without a bump.

As he taxied towards the ramp, we could feel the gusty wind hammering against the sides of the Lib. After we shut down the engines everyone piled out eagerly. As we scrambled across the tarmac we were almost blown away by the ferocious wind in the pitch-black, rain-soaked, atrocious night.

Dorval had never looked better.

Canso in for maintenance

A Good Hudson Delivery

Early the next morning Bisson, Evans and I reported to Headquarters for debriefing. We all wondered if anything would be said about our goof-up with the false Liberator engine "fire."

We needn't have worried.

"Nine days for a round trip," Group Captain Powell said with a smile, "I consider that excellent. From what I've heard most of your troubles were caused by lack of interface of the various radio setups. We'll soon fix that. What else can you suggest to help?"

Bisson said that more current weather reports were necessary. I hoped the new radio range at Goose Bay would be operational soon, and Evans said we needed more Ferry Command personnel at our Labrador base. Powell made sure his secretary noted our suggestions before answering.

"Yes, we're working on those problems right now. Goose will soon take its place alongside Gander. Sir Frederick is down at Washington this very minute conferring with the Americans. The British Air Ministry has already decided to stop shipping Douglas Bostons by sea. As far as I'm concerned I'm going to recommend we use the far north route for most of our twins."

We all nodded. The long hop from Gander to Prestwick needed plenty of helping winds to make it practical. Then Powell cleared his throat and gave us new orders.

"However, be that as it may, I want each of you to deliver a Hudson across direct from Goose to Prestwick. Apparently there are still people in high places who haven't quite grasped Canadian geography. They appear to think that Labrador to Prestwick is a lot farther than just an additional seventy-five miles compared to Gander to the other side."

Then Powell came forth with good news Evans and I had been waiting for. He smiled at us yet again.

"I see by flight reports from training that your day checks on Liberators were quite satisfactory. And now on your recent flight you've accumulated some more very valuable experience."

I twitched just a little. Well, maybe a fire in the air could be called merely valuable experience. Especially by people who hadn't been in the aircraft.

"Yes, sir," I said humbly. Let's not shoot off the mouth and screw up the four-engine checkout...he continued with the good news.

"So I've authorized your night checkout. Good luck."

I don't know how Evans felt, but I was damn proud and possibly a bit smug as we filed out of Powell's office.

Al Leeward finished Evans' and my Liberator checkout on April 17 in good old 11108. To start, we each got five more day landings and another half hour of three engines while flying under the hood. Then eight night landings each completed our course.

Finally we were genuine four-engine Captains, the highest pilot category in Ferry Command. There was a low rumble of discontent from some senior captains who thought a minimum of at least ten twin-engine deliveries should be the criterion for a four-engine checkout. Evans and I paid no attention. We were sure that one Canso flight over Greenland equaled at least ten "normal" deliveries from Gander.

Air Commodore Griffith "Taffy" Powell, RAF, CBE

There was a short delay before the maintenance people could come up with three serviceable Hudsons, so I went looking for some local flying. It came in the form of a Royal Navy Captain who had to be rushed to Washington for some reason that was never explained to me. This was normal, of course. He turned out to be a gruff, powerfully built man with eyes that matched the North Sea. As we shook hands I wondered if he would be interested to learn that I too had a naval background. After all, I had risen from Ordinary Seaman to Leading Telegraphist in the Royal Canadian Naval Volunteer Reserve. But one look into those eyes convinced me that he wouldn't care.

Eric Rush was our radio operator, and as there were no passenger seats in the Hudson, I let my four-striped passenger sit in the copilot's position, even if he wasn't sporting wings on his sleeve. I checked the weather: good. Then I filed my flight plan to the Washington National Airport.

The takeoff was normal, and soon we were winging our way along the radio range chain south of Dorval. After we passed Baltimore I checked in with the Washington National tower. My passenger was listening in. Suddenly he turned to me.

"I thought you knew I want to land at the US Naval Air Base at Anacostia."

"Nobody told me," I grumbled as I scrambled around to check my maps and radio frequencies. Anacostia turned out to be just across the Potomac River from Washington National. As I usually did, I'd been planning my approach and landing to the big airport.

So this was a major change on a short notice, and I wasn't in the proper mood to carry out the difficult landing which now faced me so abruptly. The approach path to the short runway the wind favored, and the control tower ordered, would require a unusually steep descent over a street of houses high on a nearby ridge of land.

After setting up my approach I wanted to be sure of clearing the houses, and as a result ended up coming in high and hot. The near end of the runway floated by before my main wheels touched down almost half way along. I probably should have gone around. But hotshot Ferry Command Captains don't goof up with important passengers on board, so I decided to finish off the landing.

But, due to my excessive airspeed the tail just wouldn't come down so I could get on the brakes. The waters of the Potomac River where the runway ended loomed larger and larger in my windshield. Quickly I pulled the wheel back in my belly and the tail wheel touched. Then I reached down and pulled on the brake lever roughly, and the tires left a trail of smoking black rubber on the runway. When we finally ground to a stop it seemed as if the nose of the Hudson was almost hanging over the cold green waters of the Potomac, ready for a dip.

As I taxied in I could feel the accusing eyes of the Senior Service boring into me. But he didn't say a word as he climbed out of his seat and made his way down the fuselage.

On the trip back home I had plenty of time to think. I'd recently been exonerated after my first accident in a Norseman. But the majority of pilots are skeptics where accident reports are concerned, and Taffy Powell was a pilot. So if I'd had a second accident, this one caused by plain poor airmanship, I could have quickly ended up in khaki, sloping a Lee-Enfield rifle in the ranks of the Canadian Army.

On April 21, acting as Captain-Navigator, I signed for Hudson BW410 with Rush and a green copilot named Lewis, referred to as a "one-tripper" because he'd stay over with an operational squadron. Bisson and Evans had done the same with two more Hudsons, so it looked as if Powell's plans were being carried out properly.

But out on the field at the end of the active runway, when I did my run-up, I discovered the fuel system was not working right. When I tried to draw fuel from the cabin tank there was a shower of gas in the cabin that rivaled Niagara Falls. Some valve had been hooked up backwards. So we returned to the ramp, thankful a spark from the radios hadn't blown us up.

A few hours later, we started off again, this time in Hudson FH342, and this time everything ran like clockwork. We got off Dorval in fine style and just hesitated at Goose for fuel and a hot meal, before pressing straight on.

As I started my air plot I realized that the days were getting longer, and now I had just five hours of night for astro. But this was long enough for me to get three good star fixes, using good old Polaris on each fix. We hammered through a few hours of bad weather and eleven hours after takeoff I slipped into Prestwick.

It had been a beautiful flight. Bisson and Evans were at the ramp to greet me. They reported their flights had also been good. So we'd proven in a very dramatic and convincing way that the direct Goose-U.K. flight was practical.

We now made the happy discovery that Powell had decreed that we had priority on BOAC's Return Ferry Service. Obviously he wanted to get us back in a big hurry. Now he wanted us to bring three Libs over. Naturally this arrangement suited us just fine. We jumped ahead of some other aircrew waiting to fly back to Dorval, and when they bitched I'm afraid I wasn't very sympathetic.

I caught a few hours' sleep, then paid up my bet about the one-week return to Wing Commander Jeffs, which I'd lost. He promptly bought me not one but three rounds of drinks. I began to unwind in the time-honored manner.

That night we answered the call and boarded Lib AL528 with Captain Sam Buxton in command. I had decided to carry my own insulation and unrolled my sleeping bag on the skimpy mattress on the wooden floor in the bomb bay. The black cavern reminded me of a torture cell where the prisoner can't stand up straight or stretch out full length. All stretching of cramped sinews and muscles must be done on the bias, so to speak. In order to pack in the maximum number of "bodies," as we were called, we alternated head to feet. That meant a big pair of stinking flight boots on either side of your head. Sardines had it better.

Then there was the powerful, chilling draft because the four bomb-bay doors weren't properly sealed. And the noise was right out of this world. I had plugged my ears with cotton because I knew that the four big engines with their under-wing exhausts could deafen me for life.

My session in the bar had been pretty hectic, so I was able to fall asleep in the climb. Buxton kept it low, which meant no oxygen masks, and I slept like a log for ten painless hours, waking up just as we passed over Gander. Six more hours put us down at Dorval, and I didn't even have a hangover. As I rolled out of the bomb-bay I was sure the horror tales about incompetent BOAC pilots must be greatly exaggerated.

What I couldn't know was that this flight would turn out to be just about the best flight with the Return Ferry Service I would ever make.

A Not-So-Good Hudson Delivery

At Dorval, I realized that I'd been away only 48 hours on this, my second delivery. I thought the time span was normal. How wrong I was! It would turn out to be the shortest round trip I would ever make.

I was feeling so peppy that I volunteered that very night to do another navigation flight in Ventura AE738, but I'd been out only about twenty minutes when a rough engine forced me to return.A couple of days later, while waiting for my Lib, I took the opportunity to check out on Boeing B-17 Flying Fortress FK162. Once again Moody and Leeward shared check pilot duties, and this time I had a jolly RCAF Squadron Leader from the Maritimes named "Wendy" Reid as my checkout mate.

Five landings plus three-engine air work, and one hour and 45 minutes later I was a certified B-17 captain. Compared to a Lib, the Fort's controls were feather-light. But I could see that the huge vertical tail and rudder, combined with a tail wheel instead of a nose wheel, could be a real handful in a crosswind.

© 2011 Donna McVicar Kazo

"Five landings plus three-engine air work, and one hour and 45 minutes later I was a certified B-17 captain."

Al Lilly

On April 30 Al Lilly, the chief test pilot, and I took two full hours to swing the compass and test the numerous systems of Liberator AE638. The flight was remarkably snag-free, in spite of the fact the aircraft was a bit beat-up after harsh treatment as an instructional aircraft.

On May 1 I signed RAF Form 700 accepting AE638 as my first four-engine delivery. On the ramp outside the dispatch office I did my usual walk-around inspection. It seemed to me that the nose-wheel was turned a bit too far. Obviously the man who had taxied it over from the test flight hangar line had turned pretty sharply to avoid the Admin building. While I suspected Lilly I didn't say anything; what pilot would on his first four-engine delivery?

After I got the engines started, I slowly straightened out the nose wheel and tried a fast taxi. Good. No vibration. The run-up before takeoff was flawless. But on takeoff with the throttles fully open, as the airspeed indicator passed through 70mph, all hell broke loose.

Suddenly the nose began to shake so violently that the flight instruments were just a blur. I cut back the power in a hurry and glumly taxied back to the parking line. A ground mechanic told me we had a broken shimmy dampener. It could be replaced in a couple of days. I wondered if perhaps some senior captains had set a flock of gremlins loose on me.

Meanwhile, Evans and Bisson had taken off with their Libs and disappeared to the east. I just had to get going. After all this was the final cycle of the proving flights.

After I reported my troubles with the Lib to Powell, he gave me a Hudson. There were no more Libs available. Sorry. I thanked him and went to check the Met. It looked fine, but when I went back to field operations to pick up my new Hudson, I discovered that the clown towing the Hudson over from the hangar line had managed to bang up a wingtip. Maintenance reckoned it would take a couple of days to make it airworthy again. Maybe those senior captains' gremlins were more powerful than the average?

I trudged back up the stairs and reported my sad story to Powell. Did he, by any chance, have another Hudson I could take? He scratched his head as he looked at me closely. Perhaps he thought I'd become his personal gremlin. He got a little redder in the face but came through.

In a couple of hours, ever-faithful Rush and another one-tripper, a New Zealander named Hindle, climbed aboard FP388. I'd now been actively screwing up Ferry Command's operations for just over twelve hours since early morning crew pickup. But I was determined Evans and Bisson wouldn't finish too far ahead of me.

Goose looked awfully familiar to me as I watched them refuel my Hudson. Then a night takeoff, aided by gooseneck flares on the gravel runway and I was on my way to Iceland. There was high cloud cover, but I got a good fix over Bluie West One. The skies were kind, but the winds were not, so after ten and a half hours I landed at Reykjavik. I had flown over Keflavik, the new base at Reykjavik the Americans were constructing. I noted with envy that the runways were much longer and the approaches were much more reasonable than those at Reykjavik.

In the Met. office I found that they were forecasting good weather at Prestwick. By now I'd been on the go for a little over thirty hours. But a flight plan of only four hours and twenty minutes beckoned me on. I decided I'd rather sleep the sleep of the just in the Orangefield at Prestwick than pry apart the clammy blankets in one of the local Nissen huts. I picked up two hitch-hikers, RAF couriers with the rank of Squadron Leader. With me, they'd get back to Blighty days earlier than by any other means of transport.

After punching through the usual two fronts I found that the good weather at Prestwick actually existed, just as advertised. The only problem was that it was accompanied by strong winds 90 degrees to the single runway. In addition, gusts of 45 knots were featured. The tower suggested I should divert to nearby Ayr airport where there was a runway which was closer to being into the wind. It was good advice, but a strong stubborn streak had taken over my mind. I'd set out on this exercise to land at Prestwick, and, by God, land there I would.

I had now been on duty for just over thirty-six hours.

As I made my approach the tower told me I was clear to land at my own discretion. Where had I heard that before?

The two Squadron Leaders were peering over my shoulder, watching with more than casual interest my efforts to stay lined up with the runway as I coped with more drift than I'd ever previously encountered.

After I dropped the landing gear I felt a strong inclination to go around and land over at Ayr. But stubborn Scottish pride, a very powerful emotion indeed, kept my determination to land at Prestwick when good sense should have prevailed.

I let down with just a touch of flap, having no problem in selecting the right power settings to hold a safe airspeed. A lot of crab, combined with a little wing-down, enabled me to stay lined up on the runway. So far, so good, although I found myself sweating as I concentrated. Just before I touched down I kicked off the drift and put the upwind wheel on the runway, alert for the necessary heavy rudder and braking to keep the aircraft going straight.

I was using my left hand to control the ailerons, intending to put the downwind wheel on the runway when the speed bled off. My right hand was on the throttles, ready to use a burst of power in case the rudders couldn't keep us straight.

Once again, so far, so good.

Most aircraft have toe brakes on the rudder pedals, but not this model of Hudson. The lever controlling the brakes was just below the throttles on the pedestal. To prevent a swing into the gusty wind I urgently needed full brake on the right wheel and as much right rudder as I could get.

So I had to change hands.

This put my left hand on the throttles, leaving the ailerons free to flutter in the wind. Not good, but brake was more important. I had full right rudder and full brake on as the right wheel hit the runway, leaving a trail of black, smoking rubber. My arms were crossed as I used my left hand to give the left engine a burst of power.

I thought I had it made.

It was at that exact moment I discovered that engineers who write aircraft flight manuals might just possibly be smarter than me. I was well outside the flight envelope covering cross-wind landings. Before my horrified eyes the Hudson started to swing off the runway in a classic ground loop.

I won't claim that all my life flashed before my eyes, but certainly the thought did occur that some senior bastard captains were very shortly going to get something about young McVicar to lick their chops over.

I managed to get the tail down, but my last line of defense disappeared as the tail-wheel lock let go with a nasty crack. Very quickly we swung through a whole 180 degrees and started to go *backwards.* Purely on instinct, with no conscious thought, I released the brake lever, straightened out the rudders and pushed the throttles open. The swing stopped and we began to move forward, surrounded by a huge cloud of dust and debris.

My quick, instinctive reaction had saved the aircraft, and possibly our lives as well. If I'd frozen on the brakes the landing gear would have folded forward and pierced the wing fuel tanks. We could have been trapped in the smoke and flame of the resulting explosion. It had happened to many a Hudson before us.

The control tower sounded a little irritated as he told me not to park there. As I taxied meekly away to the normal reception area, I wondered just how many Hudsons he'd seen with reversible props.

I'll never forget the look on the faces of the two couriers after I shut down. The violent gyrations of the Hudson had knocked them to the floor. After they dusted themselves off they glared at me and shot out of the door without speaking. I couldn't say I blamed them.

Up at the bar I started the unwinding exercise. It appeared that no one had noticed my stupid exhibition, which had actually lasted only a few seconds, even if it felt like a lifetime. I raised a glass of Scotch and water and told myself to never push my luck again, dummy. One nonfatal crash and you're some kind of hero. Two crashes and you become a certified asshole.

I was treading a thin line—first a near-miss at Anacostia and now a really dangerous near-accident here.

I signaled for a double.

It turned out the Return Ferry Service Libs were falling behind on returning our bodies. This meant I couldn't get back for several days, so I started a Lorenz blind landing beam course under the hood in Airspeed Oxford DF340 with Flight Lieutenant Dunn. We put in a couple of heavy days down at Silloth, where the beam was installed. It was a controlled glide slope and there was nothing as advanced in North America where we were still doing timed radio range approaches to the airports.

Then we got a Hudson and he took me around to all of Ferry Command's alternate airports. We flew into Aldergrove in Northern Ireland where Don Bennett had led the first Hudson delivery flights in November of 1940. I wasn't impressed with the airport. Then over to the Isle of Man, then down to Blackpool where I was amazed as for the first time I saw the result of German bombing raids. The more airports I saw, the more I realized what a superior setup, both weather-wise and operationally, we had at Prestwick. I was determined never to use any of our alternates if I could help it, and, as it turned out, I never had to.

May 8, 1942, turned out to be a date I'd never forget. I climbed into the hellhole of Lib AL962, Captain W. L. "Geordie" Stewart in command. I hoped his Scottish name meant capability. His flight plan was direct to Montreal in sixteen hours, the same as Captain Buxton's on my previous return flight. But other than the estimated time en route there would be no similarity between the two flights. Each BOAC captain was a power unto himself and Stewart had his own ideas.

Right off the bat he climbed up to 20,000 feet which put us all on oxygen. Why the blazes did he do that, I wondered. It wasn't the weather, because through the cracks in the walls of the bomb-bay I could plainly see the Atlantic far below. Furthermore, now he and I were up where the powerful westerly headwinds blow. And blow they did.

I might have over-trained in the bar prior to this flight, because for almost fifteen hours my body barely stirred in my sleeping bag. I finally opened my groggy eyes and checked my watch. Montreal soon. Beautiful!

I crawled out of the bomb-bay into the rear compartment where there were a few bench seats and a couple of small windows on this particular Lib. Several passengers, unrecognizable in their flying gear, were huddled together.

Then I made a horrible observation. The shaft of the sun, which was shining through the small windows, was going round and round! We were circling, because Stewart and his navigator were fresh out of ideas. In other words, this crack BOAC crew was lost.

We had to do something, so, with a couple of other Ferry Command captains I went up to the cockpit to try and straighten Stewart out. Below were the familiar outlines of the lakes and black pine forests of Labrador and northern Quebec. It hadn't sunk in to the BOAC men that therefore we must be all to hell and gone north of track. I wondered, if they had seen palm trees would they have then realized they were too far south?

After some argument we convinced Stewart to stop the senseless circling and steer a course of 225 degrees. Maybe it wasn't the direct route to Montreal, but at least we would be flying towards civilization.

After making sure Stewart was actually using our course, we captains went back to the aft compartment. A small man with a bird-like face asked me what was going on and introduced himself as Malcolm MacDonald. He was the British High Commissioner to Canada, one of the VIP who occasionally rode back and forth over the Atlantic as high-priority passengers.

When I explained to him what was going on, MacDonald shook his head. He couldn't believe that the Return Ferry Service, which he'd been told was topnotch, just about infallible, would do such a thing. No doubt no one in BOAC had mentioned their three fatal Liberator crashes back in 1941. Ferry Command had lost a lot of aircrew along with several VIP in those accidents. On the other hand, why should they?

For a couple of hours we ground along, until the St. Lawrence River thankfully came into view. Then I recognized the grain elevators at Three Rivers. Not far to go now. Now we got our first word from the cockpit. Everyone get into the rear fuselage compartment, because if we ran out of fuel we were in for a forced landing. It was a great opening message.

Most people thought that the chances of survival during a forced landing in a high wing monoplane would be about zero. We all sat looking at one another, prisoners in our metal box. No one had anything to say as the long minutes ticked away.

There was no further message as Stewart came straight onto runway 28 at Dorval with his wheels down. So we weren't going to land on our belly after all. The actual landing was brutal as we bumped down heavily on the runway. Stewart had forgotten to tell us to move forward for a normal landing. We really didn't care. Any landing you can walk away from...

We had been in the air nineteen hours and fifteen minutes, a new endurance record. A collection of fire engines and ambulances escorted us to the terminal area.

Later the gas tanks were dipped and the engineers estimated the Lib had only twenty minutes of fuel left.

Stewart had his wrist slapped by having to make just one flight as copilot with Captain Trevor Cripps.

I thought he should have been shot.

Now that our aircraft had been delivered and our three crews were back, the far-north Crimson Route proving flights were officially over. Everyone congratulated us and told us we had done an outstanding job. Maybe they were right. When I checked my logbook I found I'd flown just over 200 hours, beginning with the ski exploration flights, then proving the route in a Canso, and finishing with two Hudsons and my recent Lib delivery.

Later Bisson and I were awarded the King's Commendation.

Thousands of aircraft were to be delivered by this route which the English had christened "round-the-houses." Many of them could not have made the direct Gander-U.K. flight. If they'd been shipped by sea the U-boats would have had a feast.

Happy the pressure was off, glad to be home, I unwound in the Pic that night. There was only one black cloud in the otherwise beautiful sky. I got on the phone with the usual urgent need for sex. But it appeared that Renée had suddenly been transferred to the airport at Ancienne Lorette, near Quebec City, far out of reach. Maureen's mother wouldn't even let me talk to her. Said she wasn't feeling well. Hell!

Java Bound

That night the many, many drinks in the Mount Royal Hotel's Piccadilly Club were a poor substitute for sex, even if the conversation with a selection of other Ferry Command pilots was lively. The main topic was Stewart's goof-up, and we agreed that once again we should try to get the people in London to allow our own flight personnel to return our bodies across the North Atlantic. After all, we'd had good success in the past. However, the general opinion was that this change was quite unlikely, so I wandered off to bed in a rather bad mood.

The next morning the phone jangled me awake. Now what? With some reluctance I put the receiver to my ear to hear an impersonal voice inform me that Group Captain Powell wanted to see me. And would I mind coming immediately? That was a command, not a request. In other words, snap it up! As I showered and shaved I inquired from my reflection in the mirror what was in store for me this time.

As I drove around the airport I noted that there were several new aircraft being prepared for ferry. No doubt one of them would be my next challenge. It looked as if the American factories would actually succeed in making President Roosevelt's boast of 50,000 fighting aircraft a year ago come true. It was a welcome but rather belated response because right at this moment the Allies were losing on every front, even with the assistance of the mighty USA.

It had been just a few months ago, on December 7, when the Americans had belatedly joined the struggle against Japan. Then Hitler had made a giant mistake by declaring war on the Americans, dragging Italy along with him...

The high brass had their problems and I had mine. Putting such lofty matters out of my mind, I parked my car, entered the Administration building, then introduced myself to Powell's secretary. Without delay she conducted me inside the sacred portals.

Powell's voice was gruff. "Well, here you are, McVicar, good morning."

"Good morning," I replied obediently, twisting in my chair as I wondered what I'd done wrong. The man who controlled my destiny stared at me for an endless minute before asking the question I dreaded, even if I didn't yet know what it was.

"Were you on the Return Ferry Service Lib that arrived from Prestwick yesterday?"

So that was it! Not guilty. So I replied confidently, "Yes, sir. It was AL962 with Captain Stewart in command." He looked at me keenly.

"I've got a report from a Very Important Person that you told him the flight was lost."

Was this all the urgent call was about? But watch it, maybe they were going to try to blame the big mess on me. I began to get a little hot under the collar as I snapped back.

"Yes, sir, that is correct. That idiot Stewart was so far north we could almost see Ungava Bay."

Perhaps he hadn't expected such a straight answer. Or perhaps the mention of Ungava Bay reminded him of the good work I'd done on our recent Crimson Route survey flights. In any case his mood softened.

"Mmm," he murmured, "I see. It seems you were in the air over nineteen hours."

"Yes, and if that isn't being lost I don't know what is. Furthermore that guy Stewart is so hardheaded we even had trouble getting him to turn towards the St. Lawrence."

Powell did not reply, so I kept blasting away.

"Why can't we do our own return ferry work like we did in the beginning? Those Englishmen scare the living daylights out of me."

I felt I could say this safely because Powell's nickname "Taffy" revealed his Welsh origin. He took a deep breath before replying. I realized later that probably was nothing he himself would have liked more.

"Well, McVicar," he said patiently, "we have to do what the Air Ministry tells us to do. I'd appreciate it if you keep quiet about Stewart's flight. No doubt BOAC will look after him."

"I'll bet," I mumbled under my breath. Powell decided to change the subject.

"How many deliveries have you made in the last thirty days?"

I thought quickly. "Three in the last twenty-seven days."

He nodded. "I thought so. You don't realize it, but you're all tensed up. I'll tell Crew Assignments to give you a week off. I'm glad you're back in any case. Now let me get on with my work."

This brusque dismissal was softened by a wide smile on the old-time pilot's moon-shaped face.

After leaving his office I spotted a girl in the corridor sampling the water cooler. Her nickname was Tommy and she was one of the numerous secretaries in Admin. She had a quick tongue and a voluptuous figure. We'd had the odd exchange of wisecracks, and I'd lost most of them. But that didn't bother me because I had a feeling it was worth persevering. Her lips were wide and sensuous and her blue eyes slightly protuberant. Somewhere I'd read this meant a passionate sexual nature, commonly called "a hot piece." In any case I felt the need to experiment with this interesting theory.

"How about having dinner with me?" I inquired with my best winning smile.

"Sorry, I'm all booked up for a week ahead," she replied.

"Damn," I muttered as my face fell. "I'd sure like to get to know you better."

She was watching me closely and seemed impressed by my honest disappointment.

"I'll tell you what I can do, though."

"Yes?" I said eagerly.

"Tomorrow is Saturday and I have to work in the morning."

"And?"

"Why don't we have lunch after I'm through work?" I couldn't see how a midday lunch would lead to what I had in mind, but I was stuck, so I said, "Sure, I'd love to."

She gave me a meaningful wink as she turned and walked away. I drooled. The view from astern was as good, maybe even better than the frontal layout.

I walked down the hall and poked my head into Captain Siple's office. We'd become Wally and Don since I'd proved my mettle. I told him a little about my most recent adventures and made an appointment for that evening in my room at the Mount Royal so he could tell me about his Java-bound B-25 delivery. The one I'd missed.

That night at the hotel I found that Siple had one of the Command's old-time radio navigators, Al Loughridge, with him. Then, as he got into the story, it turned out that the famous old First World War pilot "Duke" Schiller was the first away from West Palm Beach, on Florida's Atlantic coast,

Jules Charmoz

with Siple second. The American Air Force was in its infancy on the ferrying run, and wanted only one aircraft scheduled through each day.

Siple had a marvelous memory and reeled off most of the names of the pilots who flew those B-25s: Bob Gunn, Gilbert Tobin, Bob Leroy, Ed Hightower, King Parker, Don Teel, Les Schafer, John O'Neill, Hugh Herndon, Walt Davidson, Carl Ross, Jules Charmoz, André Chatel (Free French), Charley Baughn, George Oberdorf, Bill VanDerKloot, Bud Merrill, Jack Ruggles, Carl Lange, Slim Jones, Gene Rowe, T.G. Smith, Ed Newkirk, George Hersam, Russ Jedlund (an Australian), Ted Ditton, Jack Sharpe, Jack Parkinson, Merrill Phoenix, and Al Torrey.

The flight itself was pretty routine, Siple continued, in spite of the fact they were flying Dutch aircraft into American bases with RAF civilian crews. The long haul from Natal in Brazil took almost eleven hours. Then Hugh Herndon crashed during a night landing attempt near Accra. Siple happened to be short a copilot, so he took Herndon along. Herndon was the pilot who'd flown with Clyde Pangborn in an epic flight from Japan to the USA in a single-engine Bellanca. Siple said the two old-timers hadn't talked since joining the ferry service.

Al Torrey

When I pressed him for some unusual memories he remembered Maiduguri because it was a Pan Am base complete with Coke machines, jukeboxes and ice cream. The RAF bases were rather Spartan, especially Khartoum and Aden.

He smiled as he told of the unexpected exercising of the twin .50 machine guns by Loughridge. He and Herndon were looking down at the herds of gazelle and antelope when it happened. He thought he was being attacked and took evasive action. This threw the radio man out of the turret and there were hot words for a while. Afterward on the ground they had a good laugh about it.

George Hersam

They had heard the bad news about the Japanese advancing rapidly southward through Malaysia and Sumatra, but they kept on. They arrived in Bangalore in the south of India on March 8, the day Java surrendered.

So only five B-25s were delivered, the rest were turned back, to be delivered to Australia via the Pacific. They found out that the Dutch had foreseen the debacle and six of the Royal Netherlands Air Force crews had made a hazardous escape through Sumatra and Ceylon in three KLM Lodestars. He remembered Lieutenant Andre de la Porte, Captain Rene Wittert

Gilbert Tobin

Lockheed Lodestar

and a Van Something or Other as the pilots.

I wanted to know what the Dutch did with their five lone aircraft, and Siple said he'd heard they took the turrets out—there was no .50mm ammunition available anyway—and made them into fast photo-reconnaissance ships. They'd actually flown one over Mount Everest, 29,000 feet high. The Japs couldn't catch them. Siple shook his head. He thought they would soon be grounded for lack of spare parts, but he gave the Dutchmen top marks for trying. They really had a reason to hate the dictatorships of Germany and Japan.

I said that was a pretty short story for a hell of a long flight. Did he have any suggestions in case I ever flew the South Atlantic? He laughed and suggested I stay out of Madame Zee Zee's in Belem. Of course that made me all the more determined to see this palace of pleasure.

Then he got a little serious and suggested that I never drink the local water or eat unwashed vegetables. As for Africa, it was stinking hot and humid; lots of chances to catch incurable diseases. I thought maybe I'd better stick to the chilly North Atlantic. At least it was hygienic.

Siple finished his story by telling me they'd taken a PAA DC-3 passenger flight to Accra, and a PAA flying boat to Miami. The fare of $1,640 stuck in his mind. And if I wanted to find out about the B-25 deliveries via the Pacific, he thought Don Teel would be the man to talk to. He gave me Teel's phone number and left me looking at my notes as he trotted down the long corridor.

I was lucky. Teel was in town and we made a date to meet at Dorval the next morning. This fitted in with my more nefarious plans concerning Tommy. Everything was falling into place. I still wanted to see South America and Africa, in spite of the alleged dangers. As far as I was concerned, if you've seen one iceberg, you've seen them all.

The next morning I drove my newly acquired Dodge out to the airport, pleased that it was a beautiful spring day. The air was fresh and clean, and the trees along Côte de Liesse were showing a few leaves. The snow had gone and there were patches of green showing where the grass was making its welcome reappearance after the long white winter.

As I swung around the airport I noticed a few B-25s with RAF markings. It looked as if I might get a chance to fly the smooth-looking bomber yet.

I had taken an out-of-the-way table at the cafeteria when Teel strode in. As we settled in with cups of coffee, I asked him for a little personal background. He'd started as a cadet with the Army Air Corps at Brooks Field, Texas. Then he'd been a barnstormer with his own Beech Staggerwing and other exotic prewar planes. He showed me his early number of 8627 instrument rating. I was suitably impressed.

This background, combined with his pleasant personality, tied in with the story he had mentioned to O'Neill and me about the things he did for the next-of-kin of the Prestwick Lib crashes. He shared with me the story of a fellow Texan, Andy Burke, who during one flight, had spotted a German submarine cruising leisurely along the surface off the coast. An alert to the military proved useless. Neither the Army, the Air Force, the Coast Guard, nor the Navy had an aircraft ready to go with either bombs or depth charges. Finally, one of the Civil Air Patrol pilots, Zack Mosely, had taken off with a fifty-pound bomb wired between the wheels of his Rearwin aircraft. Of course by the time he got there the sub had long gone. Teel reckoned the US military were taking an awfully long time gearing up for the U-boat attacks on American shipping.

Teel might have made the trip to India, if he hadn't lost an engine on his B-25 No. 112-472. By the time they'd given him another aircraft the routing had been changed. He'd picked up his next ship, No. 112-443, at the big modification center at Memphis, Tennessee. Then on to Hamilton Field near San Rafael, California.

From the fuel consumption figures of flights to date it was apparent they would never make the long flight to Hawaii using the Ferry Command and North American cruise control charts. So he flew over to McClelland Field near Sacramento for carburetor modifications. Consolidated Aircraft in San Diego came up with the new figures based on their long experience with PBYs and Libs in the extended range mode. Then he flew back to Hamilton for the heavily-laden takeoff. The flight plan called for minimum head winds.

Ferry Command crews stayed at the St. Francis Hotel as they waited for optimum conditions. They would be the first twin-engine landplanes to make the long flight. Martin B-26s were being transported by ship and assembled in Hawaii, and Boeing Flying Fortresses and Consolidated Liberators were making the odd flight. But the Mitchell would pioneer the route for light land bombers. Another Ferry Command first.

Teel told me his copilot was my old friend Johnny O'Neill, and his radio operator a Canadian named Charles Ayre. That brought up the name of Gordy Wightman who turned out to be R/O with the Australian Ditton. Wightman and I had been prewar friends in Vancouver. I had visited him during my tour of duty with the Royal Canadian Naval Volunteer Reserve. We had kept in touch via ham radio: he was VE5HC and I was VE4PH.

The flight crews had bought themselves a sort of uniform in case they were intercepted or shot down by Japs. It consisted of a uniform hat with no insignia and a pair of white flight coveralls with assorted rank on the shoulder straps. Depending upon the chutzpah of the owner, any rank between pilot officer and wing commander was possible. The theory was that the Japs wouldn't shoot non-civilians as spies. I wondered who dreamed that one up; as far as I could see, the Japs didn't believe in taking prisoners.

Teel was one of the first to arrive in Hawaii on March 17, surely a significant date for all people of Irish descent. I told him I'd fired a green Very pistol flare when I was up at Crystal Three, just about as far away from Hawaii as it is possible to celebrate the date. He laughed when I told him how it had drifted down dangerously close to that sole aircraft in the Canadian Arctic. I still felt a little uncomfortable as I related the story of how stupid I'd been.

The flight had been uneventful, and he'd landed with 270 gallons of fuel left with a flight time of just on thirteen hours. The new cruise control had passed the acid test. But Hickam Field still showed the effects of the Japanese sneak attack. Bullet holes in the hangars, burnt-out PBYs and other aircraft. And, of course, the biggest, saddest monument of them all, just across the harbor: the hull of the sunken battleship *Arizona*.

A couple of days later he took off for Christmas Island, a small coral speck in the ocean due south and just two degrees above the equator. His navigation was day-only, which meant he had to rely a lot on radio bearings. They tried to keep their transmissions to a minimum. The whereabouts of the most powerful naval force in the world, the Japanese Imperial Fleet, was unknown. After Pearl Harbor, no-one would ever question its striking power.

While he was waiting at Christmas, one of our B-25s blew a tire while landing on March 21. No one thought much of this at the time. Teel continued on to Canton Island, south of the equator. But, on takeoff, he too blew a tire. He was modest about what happened, but I gathered that only prompt action on his part prevented a catastrophic accident. So he lost only the tire and wheel, with some repairable damage to the wheel well doors.

He checked the pressure on his remaining tire—highly *over*-inflated.

What the hell? Turns out, it hadn't occurred to anyone that the B-25s passing through Dorval had their tires inflated during subzero weather. So when they hit the tropical air they'd built up dangerous pressures: and bang! Potentially fatal blowouts. A priority message went out to check all tires before leaving the mainland.

Canton Island is only a little over a thousand miles from the Gilbert and Ellice Islands, which the Japs had quickly occupied. Teel was concerned with the rules calling for daylight flights only. He felt that under the cover of night even the Japanese Imperial Fleet could be bypassed.

To add another layer of urgency to that present danger, on each of the three days he'd been there a Martin B-26, being flown by young USAAF pilots, was reported missing. No wreckage was ever found. The Martin was known to be a hot aircraft, one which wouldn't fly on one engine with any kind of a load, one which came out of the factory full of bugs. But was it aircraft malfunctions or Japanese carrier planes which were causing the unexplained disappearances?

Teel didn't really want to find out. The B-25 would take him through, he was sure. So why not fly at night? He approached the commanding officer of Canton, a non-flying first lieutenant, and requested permission for a night takeoff. Permission refused came the arbitrary answer, never been done before, only flare-pot lights.

Captain Don Teel (R) shakes hands with Admiral Sir Bruce Fraser, Commander of the British Pacific Fleet, in 1944

Refused.

Teel decided to force the issue. How, he said to the green lieutenant, do you intend to stop me? I'm an American civilian flying a Dutch aircraft for the British Royal Air Force. The lieutenant threw up his hands in defeat. Obviously he'd been used to mothering along inexperienced young service pilots.

So Teel got his way. A midnight departure with no trouble, and six hours six minutes later he landed at Nandi, Fiji, just in time for a nice hot breakfast. The Japs weren't all that far from Fiji. They'd invaded and occupied Bougainvillea in the Solomons just two months before. That was only about 1,500 miles to the northwest.

Teel decided to press on. It took him just under ten hours to reach Brisbane, Australia. The only sour note was that Walt Davidson ran out of fuel just on approach and wrote off one B-25. The rugged airframe protected the crew, and mercifully no one was hurt.

The Royal Australian Air Force accepted the aircraft on behalf of the Dutch. They formed No. 18 Squadron, initially based near Canberra, and took the homeless Hollanders under their wing. In the meantime the Dutch were establishing their own training school in Jackson, Mississippi. They would have their first crews trained for the delivery flight by August 10.

The Ferry Command crews now had another problem. They'd been sent to Sydney under the impression that the Americans would bring them back. But the Americans were too busy with their own little Pacific war to spare

"*The Aussie had painted the name, The Swagman, on the nose, and used it to fly his wife and family out of the Japanese invasion threat.*"

transport for the Brits, whom General MacArthur didn't like much anyway. The days went by. Sydney wasn't the worst place in the world to be stuck in. Then the weeks went by.

Eventually, Dorval got around to sending down Liberator AL514, which brought back some passengers on March 25. The Captain was an Australian named Macdonald, with co-Captain Jim Dugan, Radio-Navigator John McGrail, and Engineers Art Ryan and John Affleck. The Aussie had painted the name, *The Swagman,* on the nose, and used it to fly his wife and family out of the Japanese invasion threat. There was hell to pay about that.

Then Dorval sent another Lib, *Marvellous Minnie,* out with Captains

Gentry, Byers, and Scotty Grey with another old-time Canadian R/O "Locky" Lockenbauer. Then they sent spare crews and turned the Libs around fast at San Francisco. My old friend George Evans was one of the captains, and Charlie Rector, a darkly handsome man from California, was another.

So in the long run the Java-bound B-25 group all got back. Some had hitched rides with the USN PBY-2 Coronados. Our men had done a wonderful job in the wide Pacific and we were sure we could do the same type of job on the Atlantic, if we were given the chance.

I looked at my watch. It was almost noon, so I thanked Teel profusely, then raced over to the Admin building to meet Tommy.

She looked a little worried as she climbed into my car. Maybe she believed that my intentions were strictly dishonorable. But I also knew that if she believed my intentions were strictly dishonorable, then for sure she must know that I knew that she knew. This gave me some much-needed confidence. If I could seal up her lip-music with a quick kiss, physical contact would do the rest. After passing through the gates and saluting the airport guardhouse I turned westward in the direction of Pointe Claire and its open fields.

We both knew there were no restaurants out that way, but Tommy didn't say anything. Maybe the freshly-scented air of early summer had a soothing effect on her, although it surely didn't have that effect on me. The countryside was lush and green. As we slowly drove along, I noticed some early flowers, and this seemed like as good an excuse as any to stop.

After we got out she didn't resist when I took her in my arms. In fact, she gave me back as good as I gave. Suddenly she pulled away and I wondered what I'd done wrong. She caught her breath as she looked up at me.

"You've told me you always fly with a sleeping bag." I looked at her stupidly, without answering, so she added, "I've never seen one."

All of a sudden I got the message. In a flash, I had the trunk opened and laid the soft, down-filled bag on the ground. I had made sure, of course, that we were well-hidden from the road.

"Well, there it is," I said, unsure of my next move, and quite unwilling to believe that my seduction plan was going so smoothly.

Now she surprised me. She took off her shoes and skirt, then slipped inside the waiting sleeping bag. I was watching in a sort of deep shock, totally unused to not being the aggressor. She looked up at me, completely at ease. There was a mischievous glint in her eye as she smiled.

"These things really are comfortable, aren't they? I'll bet there's room for the two of us in it." I needed no second invitation. After I threw off my clothes and joined her in my new love-nest, Tommy proved that wide, sensuous red lips and slightly protuberant eyes were indeed reliable indicators of a passionate nature. She was terrific and I was hard put to keep up with her. There were a few early bees buzzing around and I was sure that not one of them was as busy as I.

The sun was setting when we finally tired of one another and our lovely sex-contest. When we broke camp, so to speak, we were both well satisfied. I even felt somewhat weak as I dressed and packed away my portable love-bed. Then we had our long-delayed meal at a discreet restaurant where the snoopy eyes of other Ferry Command people couldn't see us together.

Gossip is a terrible thing, especially when it is true.

That night, back at the Mount Royal, I made a purple 'X' on my navigation chart to mark the scene of our delicious encounter. I had never dreamed that when the Stores department of Ferry Command had issued me that Woods Brothers down-filled sleeping bag for the cold, cold Arctic that it would reward me in such a warm and marvelous way.

Perhaps it was my imagination, but forever after, whenever I used the bag, there seemed to linger a lovely female scent that would forever remind me of that early summer encounter amongst the flowers of Quebec.

RDX Secret Explosive

A few days later I got a welcome call. It appeared that my old friend Jack Parkinson was celebrating his safe return from his Pacific B-25 delivery. Would I care to help him?

Indeed I would.

Parky was in the new Pic, a much larger establishment in the southeast corner of the ground floor of the hotel. It was bright, well decorated with overstuffed chairs, and massive pillars, but I missed the friendly, snug, cave-like atmosphere of the old club.

Cosmopolitan Montreal provided many other meeting places, such as the Maritime Bar in the tony Ritz Hotel, the bar in the Queen's Hotel, and the discreet bar in the Windsor Hotel. The bar in the Ford Hotel was a popular hangout for our radio officers. Of course, night clubs such as the Normandie Roof, right in the Mount Royal, the Tic-Toc, and innumerable others catered to service people and civilians alike.

But, new or old, the Piccadilly Club was the Ferry Command's equivalent of a service officer's club. It was the only place in town where you could arrive in uniform or civvies and the maitre d' would always welcome you; where you could make friends with your favorite waiter; where you could be reasonably certain of meeting your friends after your and their return from trips to the far corners of the world.

It was also the place where you just might find out the destination of your next delivery flight. Tall tales, hearsay, scandal, good and bad tidings, and rumors abounded. Some were even true.

I congratulated Parkinson on getting back unscathed, and he introduced me to a swarthy, good-looking man in the uniform of squadron leader. He was a fellow Saskatchewan boy, like Parky and me. His name was L.L. "Slim" Jones and he'd just returned from his B-25 trip, where his radio officer had been none other than my prewar ham friend Gordy Wightman.

Jones wore a rare combination of decorations, a DFC and an AFC. I listened as they told of their adventures while crossing the wide Pacific. They'd liked the trip, especially the lack of icing conditions, except for the long distances and the difficulty of getting back. In fact their reaction to the Pacific was remarkably similar to that of Captain Don Teel. The B-25 was a

RAFFC aircrew: L-R, Harris, Captain Jack Parkinson, Captain Bradley, Gorman

good airplane, and the engines, except for the occasional glitch, were reliable. Once more I wished I'd taken a Mitchell for the Dutch.

After a few drinks I got up enough courage to ask Jones about his decorations. He wasn't too cooperative. I guessed it was modesty that kept him tongue-tied. But after a few more drinks, he loosened up. The Distinguished Flying Cross was for a hairy Sunderland flying boat trip from Narvik with a lot of heavy brass on board, during the abortive invasion of Norway.

He said the Germans had beaten them to the punch. The Royal Navy in particular had taken a terrible pasting, losing an aircraft carrier and several destroyers. I was impressed. The British were notoriously chintzy in giving out their decorations for bravery. The joke, if it could be called such, was that to earn the Victoria Cross, you had to agree to have it awarded posthumously.

I pressed him about his Air Force Cross. It turned out he had taken four Cats over during the winter of 1940, including the second delivery of the Command from the icy harbor of Halifax. It had been a tough winter, which tied in with what Pangborn had told me about flying boat operations.

Then Jones got onto me. He wanted to know if I didn't think I was grossly overpaid. I looked at Parky. He shrugged his shoulders. Apparently Jones, a prewar Short Service RAF officer, had a chip on his shoulder. I answered as best I could. He glared at me with his intense, dark brown eyes. I couldn't help wondering if he and Parky might not be from the same Indian tribe. I felt my scalp: still in place.

I decided a combination of the diplomatic approach and a direct attack would serve me best, so I asked him, "How much did you know about flying when you joined up?"

"Nothing, of course," he snorted. This was my opening.

"Well, I paid for my flying, and furthermore I had a twin engine rating and an instrument rating when I got into Ferry Command."

"So?" He hadn't got the message yet. It was time to make my point.

"So," I declared emphatically, "for all practical purposes, Parky and I were ready to go when we joined up."

I looked over at my monkey-faced friend. I might need help soon. But he just squirmed around in his chair without answering, caught in the middle.

"Well, maybe," Jones conceded.

I pressed my advantage.

"You can check these figures with the people who sell War Bonds. They claim that to take a civilian off the street, put him through Manning Pool, Elementary Flying Training School, then Service Flying School, and finally through an Operational Training Unit costs not less than fifty thousand bucks." I stopped to let this figure sink in.

Jones answered slowly, "What you're really saying is that the government can pay you a thousand dollars a month for over four years which is their equal investment to turn out a sprog sergeant or Pilot Officer?"

"That's right, Slim. And don't forget we come in with lots of experience while the poor guys finishing OTU are still just learning. Plus, if we slip in the bathtub and break a leg, why we're off the payroll as of right now. And we have to pay our own medical bills and hospital expenses."

"I see your point. If I have an accident my medical bills are paid, and I still draw my salary. Your sad story has touched my heart. I'll even buy you a drink."

Good men, western Canadians. Why, with a free drink, I could even take his sarcastic remark about my sad story. Jones turned out to have a great sense of humor. A little on the sardonic side, perhaps, but soon I really felt I'd made a friend.

Parky looked much relieved. At long last a bone of contention had been buried. He wanted to know what I'd been doing, so I told him about the Norseman flights. He responded with a few tall stories of his own. Jones chimed in with some about his operational flying. We really were enjoying ourselves. I've noticed pilots talk about flying on the ground, and then when they're in the air, they talk about sex.

I decided to ask Parky about his brother-in-law, Kevin Kelly, my rival for the beautiful and apparently unobtainable Maureen. He seemed to sober up instantly as he replied, "I guess you haven't read the Air Force casualty lists lately?"

I knew he was referring to the daily reports of the tragic results of Canada's war effort in the air. The Army mercifully had nothing to publish, because they'd just been marching around when they weren't rotting under canvas in England for three years. And the Navy, although doing a good job at sea, had few casualties to report.

It was the Royal Air Force with a lot of RCAF aircrew that was then carrying the brunt of the war against Germany. The casualty lists published daily in newspapers such as *The Montreal Star* announced a wide variety of misery for the next of kin:

"Killed on active service"

"Previously reported missing, now reported killed on active service"

"Missing after air operations"

"Previously reported missing, now reported prisoner of war"

"Interned"

"Previously reported missing, now for official purposes reported dead"

"Seriously injured on active service"

I felt a premonition as I looked at Parkinson. "You mean Kelly got the chop?"

"They don't know yet. For now he's been listed as missing." Parkinson stared moodily into his glass.

In a way that was the worst news. The next-of-kin would be left in the dark until the Red Cross communicated the official findings. The Germans weren't noted for quickness in reporting the fate of airmen shot down while engaged in destroying the property of the Third Reich. I gnawed my lip.

"Bad news, for sure. I guess that's why Maureen hasn't been answering my phone calls. Her mother says she isn't feeling well. No wonder."

I took a long pull on my drink, while Parky looked at me closely. It wasn't unknown for a suitor to celebrate the death of his rival. My genuine concern satisfied him and he raised his glass and joined me. In our business there was no point in thinking too deeply about death.

Bob, the Maitre d', finally convinced us they really meant to close the bar, and we staggered off to our beds.

I woke up the next day full of pep, and went out to see if I could spring some flying out of Crew Assignments. They looked at me a little askance. People who hung around their desk were liable to get some flying. I was a strange breed. I liked to fly.

I had been filling in the time by doing navigation training flights in Hudsons, until on May 29 at last got another four-engine delivery. I hoped fervently that the flight would work out better than my first abortive try when we were proving the Crimson Route.

This time I had drawn an old, rather beat-up LB-30, which stood for "Liberator-British." Except for its age it was almost identical to a current production B-24. The aircraft and its cargo were to be delivered to Prestwick.

For a copilot I had a rather arrogant American named Ted Blockley. It seemed that he was positive he was a far better pilot than I. Therefore, in his twisted mind I must have used undue political influence to attain the left hand seat so early in my career.

Somehow this belligerent attitude tended to make me a little antagonistic, so I made sure he didn't get his sticky little fingers on any of the controls. We would sit through the flight in unarmed neutrality, a poor condition for any flight crew.

Happily, I was able to secure reliable Eric Rush as my R/O. I'd decided to exercise my authority as Captain-Navigator to do my own navigation. For Flight Engineer I drew a dour Scotsman named MacLeod. He convinced me in about three minutes he knew a hell of a lot more about a Liberator than I could ever hope to learn.

When I signed out the aircraft at Field Operations I detected a somewhat strained atmosphere. Eric Dunford, the chief, took me into his office. This usually meant bad news. It was. I had a highly secret priority cargo on board! When I asked what it was, he told me it was *so* super-secret secret he couldn't tell me. I grumbled loudly and when I wandered out of his office, I was a good deal less confident than when I had entered.

Outside on the parking tarmac it was time to do a visual inspection with MacLeod. Other than exhaust and old oil leak stains, all seemed to be in order. As I climbed aboard, I looked at my cargo. Innocuous-appearing wooden crates tied securely in the bomb-bay. I wondered what my real all-up weight was. We normally carried as much cargo as the freight department dared load. Sometimes the weight and balance form didn't reflect the real weight we were carrying. Of course we, that is, the captains, would find out the hard way, either on an excessively long takeoff run, or better yet, if we lost an engine.

The weather looked good for a Gander landing and takeoff. But it wasn't to be. The takeoff was long, as usual for the weight we were carrying. But in the climb, Number Two engine started to surge. The needles of the revolution counter and manifold pressure were flicking aimlessly. At the same time it was impossible to synchronize the four engines, so the uneven commotion was very disconcerting.

Then, just a wee bit late, MacLeod informed me they'd had trouble on the test flight, but had decided to release the aircraft due to the urgency of the cargo. I didn't buy that, so I turned back and landed, even if the aircraft was quite heavy.

After climbing out and entering the Field Ops office I was aware of a distinctly cool atmosphere. It was apparent I'd tarnished my reputation as a press-on type. I even overheard Dunford getting a blast from Powell. But I stood by my guns, and insisted the aircraft was not airworthy. MacLeod backed me up. They towed it back to the maintenance hangar and I went back to the hotel.

Of course I had to wonder if I'd done the right thing. Still, if the cargo was really that important, I'd look like a real fool if I had an in-flight fire or had to make an unscheduled three-engine landing.

© 2011 Donna McVicar Kazo

"This time I had drawn an old, rather beat-up LB-30, which stood for 'Liberator-British.' Except for its age it was almost identical to a current production B-24."

It was June 1 before maintenance alleged they'd found the trouble. It was a slipping supercharger clutch. I climbed in and took off. This time the good weather had long gone. Both Goose and Gander were flat. I filed the first flight plan direct from Montreal to Greenland, that horrible strip at BW1. This time no one had anything to say. My sole alternative if the weather at BW1 went flat was BW8. It worried them, but it didn't worry me. I was one of the three captains who had been there.

After taking off, I climbed slowly up to 21,000 feet to clear the ice-laden bad weather fronts, then leveled off, with a ration of oxygen masks all around. Then Number Two engine started to surge just as before! I had a long discussion with MacLeod. We agreed it was unlikely that our ground maintenance could ever fix an internal engine problem. There was some possibility the clutch might burn up, but it only surged in high blower, which meant we could still get partial power in an emergency. I decided I'd risk engine failure to Powell's wrath if I turned back again.

The weather over the south of Greenland was clear, a truly unusual event. I could see the icecap from 100 miles out at my new lower altitude of 10,000 feet, which I had been able to settle into after crossing the fronts.

I flew over Simiutak Island, the guardian of Narssarssuaq Fjord, and started letting down between the oppressive black mountains. I passed the sunken ship and turned left. To do anything else would lead me up a blind alley, with not enough room to make a 180 degree turn back again. I got lined up on the steel pierced-plank runway which started at ten feet above sea level and ran up to 110 feet above sea level. Always land uphill and take off downhill, the manual advised.

I'd obeyed this rule, but my approach was poor, and I was too high when I passed over the sea end of the runway. There was no way to go around, so I chopped the power and hauled back. We stalled in from about five feet, I guess. There was a hell of a noise as the steel plank took the impact. A colossal cloud of dust marked the spot of my arrival. It was one of my worst efforts. I could feel Blockley's accusing eyes burning into me.

But as we taxied to the marshaling area it was apparent that nothing on the Lib was broken. I was prepared for a blast from the USAAF landing control officer, but nothing was said. Apparently lousy landings were quite common on the deceptive strip. After a performance such as mine, they just sent out a crew of engineers who replaced the bent planks.

I went up the hill to Operations and reported, "Captain McVicar with Ferry Command B-24 AE57."

"Where have you come from?" the young second lieutenant wanted to know.

"Dorval," I answered shortly, "and I filed a flight plan. Didn't you get it?"

"No, sir, nobody had told us to expect a heavy Liberator."

"Well, we're here. How about a Prestwick forecast?"

Somehow our conversation had a very familiar Greenland ring to it.

"Sorry sir, we don't have that on tap. It'll take about five hours to make one up." I thought, more bad news. In five hours the wind could switch

The inhospitable interior of Greenland
Photo © 2007 Doc Searls, used with permission

*"I got lined up on the steel pierced-plank runway which started
at ten feet above sea level and ran up to 110 feet above sea level.
Always land uphill and take off downhill, the manual advised."*

around and BW8 could go flat as a pancake. I looked at the map. If I went on a great circle course through Iceland, the distance to Prestwick was just a little longer by going direct.

"How about a forecast for Iceland?" The Ops man and his forecaster brightened up.

"No problems there. Here's a current folder. The route is good, but Iceland's weather is pretty doubtful, just on limits."

"I wouldn't expect anything different," I mumbled as I signed my flight plan.

An hour later our big black bird was perched on the high end of the runway looking down at the cold green waters of the fjord. A brisk tail wind on the rudders made the pedals fight against my feet. Operations alleged the effect of the downhill slope would counteract the effect of the following wind. I sure as hell hoped they knew what they were talking about.

Somehow, they don't teach downwind takeoffs at flying schools. I opened the throttles and then released the brakes, and we seemed to be accelerating very quickly. But the airspeed needle was creeping up with agonizing slowness as we rumbled along. Now that we were committed I forced myself to stay calm.

The engines were roaring as minimum flying speed and the end of the runway appeared simultaneously. I heaved back on the big control wheel. This was not the place for delicate airmanship, and with a groan the Lib lurched into the air. Ground effect helped as the gear and flaps retracted and I leveled off to pick up speed. I climbed slowly down the fjord to gain the necessary altitude before turning back to clear the ice cap.

My heart calmed down as it dawned on me what had happened. I hadn't told MacLeod of my change of plans, so he had taken on a full fuel load which put us right at the end of the weight and tail wind chart limits. I could have lowered the weight substantially by taking on just enough fuel for the short flight to Iceland.

I looked over at Blockley. He was still too shaken by the takeoff to realize what had happened. And I wasn't about to tell him of what I considered to be my error of judgment. There was a good ceiling and fairly good visibility at Iceland. Just a 25 knot crosswind to test my landing ability.

Thank God for tricycle gear.

In an hour we were on our way again, bound for Prestwick with a nice flight plan of only three and a half hours, mostly between layers of cloud. We got another thrill from the takeoff on Reykjavik's nerve-racking short runway, the one closest to being into the wind, as we lumbered over the city buildings on the perimeter. Keflavik had never looked better. The flight to Prestwick was uneventful with just one front to coat us with rime ice as a reminder that the North Atlantic was at all times relentless.

We passed over Stornoway, where we'd been told they hoped to build a landing strip, then over the rough northwest coast of Scotland. Good Scottish names passed below us: the Isle of Skye, Inverness, and Argyle; I could almost hear the skirl of bagpipes. Then we flew over the Firth of Clyde with its usual quota of Royal Navy warcraft.

Finally, with grimy Glasgow in the far distance off our left wing, Prestwick tower acknowledged our arrival and gave us immediate landing clearance. Tired as I was, it took all my concentration to carry out a good touch-down.

Then, after taxiing to the unloading ramp, there seemed to be an awful lot of people hanging around. It was the type of reception usually reserved for Very Important People. I was somewhat prepared because Rush had told me every time he came on the air they'd cleared the frequency. He said he'd never had such attention.

So even if I didn't know what my Lib was carrying, a lot of other people must be in on the secret. Very unusually, I could even see a photographer busily snapping away. It had to be my cargo.

I was determined to find out what was in those boxes in the bomb-bay. Jimmy Jeffs was there, making sure our cargo was sent on its way without delay. He was the man to whom I'd lost the pound bet about returning with a Hudson within seven days. He was also the man who'd spent the money immediately on three rounds of drinks. I like that attitude. A man like that could be trusted to tell the truth.

I asked him, "What in hell is going on?"

"Just a moment, Captain," he replied, "Let's make the photographer happy." The photographer was from a prominent London newspaper, *The Observer*, who insisted on snapping me in various poses. Jeffs assisted the photographer by giving him background stories while he took his pictures.

After the man had gone, he said, "You mean to say, Captain McVicar, that you don't know what your cargo is?"

I was getting more than a little angry.

"No, I bloody well don't. Dorval said it was so secret they couldn't tell me." He rubbed his chin in perplexity. If Dorval hadn't entrusted me with this knowledge, perhaps he'd better keep his mouth shut too.

I forced the issue.

"We sure get the royal treatment on the way over, and now this. What's in those damned boxes, anyway?"

"Well..." he was actually embarrassed. I tried for the humorous angle.

"I suppose, just like the husband who is the last one to find out the milkman is screwing his wife, I'll be the last one to know about my own cargo."

This brought a smile to his face. After all, the trip was over, so he decided to let me in on the secret. He looked around before whispering, "You've just brought in the first shipment of the new secret super-explosive called RDX."

My mouth fell open. For a moment I could not speak. Then I exclaimed, "Jesus, *super*-explosive?"

Jeffs seemed not to notice my dismayed expression.

"Some call it Torpex. The boffins think it's going to shorten the war." He seemed quite pleased with himself as he imparted this startling news. Then he noticed my bloodless rigid face.

"What's the matter? You've gone quite pale." I was reliving my horribly hard landing in Greenland, but managed to pull myself together.

"It's all right. Maybe I've been doing too much flying at high altitude. As a matter of fact, what does this RDX do?"

"Do? Anything dynamite or black powder can do, they claim RDX can do ten times better." I started to sweat a little.

"Does this super explosive need caps like dynamite to set it off?" He thought that one over for a few moments.

"As far as I can find out, RDX is quite inert." I breathed a heavy sigh of relief.

"But the scientists haven't really got all the answers yet." Then he kindly took my arm and said, "You look a little queer. Let's go up to the bar and I'll buy you a drink, and you can tell me about your trip."

I answered gratefully, "Best idea I've heard all day."

We walked across the tarmac to the Orangefield Hotel, then upstairs to the balcony. The hotel was one of the best features of Ferry Command. The dining room did the best they could with the war-rationed food and

Consolidated Liberator LB-30

the reception people were always glad to see us. Miss Grey could always be counted on to find a comfortable room for a weary flight crew. We felt at home when we walked in. A lot like the Pic.

I took a large swallow of my drink. I knew I needed to relax, and soon I was telling Jeffs about the weak engine. He agreed that I had made a tough but correct decision. He smiled.

"Well, Don, it all worked out for the best, didn't it?" I gazed at the ceiling as I answered slowly, "Sure...it all worked out...but what bothers me is that if I'd known what I was carrying I doubt if I would have gone into BW1." He nodded.

"Good point. I've heard some bad things about steel landing strips in the desert, and I suppose that sloping one in Greenland was even worse." I didn't bother to tell him how hard my landing had really been. I felt my own conscience would punish me enough. Besides my vanity, I had to preserve my reputation as one of Ferry Command's crack pilots; or was that cracked, I thought cynically.

Frowning, I declared, "You know, the people at Dorval outsmarted themselves. By keeping me in the dark they almost caused a hell of an accident."

"That's a possibility."

"I wonder if they thought I'd refuse the flight if they told me the truth." He looked me straight in the eye.

"Well?"

I felt my face getting red.

"Hell, no! I'll take anything they assign me. I'm not looking for easy flights." From the look on his face, Jeffs evidently believed me.

"Why don't you tell Taffy when you get back?" I had thought of doing that very thing, and now I was convinced.

"That's a hell of a good idea."

"So you're going to do it?"

"Yes, I will. I resent being treated like an adolescent." He had no response to this adolescent comment, and as I was sick of the whole subject, I asked that always-important question, "When do I go back?"

"There's a bit of a backlog right now. I'd say you'll be here about a week."

"A week!" I retorted in horror. But really, I wasn't too unhappy. It would give me a chance to explore the Scottish countryside, especially Ayr, where Robbie Burns was buried. And there was another thing I wanted to do. I'd heard of the exploits of the Air Transport Auxiliary which ferried all sorts of aircraft around internally in Great Britain.

I looked at Jeffs.

"Can you fix it up for me to ride around in some of ATA's deliveries and taxi aircraft, instead of buying me drinks here?" He grinned.

"With a proposition like that, how can I refuse? I'll get right on it."

The drink and the released tension of my difficult Liberator delivery hit me hard, without warning. I rose somewhat unsteadily and within ten minutes I was fast asleep in my private room.

The Air Transport Auxiliary

The next morning I sat down to a breakfast of powdered eggs and "bangers" which contained far more water and meal than meat. These sausage substitutes were named bangers because when they were fried, their water would expand into steam and the whole unsavory mess would explode. But what we called "ersatz" food was far from my mind as I thought back upon the history of the ATA.

The English had started the ferrying service early in the war when Gerard d'Erlanger had succeeded in getting the authorities interested in utilizing pilots who were unfit for operational flying. They were just getting into their stride, when in 1940 after the German breakthrough into France, they had to carry out the difficult and unpleasant task of rescuing the pitifully few RAF aircraft which had survived the catastrophe.

Since those early days their organization had grown to such an extent they now had pilot pools at many of Great Britain's strategic airports. Prestwick was home to No. 4 Ferry Pool. The control system was remarkably effective. It had to be to schedule hundreds of flights each day in varying weather conditions, while trying to utilize its pilots to the utmost. The pilots were from no less than twenty-six nations and flew for thirteen days solid before getting a two-day leave period. It was known that many of them spent the first twenty-four hours of their leave solidly in bed!

The main duty of the pilots was to pick up new aircraft from the factories or Prestwick and deliver them to one of twenty or so Maintenance Units scattered around England, Scotland, and Northern Ireland. After these aircraft were fitted with guns, special radio units, radar and other items essential to operational flying, the ATA would deliver them to the RAF squadrons operating that particular type.

I was hoping to ride with an American friend of George Evans named Ed Heering, who was in charge of the ferry pool at Lossiemouth, just a hundred or so miles north of Prestwick. But he was busy on other flights, so it wasn't until some months later that we got together in the cockpit of a Halifax.

Jeffs had kept his word, so after breakfast I climbed into Hudson 477 to ride with Al Krauter, an American. We visited Mollom, Barrow, Speke,

Ringway and Lichfield. He told me that ATA checked out their would-be pilots in Harvards, and we both agreed that if a person could handle a lethal Harvard they could handle any single engine type. They'd used a Bristol Blenheim for twin engine checkouts. Well, he said, they had to use something. I didn't comment.

That night I was the guest of a few of the ATA boys at Lichfield. I soon found out they were stout competitors in the drinking field. I discovered that one of the more interesting features of the ATA was that the English, whom I'd always thought of as being conservative, had welcomed female pilots into the ATA, so that they now comprised almost a quarter of the total. Of course I had to ask how they compared to males. There was a moment of embarrassed silence before Krauter spoke up and said they were as good as any man. I was impressed.

"What about Jackie Cochran?" I asked. There was another moment of silence before a senior flight captain grated, "I was based at White Waltham when she was there. Of all the ruthless, arrogant women I've ever had to deal with, she's the worst." There was a low rumble of assent.

I said, "That's what we thought when she bullied her way aboard a Hudson delivery for us from St. Hubert last year. Just to get rid of her they gave her a tame captain named Carlisle. He did the takeoffs and landings and she twiddled with the automatic pilot in the air."

Another more moderate ATA pilot said, "But she did bring over twenty-five American girls for ATA when we were short of help."

"How did they do?"

"Fine. They were a lot different from her. I think she lived just to cause confusion and pick fights. Being married to such an influential investment tycoon as Floyd Odlum gave her a lot of power which she loved to exercise." Nobody had an answer to that remark, so the rather touchy subject was dropped.

But during that evening I learned something useful that would help me all through my future flying career. It was their vital action mnemonic: H-hydraulics; T-trim; M-mixture; P-pitch, or propellers; F-flaps; G-gills; G-gas. Add U-undercarriage for the landing routine. I remembered it as "High-Tempered Member of Parliament Flaps His Gills and Gasses. Ugh." It works in every aircraft, and often when the flight handling notes for a new type were not available the mnemonic did the trick.

The next morning the weather was below their limits. These were, daylight flying only and the equivalent of our Visual Flight Rules, which meant a minimum ceiling of 800 feet and visibility of at least 2,000 yards. But the notorious English weather occasionally forced them to bend the rules in order to complete the delivery of a vital aircraft. Considering the low level of experience of only 250 hours solo—lowered to 150 after the Battle of Britain—needed to be accepted, their accident record was a reasonable twelve per cent of the average 650 pilots on staff at any one time.

I took the opportunity to tour the local countryside. It seemed the average Englishman was bearing up well. They actually thought they might win the war, in spite of the reverses their army was suffering at the hands of Rommel in Africa. But many weren't that hopeful that the island of Malta could continue to hold out against the almost 500 bombers and fighters the Germans and Italians had based on nearby Sicily.

The next morning, away I went on the taxi Anson W1707 with a cheerful chap called Stoffee. It felt just like home. After all, most of my twin engine time was on the lumbering greenhouse. We landed at Leicester.

This time I got in an Airspeed Oxford, No. T1320, with a pilot called Lane. He took me over to Hawarden, where I changed Oxfords to EB690, then up to Silloth. I was getting close to Scotland. The final leg was in a single engine Fairchild 24 HM with a dour Englishman named Privencal.

He loosened up in the Orangefield bar and I learned that pilots of both sexes were given a checkout in just one type of each classification of single, twin and heavy. The heavy types were Halifax, Lincoln and Lancaster bombers. They had proven if you could handle one example in each classification you could handle them all. Yes, he assured me, the women handled the heavies with no apparent trouble. I was more impressed, and suggested with some longing that I'd like to meet one of these talented females. Privencal stated that my chances were slim. They seemed dedicated to their work. But I still wondered what they did after dark.

I also discovered what had happened to the flock of Spitfires which had been at Prestwick when I'd brought in my second delivery, Hudson FH432, on April 22. They were to be loaded on the US aircraft carrier *Wasp*, which was berthed on the Clyde, near Glasgow, a few miles north. But there was a problem. One nearby airfield, Abbotsinch, had lovely long runways. But if the fighters landed there they'd have to be dismantled to get them to the *Wasp*.

The other airfield was a miserable little grass aerodrome called Renfrew, which had an available landing length of only 590 yards. According to the Spit's handling notes, 800 yards was the minimum landing run. But for transport from Renfrew to the dockside, only the wingtips of the Spits had to be unscrewed, a twenty-minute job.

The ATA pilots knew the Spits were absolutely essential to the defense of the island of Malta. Time was indeed of the essence. So a small band of senior pilots carried out some rather dangerous, very accurate low flying and by April 26, all forty-eight fighters were safely onto the grass of Renfrew.

The *Wasp* sailed without delay, accompanied by the Royal Navy carrier HMS *Eagle*. The two warships passed through the Straits of Gibraltar into the Mediterranean where they fought their way to within 600 miles from Malta, the maximum range of the fighters.

There the carriers turned into the wind and launched their precious cargo. The *Eagle* launched sixteen of the eight-gun Spits making a total of 64. The date was May 9; on the opposite side of the world, the Battle of the Coral Sea was being fought. No doubt *Wasp* would have helped its fellow carriers *Lexington* and *Yorktown*, but most people thought President Roosevelt had made the right decision as to its location.

The *Wasp* joined the Pacific Fleet on June 10 and fought in the Battle of the Eastern Solomons on August 25w. She then for some time was the only operational US aircraft carrier left in the Pacific. When on September 14 she was sunk by the Japanese submarine I.19, there was more than one Royal Navy officer who thought she deserved an honorary "HMS" which stands for "His Majesty's Ship."

At Malta, immediately after refueling, the Fighter Command pilots rose to challenge the might of the Luftwaffe and the Regia Aeronautica. They quickly regained control of the air and thus the torpedo and bomber aircraft based on the island were able to continue to bleed the enemy convoys dry, much to Rommel's anger and frustration.

In the Orangefield I was now officially on standby. As a member of a genuine "captive audience" it was annoying to watch BOAC play their nightly game of delayed notification of our return flight's cancellation. It seemed to us mere passengers, always referred to as "bodies," that the unwelcome news that our flight was delayed was never made until it was too late to visit nearby Ayr's theatre or skating rink. As I sat around staring at the ceiling, I hoped against hope that this flight wouldn't be a repetition of the previous debacle I'd endured with Stewart.

At long last we took off, and I found I had been worrying needlessly. Captain Trevor Cripps produced a nice low level ride straight back to Montreal. Elapsed time only fifteen hours forty minutes; no oxygen; reasonably warm in my personal sleeping bag. Even the occasional message on a slip of paper telling how we were doing came down to the bomb-bay from the cockpit. I found out later Cripps had flown in the USA with Colonial Airlines, and unlike a lot of BOAC pilots actually believed in radio ranges.

At Dorval I slowly removed my stiff body from the bomb-bay, and determined that I must buy Cripps a drink at the first opportunity. It seemed my anti-English aggression wore off in a hurry when I found a Sassenach I could trust. Too bad there were so few of them.

Powell called me into his office for a debriefing.

"Why did you go via Greenland and Iceland in a Lib?" was his first question.

"Well, the weather really screwed me up, and I probably wouldn't make the flight just that way the next time. But they said the cargo was most urgent, so after my delays with that lousy engine I decided that the Bluie West One landing was an acceptable risk."

"Well, under the circumstances, I suppose you made the right decision," he rather reluctantly admitted.

That settled, I asked, "Why wasn't I told that my cargo was RDX?"

"Well..." he seemed to be having trouble coming up with a reason.

I continued my attack.

"Don't you trust me?" He looked at me with a puzzled frown, and I wondered if I'd overstepped his limits of friendship.

"You should realize, McVicar, that ordinary captains like you actually shouldn't come into my office and talk to me in the manner you've just done." There was heat in his tone.

But I knew I had a good point, so I stuck to my guns. "How else will you find out what goes on in the real world if people like me don't tell you?"

"Harrumph," or some such noise issued from his mouth. Then slowly he said, "I suppose you could be right." I took this as the closest a Welshman could ever come to apologizing to a Scottish Canadian, and we shook hands as he escorted me out of his office.

I was appeased. I suppose all I really wanted was a little recognition for successfully completing a rather dangerous and difficult flight.

I decided my life would be perfect if I could just pierce the mother-barrier and talk to Maureen. But she refused to establish communication.

Tommy did, though.

The Mitchell

A few days later Crew Assignments advised me my next delivery would be one of the first B-25s to Prestwick. The RAF were starting to get their share. This suited me fine. I liked the fast twin and I'd made a study of the career of General W. L. "Billy" Mitchell, after whom the aircraft was named.

He had been a real old-timer, taught to fly by none other than Orville Wright. He'd been in the original Army Air Services, a branch of the Signal Corps of the US Army in the First World War. After the war he tried to bring some original thinking into the stuffy military minds of that era. But he'd hit a lot of resistance with every new idea he brought forward.

Then he claimed an aircraft could sink a battleship. It was the captured German battleship *Ostfriesland*, a big one of 29,000 tons. He used eight Martin bombers, each carrying a 2,000 pound bomb. The Navy said he'd cheated! He should have used only 1,000 pound bombs.

His enemies finally got him and he was reduced to colonel in 1922, but he refused to quit. A court martial in 1926 under General Douglas MacArthur kicked him out of the service. The charge was insubordination. He continued his crusade for the proper use of air power as a civilian until his death in 1936. He died a bitter and disillusioned man.

You would wonder why they had named an aircraft after him, if he was so unpopular. Well, it seemed that after the Luftwaffe struck, his ideas were recognized as being not so stupid after all. Thus the belated honor.

Then, just a few weeks before my flight, the US Congress had voted to restore his name to the Army rolls with the rank of major general. Six years dead before he got some recognition of his life's work.

There was another reason I held the Mitchell in such high regard. On April 18, 1942, the electrifying news that Japan had been attacked appeared in "war extras" from newspapers all over the country.

President Roosevelt stated that the attack had been mounted from Shangri-La, that wonderful, timeless place located in the wastes of Tibet, described in the novel *Lost Horizon* by James Hilton.

Most informed people, including the Japanese, realized the attack must have actually been launched from an aircraft carrier, especially as the USS *Hornet* had steamed out of San Francisco harbor on April 2nd with sixteen B-25s lashed to her deck. And in broad daylight, too!

But the Japs didn't react in time. Then came the exciting news that the famous racing pilot Jimmy Doolittle had led the raid. On May 19 he was promoted from lieutenant colonel to brigadier general and awarded America's highest decoration, the Congressional Medal of Honor. He said he really didn't deserve it. I could not have disagreed more. Somehow flying the same type of aircraft as the heroes of the Tokyo raid made me feel more than a little proud.

Jack Dalton

I had made a new friend, Jack Dalton, from Toronto. He was a burly, good looking man with a set of sugar-cube-white teeth and a great sense of humor.

I discovered my B-25 was FL210 and that he had the one right next to it. We decided to try to stick together on the delivery for two good reasons: firstly, if either of us went down the other could call for help; secondly, if we were stuck someplace due to weather or maintenance, he would be a hell of an interesting social companion.

The weather was beautiful on June 18 when we pulled out of Dorval. This time I had another American copilot, named Brown, a slightly built youth with a gaunt face. His personality was acceptable, but just like Blockley, he had one great fault. As an American he was paid in tax free US dollars with a ten per cent differential exchange rate going his way, of course. That meant he was getting more for sitting in the right hand seat, knowing and doing nothing, than I was, being captain with all the responsibility.

I didn't like the arrangement and had complained loudly. The response was not unexpected. Americans told me to mind my own business. Canadians agreed wholeheartedly. Englishmen, Australians, South Africans, Poles and other nations who were paid less than Canadians just laughed. I decided to forget about it.

Again, the dependable Eric Rush was my R/O, and this time they'd given me a Service navigator named Swain. I was told to let him do the navigating. Of course if he goofed it up I would be expected to take over. I smiled to myself. Just like back home in the Air Observer School.

After an uneventful flight of four hours and thirty-five minutes we landed at Goose and decided to stay overnight. The days were very long and I wanted to get a daylight fix over Greenland instead of trying for a star fix during the short night.

Early the next morning, Dalton got away with me right behind. We climbed up to about 10,000 feet and set course. About half way across the Davis Strait he decided to formate on my right wingtip. Brown had a camera, so I held a steady course while Dalton tucked in tight. Then we got the shock of our lives. We'd heard about the ice-collecting tendencies of the Holley carburetor fitted to the Wright engines. Now we got a dramatic demonstration.

My right engine cut out just as Dalton's left engine gave a big cough and a backfire. I pulled up and rolled away to the left. I hoped he'd have enough sense to dive away. When I finally got straightened up, I found him below and half a mile away on my starboard side. Right then and there we both decided that any formation flying we'd do in a B-25 would have nice separation. Half a mile would be fine and dandy.

We landed, refueled, and then got the hell out of Iceland. Good weather and long days were not to be wasted.

At Prestwick, we attracted a lot of sightseers with our spanking new Mitchells. The manufacturer, North American Aircraft, should have paid us for being their two best salesmen. Afterwards, we unwound enough in the bar and lumbered off to bed.

The next morning we discovered that because we were the first B-25s to arrive in the U.K. on June 19, the ATA hadn't yet printed their usual *Pilot's Handling Notes*. So would Dalton or I like to ferry one to Aston Down, where a flock of RAF engineers were eager to inspect their latest light bomber?

We tossed, and I won. Or at least I thought I'd won, because there was supposed to be a big backlog for return flights. However, just as I was filing my flight plan I learned Dalton was scheduled to go back on Return Ferry Service that very night. So maybe I'd lost.

But maybe I'd won after all, because they, those mysterious "They" people, finally got around to telling me that after my delivery I'd have to get to London somehow, check into a hotel and stand by for further orders. London! Oh boy!

As I laid out my course on the English map with its strange contour coloring, I was glad I'd been able to map-read while on my flights with the ATA. Aston Down was located in the south of England near Bristol. For some strange reason it had been built on a hilltop between the towns of Cirencester and Stroud, about 500 feet above the surrounding countryside. So it shouldn't be hard to find, provided it wasn't sticking into a deck of low cloud.

© *2011 Donna McVicar Kazo*

North American Aircraft B-25 Mitchell in RAF camouflage

The barrage balloons over the major cities were marked and to avoid them my track had a lot of bends in it. I had to stay low, in sight of the ground, so I decided the best way would be to follow the main roads, which were well marked.

I also knew to stay well away from the coast, where the Navy gunners shot at everything in the sky. This was the first Mitchell to fly over England, and the thought passed through my mind that it looked like a Junkers Ju88 which had sown many tons of destruction. I hoped fervently that the anti-aircraft guncrews didn't suffer from itchy trigger fingers and had lots of aircraft recognition experience.

After taking off I cut across the rugged hills of southwest Scotland until I picked up the Solway Firth, then identified the border city of Carlisle. A prominent highway and a railroad pointed the way south. Now I had to do a little contour chasing to stay below a deck of stratus cloud. I peered out intently through the usual industrial smoke and haze as I dodged the barrage balloons of Liverpool and Manchester. Staying away from major cities lessened the chance of getting shot at.

Now the weather began to improve and the balloons around Birmingham passed to my left. I had intended to use military airports along the track for check points, but found that in many cases their camouflage was too well done. No wonder the Germans had dropped their loads on many an open field!

When I circled around Aston Down on its hilltop on the Cotswold Hills, just as advertised, I thought it should have been named "Up-and-Down."

The main runway ran right over the top of the hill. I got a green light from the control tower and stuck the Mitchell down in the first hundred feet of the rather narrow strip. It was eerie to look ahead, because the macadam disappeared from sight over the brow of the hill. Like a roller coaster, we went up, over, and down the other side. The B-25 just barely fitted in and I had to use heavy braking.

After parking it was a relief to climb down, using the ingenious ladder which folded up to become part of the fuselage. I reached down to feel the brakes. They were so hot I couldn't touch them, so I left the parking brake off and asked for chocks. The RAF sergeant looked at me strangely when I explained I didn't want the brake discs and blocks to weld together. Maybe pilots who cared that much about their aircraft were unusual birds to him. Or maybe the fact that I was dressed in civilian clothes threw him for a loop.

But soon those problems were far behind me. I was on board an English train hustling along at an alarming speed bound for "The Big Smoke." London! There were five other occupants in my compartment. One of them, an Australian, pulled out a bottle and offered everyone a drink. This broke the ice, and I found myself accepted after I told them I was with the outfit which brought them those nice American aircraft.

I learned from my new chum that the place to stay is the Strand Palace, lots of action there, the Aussie gloated with a big leer. I told him I'd remember, then added how much I admired the way the Anzacs were fighting in Africa. Naturally this made me his friend for life, and we decided to get together in London.

The engine's high-pitched whistle was almost continuous as we rattled through Reading, then Windsor and Eton, all familiar names from my experiences with English novels. As we passed through the outskirts of London, the sight was grim and sobering. Rows of houses lined the rail embankment, tightly packed, shoulder to shoulder, but with strange gaps in unexpected places. I saw the open side of one with pathetic remains of the unlucky family still hanging out in space.

With a shock I realized that I was seeing the results of the Luftwaffe's bombing raids. Londoners had suffered constantly, especially during the "Blitz." As we slowly drew into Paddington Station, I saw more evidence of the pasting London had taken. There were no glass panels left in the spacious roof. On the platform were little piles of rubble and shards of shattered glass which would be cleaned up when the station attendants had time.

I fought my way into one of the comical little taxis. When the driver made a 180-degree turn in the narrow street I realized how efficient the cars really were. Much argument and talk got me a room at the Strand Palace Hotel. My Australian friend was right. The lobby was actually seething with people, the majority of them young men in uniform. There was an air of forced gaiety and some singing, even at five o'clock in the afternoon. Not many women around, I noted. And those who were in sight seemed to be under close escort.

During the long twilight I wandered around like a typical tourist. First, Nelson's Column, then Buckingham Palace, Piccadilly Circus, the outside of the Windmill Theatre. Interesting girls in there, according to the play-bills.

Later that evening I was having a pink gin in the hotel lounge when everything ground to a halt. Horrors! They'd run out of liquor! My Aussie friend wasn't around, and I had a feeling he'd gone to ground with some private stock. I went outside for a breath of air and was accosted by one of the numerous "Piccadilly Commandos" on patrol around the hotel.

"'Ello, Guv," she said as she sidled up to me. "'ow about a bit o' fun?"

"No thanks," I said and lengthened my stride. She wasn't exactly what you'd call ugly, but she wasn't very attractive either. But maybe after you'd spent a month or so at sea, or a year or so in the desert...

Next day I played tourist again, strolling along the narrow twisting streets. My thoughts turned to the Ferry Command pioneer Don Bennett, who, after leaving our ferry service, had endured a difficult struggle before rejoining the RAF at the relatively low rank of Wing Commander. But eventually he had been promoted to Commanding Officer, No. 10 Squadron.

On a recent operation he had been flying a Halifax whose bombs were supposed to destroy the German battleship *Tirpitz*. It was an almost suicidal mission and the hellish antiaircraft fire as he flew up the narrow Norwegian fjord had set his Halifax ablaze and shot off half a wing. He and his crew bailed out and he made his way from Nazi-occupied Norway to Stockholm in neutral Sweden. From there, in his usual forceful style, he convinced the RAF to provide him with a Hudson which flew him back to England. He was awarded with a well-deserved DSO for his efforts.

Air Vice-Marshal Donald Bennett DSO

That night the Germans put on an air raid. It wasn't a very big raid according to the bomb-hardened "Blitz" standards of the average experienced Londoner, but it impressed the hell out of me. The sirens emitted their peculiar mournful wail, and I could see searchlights probing the skies far to the south. Naturally, I had disobeyed standing orders and had gone outside to see better.

Soon the guns at Hyde Park started to boom, and high in the air I could see the silvery reflections of half a dozen Heinkels or Junkers which had broken through. They dropped their sticks of bombs a comfortable number of blocks away and shortly afterwards the noise died down, except for the clamorous bells of the fire fighters.

After the sirens had wailed the more cheerful tune of "All Clear," a warden came along and scolded me for my foolishness. I was forcefully informed that a bit of shrapnel from the AA guns could be bad for my health.

The next morning there were only about three lines in the local paper about the raid. One Jerry had been shot down by a Beaufort night fighter and one by Ack-Ack. To me it was a really big event in my life. To Londoners it was, sadly, routine.

My Aussie friend finally showed up and I told him he'd missed my June 21st birthday party yesterday. No trouble, he replied, we'll do it up tonight. And that was when I learned the big secret: the so-called private bottle clubs. Ten shillings made you a member and in you went. The noise and the crush in the well-stocked bar from the men and women in many uniforms was tremendous. A little smooth talk resulted in our having two neat-looking WREN officers at our table. I always was a sucker for a blue uniform and the Women's branch of the Royal Navy had a nice setup, especially their tricorn hats.

We started to get along really well after I made my usual explanation of being in Ferry Command. My girl had told me to call her Pamela. After we had left the club she allowed me to slip her past the house detective into my hotel room. Then she seemed to enjoy the action as much as I did. So maybe those jokes about the lack of sex drive in English girls wasn't true. More research was called for...

As she got dressed, I tried to get her name and phone number for a return engagement. But she refused, looking at me with a quizzical expression as she remarked that if I knew who she really was I'd be very impressed. Why was she being so secretive? It wasn't against the law, or for all I knew, against a WREN regulation to sleep with a man, after all. Was she Lady Something, or perhaps held a higher title in the stuffy ranks of British aristocracy? The question would bother me for the rest of my life. How was I to know there were so many "Pamelas" in the world? Impossible to track them all down.

The next day the news of the fall of Tobruk came as a stunning shock to the people of the British Isles. My Aussie friend said it never would have happened if his division had still been there.

The bad news was partially balanced by the good news that RAF Bomber Command had duplicated their first 1000-bomber raid on Cologne. This time it was Bremen that took the pounding. The newspapers said the flames of the burning city could be seen for a hundred miles. I wondered how many of the aircraft on the big raid had been delivered by our people. Probably not many, but given time, we'd do our share.

I was getting bored with London when I was given a transport warrant and told to report to Poole, a seaplane base on the south coast of England near Bournemouth. RCAF crew were stationed there prior to reporting to an operational squadron. After the usual crowded train ride, I was placed aboard a Sunderland flying boat. As it positively bristled with turrets, it was called "The Hedgehog" by the German fighter pilots who tried to shoot it down. I was impressed by the size of the machine and how it handled in the water.

It was an uneventful three-hour flight across the Irish Sea. Some of the passengers were obviously military, although like me, were in civilian clothes. We landed on the River Shannon at Foynes in the neutral Republic of Ireland. After the four engines were shut down, all the passengers were again warned not to talk when ashore. It was typical of the Irish to be more "neutral" to one side than the other.

A launch took us to a wooden dock and we walked to a convenient pub where we were served a pre-departure meal. The servings were generous, nothing was rationed, and the beer was excellent. But it sure was hard for me to keep my big mouth shut as I observed the layabouts emptying their steins while complaining about Englishmen and how badly they were being treated. Some were still even moaning about Cromwell.

Just before sunset we were loaded aboard another launch which took us out to the river where we boarded a Boeing Clipper, G-AGCA, Captain Peacock in command. After a beautiful low-level trip with just a touch of turbulence, fourteen hours later we landed at Botwood, in good old Newfie.

To contrast this to the bomb-bay of a Liberator was like night to day. No drafts, lights to read by, no engines roaring. Instead of sawdusty sandwiches we had digestible meals served by a steward. Instead of a hard wooden floor we sat in roomy upholstered seats.

In the dawn's early light a shore tender refueled the aircraft while the ground people supplied sandwiches to the passengers. Across calm waters, the big flying boat helped itself to a long, long takeoff run, then climbed with tranquil, powerful grace through many layers of turbulent cloud before leveling off. I caught glimpses of the dark green forests of New-foundland before we crossed the Cabot Strait.

Canada's maritime provinces slowly fell behind as our shadow slipped over the east coast of North America. We flew over Long Island with the skyscrapers of New York City lining the western horizon. Traveling a day, a night, and now well into the second day had thoroughly bored me to the extent I was actually squirming in my seat. I wished that the tedious trip would end with a landing in that harbor of that exciting, cosmopolitan city. But we just flew on and on.

So it was eleven long hours from takeoff until we were over the harbor of

Baltimore, Maryland. Just before the steward covered the aircraft's portholes with blackout curtains, I saw the hulk and masts of a sunken ship right in the harbor. In the distance was a column of black, oily smoke marking another ship which had recently been torpedoed, in the process of joining many, many others on the bottom of the Atlantic. It was painfully apparent that the Americans hadn't yet figured out how to handle the Nazi U-boats.

After an uneventful landing, my next goal was to get to the land airport. Then a DC-3 of Pennsylvania Central Airlines took me to New York's LaGuardia airport. Once there, I had to change airlines, and dreaded yet another damned delay. But I caught a lucky break, powerfully aided by my high-priority travel status, which enabled me to bump some unlucky fur salesman.

The DC-3 of Colonial Airlines did not have one square inch of its fuselage which wasn't crammed with passengers. At Dorval, I popped out of my aluminum prison cell into good Canadian air. As I looked around, surveying the Ferry Command aircraft waiting, I reflected that it had been the nicest return flight I'd had to date.

Slow, yes, yes, but oh! So safe and comfortable.

From Flight Test to Marauder

After returning from my Mitchell delivery late in June, 1942, there was a slowing of aircraft from the American factories to be ferried overseas, so I'd volunteered to join the test department. I would wring out the systems of a variety of aircraft, feather each engine in turn, and most importantly, swing the magnetic compass while a radio man calibrated the direction finding loop. The work demanded close attention and also kept me in the swing of things.

After a couple of weeks testing various Mitchells, Libs and Flying Fortresses, I was ordered by my old instructor Captain Hunter Moody to report to his new office in the Admin. building. He had been promoted to Chief of Civilian Pilots. Of course I responded promptly.

Now, after a handshake and a short exchange of typical pilot wisecracks, I found his button-like blue eyes to be regarding me intently.

"How're they treating you in Flight Test, Mac?" I moved uneasily in my chair. Moody was a nice guy, sure, but he hadn't taken the trouble to have his secretary track me down just to pass the time of day.

"It's okay, I guess. It's not very thrilling, but at least I get enough flying to keep my hand in. You know I figured out I was getting rusty because on deliveries I was averaging only about a landing a week."

He understood. "Same here. But when I get tired of flying this desk I threaten to quit. Then Powell lets me do a delivery or a Comm. Squad flight."

"So that's what they're calling it now. I sure have done a lot of their type of flying." The preliminaries completed, he got down to business.

"Have you seen our new Martin B-26 Marauder FK111 that's just arrived?" So that's the way the wind blows, I thought.

"Yeah, it's a beautiful machine. Perfect streamlining, for sure. But I can see why they call it the 'Flying Prostitute'."

He smiled. "Because its wings are so short it's got no visible means of support?" I nodded.

"Right. The grapevine says it's the hottest thing in the air. The grapevine also says they've killed a hell of a lot of pilots on training."

Moody looked a little uncomfortable. Maybe the interview wasn't going exactly the way he'd planned.

"I suppose that's true, but most of the pilots who got into trouble were young second lieutenants with no flying time to speak of." Again I moved around nervously as I began to see where the conversation was heading.

"I've heard it won't fly worth a damn on one engine. A guy could have ten thousand hours and he'd still be in trouble."

"No, no, Mac. I'll bet you wouldn't have any trouble with it at all." He paused to see what effect this outrageous flattery—very unusual from Captain Hunter Moody—was having on me.

"I don't intend to find out, thanks," I replied firmly. His attack on a pilot's weakest spot, his vanity about his flying ability, wasn't going to change my mind. Moody scratched his head. I was making it pretty tough for him, so he tried another tack.

"I've got to come up with six civilian crews. The service boys will qualify another four. We need ten because the Americans have given us ten to start with."

"So?"

"So I want you to be the first civilian captain." This made me think. To be "first" must mean those mysterious powers-that-be actually had a fairly high opinion of me.

"Well, maybe later," I mumbled, in my best procrastination act. He threw his clincher.

"We want them delivered all the way to Cairo, Egypt." I straightened up.

"That's more like it! Cairo. Belly dancers. The mysterious East. The pyramids. And I'll get to fly through Africa and South America. Oh boy! It'll be like a...South Atlantic safari."

Moody smiled as I rambled on. I was doing a good sales job on myself. Better than he could have done, probably.

"Well, so what do you say?"

"Why not?"

"Good." Then he gave me my marching orders. "It's a bit unusual, but there's a New Zealand service pilot in charge. Why don't you go over to Service Flight Training and ask for Wing Commander Adams."

"Service Flight Training?" I repeated incredulously. Most of the Air Force pilots had very little flying time in their log books compared to mine.

Moody decided the time was ripe for a little more psychology. He leaned forward, even lowered his voice. "Adams has an assistant, Flying Officer Dennis Robinson, an Australian, and they've both got DFCs. I've been told they're pretty hot pilots."

He leaned forward even further in the best confidential manner as if he was about to confer a great honor on me.

"I want you to check out on the Marauder, then report back to me just how good these two service guys really are." He leaned back to observe my reactions.

I took the bait. Gobbled it down, in fact.

"Sure, Hunter. Glad to oblige."

I jumped up and trotted over to the Service Training office. I was thinking that the B-26 might be hot, and have a hell of a reputation, but it was the latest and most modern aircraft I'd ever seen. Now I was going to fly it, and as well I was No. 1 Spy for Moody. I was proud of myself.

And so I merrily volunteered to fly the aircraft which had already killed many men and which would come damn near to adding me to its lengthy list of victims.

B-26 Martin Marauder

*** END ***

And now, Chapter One of *South Atlantic Safari*, the next installment in the thrilling flying career of Captain Don McVicar.

South Atlantic Safari

The Widow Maker

66 Dorval tower, this is Marauder FK111. Takeoff clearance, please." So spoke Radio Officer Russ Holmes on that sunny morning of July 16, 1942. The man in the control tower gave us the wind direction and take-off clearance.

This was to be the final circuit of my B-26 checkout, and my instructor, Flying Officer Dennis Robinson, RAAF, watched me closely as I released the brakes and let the beautifully streamlined bomber roll smoothly onto runway 24.

When I opened the throttles fully, we were rewarded by a satisfying surge of power as the big Curtiss-Electric props bit the air. Then the tedious and dangerous long run to attain the minimum 135mph takeoff speed began. As I felt the elevators come alive I eased back the control wheel to extend the nose wheel oleo and change the angle of attack of the wing.

Then, rather quickly, I let the nose down to a more normal angle. This unusual maneuvering was necessary only on the Martin Marauder. Meanwhile, the airspeed was steadily increasing as the 5,000 foot runway disappeared under our nose at a truly astonishing rate.

The wheels had just left the runway and I had signaled for landing gear up when suddenly a weird howling sound filled the cockpit. At the same time, in spite of all my efforts, we veered off the runway to the left. I wrestled with the control wheel and rudder pedals, fighting with every ounce of my strength to keep airborne.

The worst possible malfunction of the tricky aircraft had occurred at the worst possible time. The four-bladed port Curtiss propeller was speeding wildly out of control.

The rogue prop blades were acting like a big flat disc, slowing us down as they pulled us to the left. Left wing low, we were now heading directly to the Administration building, actually below the level of the second-story windows. I considered cutting the other throttle and trying to force the aircraft into the grass of the infield in order to save the lives of the people in the building.

But out of the corner of my eye I could see Robinson's quick hands darting around the pedestal. He had already pulled the prop pitch control back, and when that had no effect he had hit the manual safety switch. This time the electric motor decided to work and the prop began to bite the air again. The change was violent, and I had to be quick on the ailerons and rudder as the aircraft tried to roll the other way and force us down into the grass and dirt of the infield.

The small but vital increase in airspeed allowed me to pull the wheel back so that we just skimmed over the roof of the Admin building.

The airspeed was still dangerously low. If the landing gear had not retracted we could never have made it. I signaled Robinson to bleed the flaps up, but even with my most careful efforts the aircraft sank sickeningly and almost crashed into the trees surrounding the airport.

Holmes screamed, "The tower wants to know what's going on!"

As we slowly began to climb I shouted over my shoulder. "Declare an emergency! We've got a runaway prop! Get priority landing clearance!"

He spoke urgently into his mike and then gave me the thumbs-up signal. The tower was cooperating.

As I flew around the circuit, Robinson was controlling the rogue prop by skillful use of the electrical prop control switches on the pedestal. The blades of the prop were actually in the fixed pitch mode, the failed electrical control motor having lost its constant speed function. My instructor/copilot was now manually selecting the revolutions we needed by manipulating his switches.

As I called for landing gear and then flaps down, I still wasn't quite sure we were going to make it back safely. But my experience with previous landings with the hot aircraft allowed me to arrive at the end of the runway at just the proper height and airspeed. I really put out my best efforts on the landing, with the result that we greased on in good shape.

After we had slowed down, Robinson hit me on the shoulder.

"Great work, Mac!" he exclaimed, obviously much relieved.

"Yeah," I grunted, and then said something not too smart.

"Am I checked out now?"

He stared at me for a second or two. "You bet," he said with a grin. Then it was his turn to exercise his sense of humor.

"Do you think I should teach the runaway prop on every checkout?"

With no hesitation I replied, 'I think you're crazy."

There was a guard of honor for us at the end of the runway. We passed an impressive lineup of emergency vehicles.

"Well, we've stirred up the fire department and the meat wagon, anyway," I commented. Robinson, the cool one, just laughed.

The fire trucks and ambulance followed us to our normal parking spot on the ramp in front of Training Hangar No. 2. After I shut off the engines we actually jostled one another in our hurry to get out of our metal coffin. Holmes was the first out.

"Goodbye forever, I hope," he proclaimed as he scuttled away. Robinson and I both grinned. To us this was a perfectly natural reaction.

Later, Holmes told me that he had frozen when he heard the strange noise of the runaway prop. The first thought that flashed through his mind, he recalled, was how stupid he had been to volunteer for a flight in an aircraft which was often called "The Widow Maker." He'd been possessed by a terrible feeling of helplessness as the Administration building loomed up and was sure he'd left his fingerprints in the metal stanchions he was gripping so grimly. He'd had time for one short prayer, just a "Dear God," before we flashed safely over the buildings. Then the voice from the tower had brought him back to reality.

Robinson and I started to talk about what we had just gone through. We thought we had ourselves well under control, but later it would turn out we were both shaken up more than we realized.

Soon we were surrounded by maintenance personnel who had been attracted by the wailing sirens of the crash squad. The Chief Maintenance Inspector began questioning me.

"Well, what happened?"

"The prop ran away. Didn't you hear it on takeoff?" I replied, somewhat defensively.

"That's unusual. Couldn't you control it?" I felt my temper rising as I saw a slightly incredulous look on his face.

"Robinson here did a hell of a good job," I snapped. He didn't answer. It was apparent that he believed that it couldn't have been one of the aircraft under his charge which had given this trouble. Very probably, like a lot of maintenance people, deep down he felt we pilots must be at fault. I sensed this ever-present doubt, and had to shoot back.

"It's too bad you people don't maintain the training aircraft better." This was an ongoing argument between the ground people who serviced the aircraft and the airmen who had to fly them. The inspector looked at me, obviously about to snap back, but then he must have realized the strain we had just been under.

"We do the best he can," he said.

"Oh sure," I replied, surly to the end. He couldn't resist firing a parting shot.

"Oh, by the way, Group Captain Powell wants to see you right away." He tried to hide his grin behind his hand as he turned away.

I'd lost that round.

"I just love those, 'Oh by the way' messages," I grumbled to Robinson. "Well, let's get it over with."

All too soon, the familiar red countenance of Group Captain 'Taffy' Powell glowered at us across his desk. I recounted my harrowing tale and was relieved to see that he seemed to believe me. There was no doubt in my mind that he had heard tales of the Widow Maker's numerous maintenance problems. Robinson stood by me loyally and assured the Senior Air Staff Officer that I'd done a hell of a job. Mentally I put him down for several free drinks.

Then it was my turn to tell our boss that without Robinson's efforts they could have been picking the remnants of the Marauder out of the woods behind the Administration building. Powell nodded without replying. I thought we were out free and clear when Powell glared at me and made a sudden accusation.

"Are you sure you just didn't feel like shooting up the place?" I was so flabbergasted by this suggestion that I blurted out the first thing that came to my mind.

"If I wanted to shoot up the place I sure as hell wouldn't use that bucket of bolts." He didn't reply, and for a moment I could have sworn a grin scooted across his face. Group Captains must have the last word, of course, so he summed it all up.

"Well, I'm glad you saved the aircraft. Don't let it happen again. Help is hard to get out here at the airport and sixteen secretaries resigned right after you shot over the roof and shook their coffee cups out of their hands. Dismissed."

We turned on our heels and made our escape before he had a chance to change his mind.

Once outside the office I felt a little upset.

"Christ, what an attitude. 'Glad you saved the aircraft,' he says. Not one word about our precious skins. On the other hand he must have believed our story or he wouldn't have made the joke about sixteen secretaries quitting, so I guess we're in the clear."

Robinson was puzzled by what he'd just seen and heard. "You know, Mac, if I'd spoken to a Group Captain like that I'd be back to an Acey-Ducey on hangar floor-sweeping detail. Why did he let you get away with it?"

"Acey-Ducey" was Air Force slang for the rank of Aircraftsman Second Class, the lowest of the low.

"Well," I started slowly, "he's an old-time pilot himself, so he understands us a lot better than most of the other ground bods. And maybe he really thinks we did a good job of saving the aircraft. Who knows what goes on behind those scrambled eggs anyway?"

"Right, who does know?"

I was becoming impatient. "Let's forget it ever happened. I'll drive you downtown to the Mount Royal Hotel and we'll meet in the Piccadilly Club for a few belts, okay?" Robinson's face lit up.

"I say! That's the best idea you've had all day! The billeting people booked Adams and me in there too, because the RCAF Manning Pool at Lachine was full up, or something."

On the way to Montreal I noticed that I was driving much more slowly than I usually did. Robinson was quiet. The full realization of our narrow escape was just beginning to sink in.

Once at the hotel, for a moment I fumbled with the key to my door. Once in my private sanctum I began to strip off my sweaty flight clothes. It was then that the reaction really hit me—hard. I broke into a cold sweat and my knees started to shake. I flopped weakly into my big easy chair, thinking that this sort of thing happened only to other people—in novels, or the movies.

Suddenly a succession of violent shivers racked me. It was time for the only cure I knew of. I uncorked my 26-ounce bottle of Canadian Club rye whiskey and took a deep swallow right from the bottle. The raw alcohol made me choke and splutter, but I was able to hold it down. In a short time I began to feel warm again and the violent shivers became just occasional spasms.

My radio was playing a selection of pleasant Western tunes as I drew a hot bath and slipped into the steaming water. Then I laid back and reconstructed the series of events which had led to me damn near getting killed in Ferry Command's newest and most dangerous aircraft.

I realized it had really started when Captain Hunter Moody had talked me into becoming the first civilian Ferry Command pilot to be checked out on the Marauder. The thought of delivering a bomber through South America, across the South Atlantic and then across Africa to mysterious Cairo had strongly influenced my decision to meet the challenge. Then he'd suggested it would be a good idea to report to Wing Commander Adams RNZAF in Service Flight Training, and I'd complied...

*****

Look for *South Atlantic Safari* in its entirety, soon to be released by Words on Wings Press.

Index

RAFFC Aircrew in
Ferry Command Pilot

King, W.M.
Lange, Capt. Carl
Leeward, Capt. Al
Leroy, Capt. Bob
Leroy, R.S.
Lewis, copilot, "one-tripper"
Lilly, Capt. Al
Lockenbauer, R/O "Locky"
Longhurst, F/L William "Bill"
Loughridge, A.M. "Al"
Lyons, W.B.
Mackay, D.
Mackey, Capt. J.C.
McGrail, Radio-Nav. John
McIntyre, J.D.
McVicar, Capt. Donald
Meagher, R/O C.P.
Mellor, W.T.
Merrill, Capt. Bud
Meyers, H.G.
Mitchell, F.
Moody, Capt. Humphrey
Moody, Capt. Hunter
O'Neill, Capt. John
Page, R.H.
Pangborn, Capt. Clyde
Parker, Capt. King
Parker, H.F.
Parkinson, Capt. J.T. "Jack"/"Parky"
Pearce, F.
Phoenix, Capt. Merrill
Pollock, Radio-Navigator Gerry
Powell, Group Captain Griffith "Taffy"
Pringle, Capt.
Raine, D.
Rector, Capt. Charlie
Reeves (aircrew)
Rennie, D.N.
Rodgers, W.C.
Ross, Capt. Carl
Ross, W.C.
Ross, Wing Commander Don, Senior Air
    Staff Officer
Rowe, Capt. Gene
Ruggles, Capt. Jack
Rush, R/O Eric
Ryan, F/E Art
Schafer, Capt. Les
Schiller, Capt. Clarence A. "Duke"
Sharpe, Capt. Jack
Siple, Capt. Wallace "Wally"
Smith, Capt. Ian

Smith, Capt. T.G.
Smith, N.E.
Snailham
Spry, R/O
Steen, N.
Store, A.G.
Swaney, F/E Gayle
Sweet, H.A.
Teel, Capt. Don
Tobin, Capt. Gilbert
Torrey, Capt. Al
Tripp, C.M.
VanDerKloot, Capt. William "Bill"
Wakeman, Squadron Leader
Webber, J.A.
West, R.L.
Wilson, J.N.
Wheeler, R/O Lloyd
Wightman, R/O "Gordy"

Made in the USA
Monee, IL
07 October 2020

44185551R00125